Ultrasocial

Ultrasocial argues that rather than environmental destruction and extreme inequality being due to human nature, they are the result of the adoption of agriculture by our ancestors. Human economy has become an *ultrasocial superorganism* (similar to an ant or termite colony), with the requirements of the superorganism taking precedence over the individuals within it. Human society is now an autonomous, highly integrated network of technologies, institutions, and belief systems dedicated to the expansion of economic production. Recognizing this allows a radically new interpretation of free market and neoliberal ideology that – far from advocating personal freedom – leads to sacrificing the well-being of individuals for the benefit of the global market. *Ultrasocial* is a fascinating exploration of what this means for the future direction of humanity: Can we forge a better, more egalitarian, and sustainable future by changing this socioeconomic – and ultimately destructive – path? John Gowdy explores how this might be achieved.

John Gowdy is Emeritus Professor of Economics at Rensselaer Polytechnic Institute, where he served as Chair of the Department of Economics and Graduate Director of the Ecological Economics program. He was a visiting Leverhulme Professor at Leeds University and Fulbright Professor at the Economic University of Vienna.

"Building on fresh understandings of evolution, this amazing book revolutionizes our understanding of the past and explores a future in which our humanity may be rekindled on a planet likely to be too hot to sustain conventional agriculture. A *tour de force*."

Peter G. Brown, McGill University

"The evolutionary economist John Gowdy has written a grand narrative tracing how over thousands of years the global human society has become complex, stratified, and interconnected, turning into a vast self-regulating superorganism. And now this superorganism has fallen prey to the ideological virus of neoliberalism, which subordinates the well-being of individuals to the needs of the global market. Ultimately, *Ultrasocial* is a scathing indictment of neoliberal ideology and market fundamentalism from the evolutionary point of view."

Peter Turchin, University of Connecticut and author of
*Ultrasociety: How 10,000 Years of War Made Humans
the Greatest Cooperators on Earth.*

"Gowdy puts forward the provocative case that as we came under the yoke of states, humans became closer to ants and termites. Individually we may still be social primates, but collectively we are now closer to a leafcutter ant colony. A stimulating read that reworks the fabric of history away from a simple narrative of increasing complexity and prosperity, to one in which we have traded autonomy and humanity for power. A book that might just change your mind on what it means to be human."

Luke Kemp, Centre for the Study of Existential Risk,
University of Cambridge

"In this highly original, stimulating, and provocative interdisciplinary analysis, John Gowdy bridges the agricultural societies of African mound-building termites and fungus-gardening ants with human nature to generate deep insights into modern economics and sustainability."

James Traniello, Boston University

Ultrasocial

The Evolution of Human Nature and the Quest for a Sustainable Future

John Gowdy
Rensselaer Polytechnic Institute

CAMBRIDGE
UNIVERSITY PRESS

University Printing House, Cambridge CB2 8BS, United Kingdom

One Liberty Plaza, 20th Floor, New York, NY 10006, USA

477 Williamstown Road, Port Melbourne, VIC 3207, Australia

314–321, 3rd Floor, Plot 3, Splendor Forum, Jasola District Centre, New Delhi – 110025, India

103 Penang Road, #05–06/07, Visioncrest Commercial, Singapore 238467

Cambridge University Press is part of the University of Cambridge.

It furthers the University's mission by disseminating knowledge in the pursuit of education, learning, and research at the highest international levels of excellence.

www.cambridge.org
Information on this title: www.cambridge.org/9781108838269
DOI: 10.1017/9781108974264

© Cambridge University Press 2021

First published 2021

Printed in the United Kingdom by TJ Books Limited, Padstow Cornwall

A catalogue record for this publication is available from the British Library.

ISBN 978-1-108-83826-9 Hardback

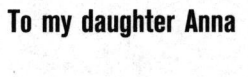

To my daughter Anna

CONTENTS

FIGURES

TABLES

PREFACE

I have been lucky to have been exposed to intellectual conflict my whole life. I was born and raised in the wilds of the Arkansas Ozarks where I came of age in the 1950s and early 1960s. My mother was a fundamentalist Christian and my father was a country doctor and freethinker. At prayer meetings and tent revivals I learned to appreciate the power of community, the camaraderie of sharing belief systems, and the importance of ritual and tradition. In the church I also gained a lifelong appreciation of music as a cultural unifier and, more importantly, as a common denominator for all people. But the dark side was there too, the anti-intellectualism and the stultifying ignorance and intolerance. From my father, I gained an appreciation of the power of science and reason and the joy of learning.

The subject of evolution drove a wedge between me and the church and I gradually came to the conclusion that the prevailing beliefs of religious fundamentalists about established scientific facts were clearly wrong. Science and the accumulation of knowledge and understanding the world beyond my immediate experience became an almost spiritual force as powerful as any religion.

In 1962 my father took a job with the Food and Drug Administration in Washington, DC and I was thrust into a new and different social and intellectual environment. During high school and college in the DC area I was drawn into the civil rights and anti-war movements. As with the conflict between religious fundamentalism and evolution, the lines were clearly drawn. People were beaten for trying to go to public schools or eat at a restaurant. A bloody and incomprehensible war was raging with the support of the most powerful politicians and business leaders. Again, conventional wisdom and the belief systems of the establishment proved to be wrong.

My interest in science and evolution led me to major in anthropology at American University where I focused on archaeology and human evolution. Several field trips on archaeological digs gave me indispensable training in the scientific method and showed me the benefits of interdisciplinary research and the power of the past over the present.

1968 was an eventful year. I married the love of my life, Linda, and the other love of my life, my daughter Anna, was born. I was drafted and sent to Vietnam. After returning home from Vietnam I completed a degree in community planning at the University of Rhode Island where I began to appreciate the importance of economics in understanding politics, society, and public policy. A few years later, with the help of the GI Bill and a very generous foundation fellowship, I completed a PhD in economics from West Virginia University (WVU).

At West Virginia University I was fortunate to have three teachers who helped me set the stage for my academic career. My PhD advisor Walter Page taught me neoclassical microeconomics as a system of thought, not merely a collection of tools to analyze narrow questions of production and distribution. Like any religious or political system of thought, the prevailing economic theory depends on using a few basic assumptions to establish what Marshall Sahlins calls a "cosmology" – a way of organizing the world into a coherent whole that can be easily understood and applied to almost any situation. Another economics professor, William Miernyk, introduced me to the "heretics" of the profession who rigorously challenged the ideology of neoclassical theory.

While registering for my first classes, my advisor told me about a visiting professor, Nicholas Georgescu-Roegen. I had never heard of him but I quickly learned that he was one of the premier economic theorists of the twentieth century and an authority on energy and resources. I bought the text for the course, *The Entropy Law and the Economic Process*, and met Georgescu the next day. My intellectual life was changed forever by this accident of fate. Georgescu was at WVU every other semester while I was there and I am grateful for his wisdom, warmth, and generosity toward me.

The 1970s were exciting times to be an economist focusing on energy and the environment. Spiking energy prices and long gas lines seemed to confirm the work of Georgescu-Roegen and Kenneth Boulding and the limits-to-growth movement. The environmental movement was having a major impact and enjoying wide public support. The inequities of American society and the scourge of institutional racism were finally being seriously addressed. It seemed certain that radical changes in both economic theory and public policy were on the way. Unfortunately, fundamental change never happened. Explaining the gulf between understanding the problems and translating this knowledge into the political action required to address them became the major focus of my academic career.

After completing my PhD, I worked for three years at the New York State Energy Office as an econometric modeler forecasting energy demand. In 1982 I began teaching at Rensselaer Polytechnic Institute (RPI) in Troy, New York. During my thirty-five-year career at RPI I buried myself in reading, writing, publishing, and thinking about subjects as diverse as energy; the mathematics of utility theory; the representation of the economy using input–output analysis; behavioral economics; the economic structure of hunter-gatherer societies; and of course, the facts and theories of evolutionary change.

While at RPI, with the help of colleagues Faye Duchin, Jon Erickson, and Sabine O'Hara, I established the world's first graduate program in ecological economics. The many RPI graduate students I worked with over the years made all the trials and tribulations of academic life well worth it.

The last decades of the twentieth century and the first years of the twenty-first century were a period of ambiguity. There were some important successes. Energy and the environment became a major focus of government policy. The first African American was elected president. More women were entering academia (except for the field of economics) and being elected to public office. Structural racism was at least being recognized and discussed. In the field of economics, important new empirical and theoretical work was documenting how inequality is generated by capitalist accumulation and the power of hereditary wealth. But fundamental change was missing. Some policy successes were there but the limits to liberal reforms became more and more apparent.

What I learned from studying evolution is to keep digging deeper and deeper, whether it's about biology or economics. It's not enough to document how a particular species evolves in a certain environment. What are the general patterns common to evolutionary change? The same applies to the social sciences. It's not enough to explore why the US political system has been captured by far-right extremists. Why is the same thing happening the world over? The Internet may be facilitating the spread of conspiracy theories, but why are people so susceptible now to the message?

Today, in the era of Donald Trump, it seems as if we have returned to the black-and-white clarity of the 1960s. On one side are the forces of anti-intellectualism and repression backed by fundamentalist religion, the growing power of the billionaire class, and the underclass of desperate people left behind by globalization and market "rationalization." On the other side is a growing and energetic movement demanding fundamental structural change and an end to domination by an elite few. This is a time of despair and a time of hope. Never in my lifetime has the future seemed so uncertain. The neoliberal world is in tatters. Will it be replaced by fascism or by progressive democratic change that reshapes the world order for the common good?

ACKNOWLEDGMENTS

During a lifetime thinking about the issues raised in this book, I have been fortunate to have been taught by outstanding teachers and colleagues throughout my intellectual journey via the joys and tribulations of an academic career. Among my professors I would like to single out William Harrison, who introduced me to archaeology and the scientific method; Walter Page, who taught me to appreciate the logic and rigor of neoclassical economics as a system of thought; William Miernyk, who introduced me to the limits of neoclassical economics; and, most of all, Nicholas Georgescu-Roegen, whose intellect and ideas changed my life. Among the many colleagues I have worked with over the years I would like to thank two biologists, Carl McDaniel and David Sloan Wilson, who gave me a deeper understanding of the beauty of evolution and evolutionary theory. A special thanks goes to my colleague in ultrasociality Lisi Krall, the only person who got it right from the beginning.

I would like to thank the following people who patiently read draft after draft of the book and gave valuable suggestions throughout: Ken Blumberg, Micha Brym, Faye Duchin, and Kathy Keenan. Thanks to Linda Gowdy for the arduous task of tracing down permissions for the figures used.

Part I

THE EVOLUTION OF
HUMAN ULTRASOCIALITY

[R]ecent discoveries suggest that the adoption of agriculture,
supposedly our most decisive step toward a better life, was in many
ways a catastrophe from which we have never recovered. With
agriculture came the gross social and sexual inequality, the disease and
despotism, that curse our existence.

> Jared Diamond, 1987, The worst mistake in human history,
> p. 91

Homo sapiens has been present on planet earth for at least
300,000 years. For almost all that time we lived as immediate–return
hunter gatherers. During this period we evolved the basic traits that
make us human. We lived in small bands where virtues like altruism,
sharing, and the preservation of nature were essential to group
survival. Our societies were sustainable and egalitarian. Hunter-
gatherers show us that neither environmental destruction nor
extreme inequality is due to human nature. Both are the result of
the requirements of production for surplus that came with agriculture. Over the last 10,000 years human society became *ultrasocial*,
that is, it became so complex, stratified, and interconnected that it
began to act *as if* it were a single self-regulating superorganism. The
parallel evolution of agriculture in humans and social insects was the

product of natural selection operating on groups. The transition to agriculture was set in motion by economic drivers that came into play with production for surplus – a complex division of labor; economies of scale in production; and the advantage of larger sized communities. With intensified group-level competition, larger populations and intensive exploitation of nature and people became the norm. The "social conquest of earth" was underway.

1 THE ULTRASOCIAL ORIGIN OF OUR EXISTENTIAL CRISIS

> Humanity today is like a walking dreamer, caught between the fantasies of sleep and the chaos of the real world. The mind seeks but cannot find the precise place and hour. We have created a Star Wars civilization, with Stone Age emotions, medieval institutions, and god-like technology. We thrash about. We are terribly confused by the mere fact of our existence, and a danger to ourselves and to the rest of life.
>
> E. O. Wilson, 2012, *The Social Conquest of Earth*, p. 7

Professor Wilson eloquently describes the mismatch between evolved human emotions and the institutions and technologies we depend on today. There is indeed a conflict between human nature and the technological civilization we are embedded in. But Professor Wilson's quote is misleading. The fault lies not in our Stone Age emotions but rather with the Star Wars civilization we stumbled into through a quirk of social evolution. With the reorganization of the economy that accompanied the adoption of agriculture, human society became *ultrasocial*.[1] It began to resemble a superorganism – an autonomous, highly integrated network of technologies, institutions, and belief systems dedicated to the production of economic surplus. The human economy began to operate *as if* it were a self-referential organism whose requirements take precedence over the well-being of the individual humans within that system. Our current social and environmental crises are not the fault of human nature but rather the fault of the surplus-producing economic system that came with the agricultural revolution some 10,000 years ago.

The accomplishments of civilization are impressive. We have answered many of the questions that puzzled us for ages. We have a good understanding of the origin of the universe and the evolution of *Homo sapiens*. We know the structure of the human genome, we have sent scientific instruments to the far reaches of the solar system and beyond, and we are on the brink of solving the riddle of the origin of life itself. On the other hand, our rapacious economy and our burgeoning population are destabilizing earth's biophysical systems and now threaten the continued existence of the complex technological world we are so proud of. We recognize and carefully document the existential threats of climate change, biodiversity loss, and increasing inequality, and we formulate feasible solutions to these problems. Yet so far, with a few limited exceptions, we have been incapable of effectively dealing with any of them. Why is there such a disconnect between understanding and action? The answer lies deep in our evolutionary history. For some 300,000 years *Homo sapiens* lived in small groups of a few dozen people within the confines of local ecosystems. Humans lived, as other animals do, from the day-to-day flows from nature. The human population grew and shrank with changes in climate and in the resources flowing directly from the natural world – the hundreds of plants and animals our hunter-gatherer ancestors depended on. The human presence on earth, and our place within the web of life, changed dramatically with the Holocene, a geological epoch that began about 12,000 years ago. An unprecedented combination of climate stability and warm temperatures made possible a greater dependence on wild grains in several parts of the world. Over the next several thousand years, this dependence steadily increased and eventually led to permanent agricultural settlements and large-scale state societies. It took only a few thousand years after sedentary agriculture began for it to spread and become dominant.[2] Within that relatively short time period, the human population exploded from a few million to more than 200 million by the beginning of the Common Era (CE) 2,000 years ago.[3,4] Such a large population required radical changes in economy and society.

The economic structure required to support agriculture changed the place of individuals in human society and the relationship between humans and the natural world. Social evolution took a path in many ways inimical to the evolved characteristics that made us human – compassion for others, sharing, cooperating for the common good, and a spiritual connection to the natural world. The agricultural way of life created a mismatch between the demands of the ultrasocial system and the well-being of most individuals within that system. The last ten thousand years of human history can be seen as a struggle between the requirements of the surplus-generating economy and the fundamental human biological, social, and psychological characteristics we evolved during the Pleistocene.

Agriculture and the resulting population explosion dramatically changed the human impact on the natural world. Competing species were driven from human settlements or exterminated altogether. Diverse local ecosystems were radically transformed and simplified as humans cleared forests and meadows to produce crops. The effect on human society was also dramatic. As agriculture evolved, small-scale egalitarian bands were eventually replaced by large-scale, hierarchical, economically integrated, and interdependent city-states with extremely complex divisions of labor. These rigidly hierarchical societies were reinforced by caste systems, state religions, and the economic and military power of elites. Ironically, as the Darwinian fitness of *human groups* increased (as evidenced by the huge population increase), the well-being of most *individuals within the group*, as measured by health and quality of life, decreased dramatically.[5]

• • •

With agriculture and the active control of food supply, humans followed the path of the ant and termite civilizations that came some 40–60 million years before us to evolve societies so complex, stratified, and interdependent that they act as if they are single organisms. The evolutionary drivers of ant, human, and termite ultrasocial societies were the same – the economic requirements of surplus food production. The results were also the same – the domination of planet earth and the subjugation of individual autonomy to the needs of the new economic order.

Species populations rise and fall with external changes in the flow of food from the natural world. Individuals can catch or gather more or less food, but they cannot augment the flow. With the adoption of agriculture the food supply became endogenous, that is, under the control of the species engaging in it. A complex level of economic organization enabled agricultural societies to aggressively manage their environments to produce an abundance of food. Economic activity was transformed from using resources directly for immediate livelihood to large-scale resource management to produce future surpluses. Human groups began to actively manage food production by tapping into the stock of fertile soil that had built up over eons, extracting water for irrigation, protecting crops from predators, and redirecting the flow of solar energy away from nonhuman nature in order to grow crops. Agriculture allows a species to create its own food supply.[6] The need to produce surplus food to meet unexpected emergencies means that there is usually more food than the existing population needs to survive. Surplus food triggers population growth, which requires further expansion of agricultural production. This positive feedback loop is how agricultural ants, termites, and humans came to dominate the planet in terms of sheer numbers and total biomass. Most of the earth's land area animal biomass consists of ants, termites, and humans. Why do these three lifeforms dominate the natural world? Their incredible success is due to the direct control of the birth, growth, and management of food sources.

The resemblance between social insect and human agriculture is remarkable.[7] Leafcutter ants, for example, (1) produce a specific kind of fungi using a variety of complex management techniques and organic inputs; (2) use manure to stimulate growth; (3) eliminate weeds mechanically and with carefully manufactured antibodies; and (4) trade crops and antibodies with other ant colonies, sometimes with different species. Like humans, the insect farmers became dependent on cultivated crops for food. They developed carefully articulated task-partitioned societies cooperating in gigantic agricultural enterprises. Agriculture ultimately enabled the social insects to rise to major ecological importance. Ants account for 15–20 percent of the world's terrestrial invertebrate biomass.[8] In the Brazilian rainforest, ants and termites comprise about 75 percent of the insect biomass.[9] Ants and humans have roughly the same total global weight.[10,11] Like humans, agricultural insects have complex societies dominating the ecosystems they reside in. As Bert Hölldobler and E. O. Wilson[12] put it, "Social insects hold the ecological center; solitary insects occupy the periphery."

Human and Social Insect Behavior

Ant, termite, and human societies are unique on planet earth. They dominate in terms of total population, the size of their cities, and the number of occupations in their colonies. They are also unique in terms of the complexity of their social organization dedicated to the production of economic surplus. Their societies have key features in common originating from the existence of surplus. Like human societies after agriculture, social insects must defend their stores of wealth. Ant wars between colonies can last for decades resulting in battle deaths numbering in the billions. Ant suicide bombers rush into enemy lines and blow themselves to pieces to inflict casualties. Ant warfare tactics are so sophisticated they are used as models for training West Point cadets. "Untouchable" ants dispose of the waste products of the colony and are not allowed to come into contact with other ants. Because of a slight genetic modification, ant societies are now experiencing globalization. Argentine ants are forming global communities numbering in the trillions, such that ants from North America, Europe, and Japan are accepted in each other's colonies.

"But wait," you say, "How can ant behavior be relevant to human behavior? Human behavior and indeed human society are the products of biological evolution, how can our behavior be compared to that of distantly related insects? We should learn about human social evolution by studying our genetically closest relatives, the great apes and other primates. Similarities with insects are coincidental and irrelevant." The study of primates has greatly enriched our understanding of human behavior but consider this thought experiment. Suppose we discovered, deep in the Congo, a chimpanzee society with complex agriculture including the sophisticated use of antibiotics and monoculture, a complex division of labor, occupational castes, highly organized warfare with other agricultural chimp groups, cities, and a sophisticated communications network to manage their economy. Such a discovery would shake the foundations of the social sciences. Why are ants and termite societies with these characteristics relegated to the category of mildly interesting analogies with little relevance to human society?

• • •

The human economy after agriculture became a kind of self-organized ultrasocial system with its own dynamic of expansion, resource exploitation, and control. But human society has not yet become an ant colony. Human societies have one critical difference from those of the social insects. Ant and termite occupations are based on differing phenotypes and life cycle stages. Unlike ants, human societies have castes based on hereditary wealth. Human classes are the result of social institutions and the consolidation of entrenched political and economic power, not genetics.

Just as an ant colony acts as if it is a single organism, so too does the global market economy act as if it is a single living entity constructing its own ecosystem niche within which to survive and flourish. One need not be a rigid historical materialist to recognize that the parallels in human, ant, and termite societies were driven by similar evolutionary forces and similar economic drivers. The most important consequence is the fundamental conflict between the rules that favor the requirements of the global market superorganism and the basic needs of individual humans embedded in that system. The dynamics set in motion by early agricultural state societies led directly to today's global market economy. The history of state societies shows regular patterns of environmental overshoot, and increasing inequality leading to deterioration and sometimes a total social collapse. Early state societies the world over showed similar patterns of intensive resource exploitation and a concentration of wealth and power.[13,14,15] The rapacious exploitation of nature frequently led to the demise of early state societies, but these collapses were regional. Populations were able to regroup, move to other areas, or were absorbed by outside conquests.[16] Some societies were able to change the course of their histories, but most did not. Agriculture did not inevitably lead to global capitalism. Agricultural societies followed many different paths. But today's global socioeconomic system arose directly from the early state societies of the Middle East.

Today we face two broad existential crises: the rapacious economic exploitation destabilizing the natural world and staggering inequality. Individual well-being and the health of the earth's ecosystems are being sacrificed to the needs of the global market. With agriculture, nature and people became impersonal inputs to support the production of economic surplus. Agriculture dramatically changed human society and the natural world. Another dramatic change came with the intensive use of fossil fuels that ushered in the industrial age. This intensification accelerated after World War II with the globalization of the market economy and explosive increases in population and economic growth. This period, termed the Great Acceleration, has been characterized by unprecedented changes in the earth's atmosphere, geochemical processes, and the annihilation of the nonhuman biological world. Impacts are now global, not merely regional. These impacts will change the course of biological evolution and the earth's geochemical processes for millennia.

The Absorption of Nature by the Human Economy

The first major consequence of agriculture was the human domination of local ecosystems. For most of human history we were a minor player in the earth's biosphere. Human biomass was a tiny fraction of total terrestrial vertebrate biomass. At the beginning of agriculture, the human–wild animal biomass ratio overwhelmingly favored wild vertebrates. This changed dramatically when humans began to control food production. By 1900, humans and their farm animals made up the bulk of terrestrial vertebrate biomass. The total biomass then was about the same as it was before agriculture, but by redirecting the flow of solar energy, water, and soil fertility, humans expropriated the bulk of the land's productive potential. Another major transition in the relationship between humans and the biosphere occurred with the fossil fuel revolution. With the fossil fuel supplement to solar energy, the ratio of humans and their livestock compared to wild terrestrial mammals is now 23:1 in favor of humans and their livestock. The biomass of domestic poultry is three times greater than that of wild birds.[17] Moreover, the total land vertebrate biomass increased severalfold as fossil fuel–driven agriculture came to dominate the solar-powered biological productivity of the planet.[18] Today, the human impact on planet earth is so unique that the present era in earth history has been dubbed the Anthropocene, the age of humans.[19] Humans are now changing basic atmospheric and biophysical processes on every part of the planet.[20,21,22] Furthermore, with the Great Acceleration of the economy since World War II we seem to be entering a new, more virulent phase of the human impact on planet earth. The numbers of birds, fish, insects, and mammals have declined by more than half since the 1970s. The human population is now 7.7 billion and is projected to reach 9 –10 billion by 2050. Catastrophic climate change looms as an existential threat.

The Subjugation of Individuals to the Requirements of the Economic Superorganism

The second major consequence of agriculture was a loss of individual well-being and autonomy resulting from the regimentation, fragmentation, and hierarchical control of food production. The complex division of labor increased the productivity of food production and supported the evolutionary success of humans in terms of sheer numbers. But individual autonomy and self-reliance were suppressed to support easier control and coordination of food production. In contrast to hunter-gatherers, a large part of the day-to-day lives of agriculturalists was spent in specialized, monotonous activities. Although the variety of occupations increased, the roles of individuals were much more narrowly defined. People were born into rigid and distinct hereditary classes that determined their occupations and life prospects. The economic structure of human society began to resemble that of an ant or termite colony. Of course, humans have only recently started down the path to ultrasociality and the suppression of individual autonomy is far from complete compared to social insects. The physical type and age of ants and termites determine their occupation. The proportion of different occupations in social insect colonies is adjusted according to the requirements of the colony. Ants do not have hereditary castes. By contrast, human societies are divided into castes and occupational classes based on culture, customs, social institutions, and political power.

A common feature of human and insect agricultural societies is that individual behavioral complexity and flexibility, what insect biologists call *totipotency*, is in general not as great as individuals living in societies relying on foraging alone. Individual behavior in human and insect societies with an elaborate division of labor is simpler even as the society itself grows more complex. Increasing social complexity is associated with a decrease in individual behavioral complexity. There is no conscious "hive mind" in ultrasocial societies. Humans, ants, and termites are not evolving into Star Trek Borgs with the ability of individuals to tap into a kind of collective intelligence. Complex agricultural ant and termite colonies are successful because they evolved, through natural selection working on groups, incredibly efficient social structures to produce and manage agricultural surpluses. But individuals within the system come to resemble cells in a body, doing simple tasks within complex systems. Individuals are expendable cogs in an ultrasocial machine. With agriculture, the human species started down the same path as social insects toward increasing societal complexity and decreasing individual autonomy.[23,24,25]

In human ultrasocial societies individuals are dependent on the economic superorganism for employment and well-being. This loss of autonomy and individual independence has led to socially constructed hereditary class and caste systems. Inequality is a human phenomenon. There are no genetic reasons why an individual human should be a king or laborer. But extreme inequality has plagued our species for millennia and is one of the most well-documented consequences of the agricultural revolution. It seems to be an inevitable consequence of production for surplus.[26] Walter Scheidel has documented the existence of inequality over the past 10,000 years and makes a convincing case for a near-universal tendency for inequality and exploitation to increase until it is halted by natural or human-caused catastrophes like wars, depressions, plagues, climate disruption, and resource depletion.[27] The level of inequality seen in past and present human societies is remarkable. Today, the sixty-two richest individuals have as much private net wealth as the bottom half of the human population, some 3 1/2 billion people.[28]

Although the beginnings of inequality can be seen in some hunter-gatherer societies, egalitarianism was the norm before agriculture. Extreme and persistent inequality is a defining feature only of the last few thousand years. This is important because it shows that rapaciousness and greed are not the result of human nature. For most of human history we lived in harmony with nature and not under the domination of an elite few. We lived as immediate-return hunter-gatherers with simple technologies and a limited division of labor based on age and gender. It was during our pre-agricultural Pleistocene past that we evolved our basic human characteristics – large brains, language, complex culture, and an ability to cooperate extensively with nonkin. Judging from archaeological evidence and historical accounts of hunter-gatherer societies, our Pleistocene ancestors lived equitably and harmoniously without destabilizing their habitats.

• • •

The adoption of agriculture caused human and social insect societies to evolve broadly similar characteristics for the same reasons – the economic requirements of food production. Economic drivers highlight the importance of mechanistic forces in the social evolution of our species. They suggest that the broad structure of current human society is the result of forces not under conscious human control. This leads us to question the degree of human intentionality and control over society and its economy. The similarities between ants and humans are not merely interesting but inconsequential analogies. The ultrasocial forces that took hold when agriculture began 10,000 years ago continue to mold, constrain, and direct human society in the twenty-first century.

The drivers behind the evolution of large-scale agriculture were the physical laws of economic production. The agricultural transition was propelled by the selection of groups that could best capture the advantages of (1) more efficient management of food production; (2) a more complex and economically efficient division of labor; and (3) increasing returns to a larger scale of production and to larger group size. After the establishment of agriculture, populations expanded as these economic drivers opened up new opportunities for the exploitation of resources and a more intensive management of economic activity. Group-level competition encouraged larger populations and more intensive resource exploitation that provided competitive advantages. The result was what E. O. Wilson termed the "social conquest of earth."

The economic origin of ultrasociality has significant implications. It shows the importance of evolutionary processes in the human economy and the current human predicament. It also demonstrates the importance of moving the analysis of social evolution away from an obsession with individual autonomy and voluntary choice. It leads to a greater appreciation of the group itself as an evolutionary force and the importance of the physical and social organization of production as a driver of social evolution. The agricultural revolution transformed human material and social culture. The ultrasocial group became the dominant unit of natural selection. The complex relationship between humans and the biosphere changed as the nonhuman world was reduced to a one-dimensional input to surplus production. The interactions between individual humans changed from personal face-to-face cooperation to large-scale impersonal coordination of economic activity. The human propensity to cooperate was harnessed to facilitate the coordination of economic activities. Human embeddedness within the confines of local ecosystems was replaced by the domination and exploitation of nature for economic gain. The value of individuals and nature was reduced to being mere economically productive inputs. The door was open for rapacious environmental exploitation and social hierarchy and inequality.

Understanding the economic mechanisms behind the transition to agriculture is key to understanding the forces behind past and current episodes of explosive population growth, the ravaging of the natural world, the expansionary tendencies of human societies, and extreme material inequality. Complex human societies are the products of coevolutionary processes that are entirely consistent with the principles of biological evolution, especially the principles established in recent work in extended evolutionary theory.[29,30] Groups that could best capture the economic factors driving efficiency in production had a competitive advantage over other groups. As agriculture took hold, those societies having group traits most favorable to surplus production outcompeted other groups. Some groups gained a competitive advantage through the evolution of institutions – from religion and divine right to rigid caste systems – that supported surplus production. The requirements of the higher-level superorganism began to override the behavior, organization, and functions of hunter-gatherer customs, human relationships, and ethical values that made us human. Complex human societies are integrated systems consisting of technologies, power relationships, institutions, and belief systems that act to ensure the coherence and survival of the system as a whole, not necessarily for the benefit of individuals. These social variants are the products of evolution. Natural selection favors those variants that are successful at a particular time in a particular place. Evolution cannot see ahead. Successful variants in one context can become dysfunctional in another.

Post-agricultural belief systems have taken various forms from the early beliefs in the divine right of humans to "subdue and conquer the earth" to the more recent faith in the upward path of human progress and technology. One of the most powerful institutions to come out of the agricultural mode of production is the market that has become the worldwide embodiment of human ultrasociality. A variety of belief systems have sprung forth to support and protect the market as the ultimate organizer of human affairs. Today, neoliberalism is the dominant ideology promoting the market economy as a kind of superorganism whose information processing ability is far beyond that of individual humans.[31,32]

If we step back and look at the world around us, it is apparent that the increase in material well-being has come at considerable cost. In spite of our awareness of our precarious situation, we are unable to take control of the economic trajectory we find ourselves on. The expansive and highly integrated production economy that characterizes us as an ultrasocial species makes it difficult to disengage from it, even as it becomes increasingly unstable. The superorganism doesn't care about fairness or the environment because it is not a conscious, morally concerned entity. As we look around we tend to see everything as examples of human choices. As individuals we make choices every day, sometimes life-changing choices. But what if the social "we" does not choose? What if blind evolutionary mechanisms are largely responsible for human civilization and its consequences. This leaves us to question what we have become as a species and how much meaningful control we have over the direction of human society. It also points to the need to gain control of the evolutionary path we have stumbled onto if we are to survive the coming centuries. As individuals we can clearly see the consequences of climate change, the loss of the natural world, and the other existential threats we face. But even though the ultrasocial system we live under acts *as if* it is an individual organism, it is not a sentient being. It cannot see the long-term consequences of its immediate behavior.

• • •

Even though the market superorganism is the result of natural evolutionary forces, that does not mean it is good for humans. "Natural" does not mean "good." In advanced ultrasocial systems such as those of ants and termites, individuals are expendable, like cells in a body. Moreover, natural selection cannot see ahead to avoid distant dangers that do not affect current fitness. An immediate and practical implication is that we cannot rely on a product of amoral natural selection, the global market superorganism, to save us from the destabilizing effects of environmental disruption and material inequality. In fact, to survive and flourish in the coming decades we must come to a radically new understanding of economic life. If we are to save ourselves from a bleak future, we can no longer accept horrific inequality or the rapacious exploitation of nature. To avoid ecological and social disaster we must get control of the superorganism that has evolved into the global market economy. Minimal first steps include global controls on carbon emissions, enforceable protection of the earth's remaining biodiversity, and insuring an equitable access to the world economy's material output. Is such intentional change possible? Do we have the collective ability to change? Democratic socialist economies, most notably in the Scandinavian countries, have been successful in modifying the excessive inequality generated by capitalism. We can modify the existing system to make the world a better place – such a "minimal bioeconomic program" is suggested in Chapter 8. But this is not enough. Without addressing the structure and evolution of our current expansionary system we cannot achieve a stable economic order or the stability of nonhuman world. We cannot change overnight but we can start down a new evolutionary path compatible with basic human needs and our place in nature.

Evolutionary theory has been used successfully to modify individual behavior, and to shape decision-making in small groups. But the task is to change our global collective behavior. How can nations with widely varying material needs, and very different social and environmental values, agree to common rules that limit national sovereignty? And how can we fundamentally change economic structure while we humanely establish these binding global rules? We have entered the realm of what has been called "post-normal science" – characterized by extreme uncertainty and the possibility of catastrophic consequences of inaction.[33]

Human society has taken on many of the characteristics of an insect superorganism. The dynamics of ant, termite, and human ultrasocial systems show strikingly similar commonalities. The convergent evolution of agricultural societies in widely dissimilar species is the result of natural selection acting on groups. As the group becomes the focus of natural selection, the components of the group – individual humans, ants, and termites – become expendable for the good of the superorganism. What is good for the group may no longer be good for the individuals that comprise it. The question raised by human ultrasociality is whether our fate as a species will be left to blind evolutionary forces or whether we can use ethics, science, and reason to collectively change our present trajectory. Can we alter the path of social evolution? Can our global civilization return to the sustainable and egalitarian world of our hunter-gatherer ancestors based on collective responsibility for the well-being of every individual?

The vision of the market economy as a highly integrated, self-organizing system is not new. In fact, it is widely accepted. The crucial difference in the vision presented here is that this system operates as if it is a sentient entity advancing and protecting its own narrow interests. Individuals within the ultrasocial system are mere tools – pawns to be used to further the "goals" of the superorganism. Recognizing the inherent conflict between individual well-being and the workings of the global market is a critical first step if we are to move toward an equitable and environmentally sustainable human presence on planet earth. Understanding the evolutionary origins of this conflict is crucial.

2 THE EVOLUTION OF ULTRASOCIALITY IN HUMANS AND SOCIAL INSECTS

Ants, termites, and humans dominate planet earth. Ants and termites comprise over 50% of the world's insect biomass and humans and their farm animals make up over 95% of terrestrial vertebrate biomass. Yet ant and termite species represent only about 2% of all insect species and humans are only one species among over 4,000 species of mammals. Why are these lifeforms uniquely successful in evolutionary terms? What do they have in common? It is not their genetic similarity. The last common ancestor (LCA) for all three (the precursor of both arthropods and chordates) existed more than 530 million years ago. The LCA for ants and termites lived more than 100 million years ago. Ants, termites, and humans are not closely related, but their social characteristics are strikingly similar and unique in the animal kingdom. Each dominates the ecosystems in which they occur. Each has a complex division of labor with individuals doing very specific interrelated tasks within the group. Each live in very large-scale societies devoted to the production and protection of food. Until recently these similarities have been dismissed by biologists and social scientists for a variety of reasons, especially the belief that genes alone are the focus of evolution. With the broadening of evolutionary theory to include natural selection at multiple levels – genes, individuals, groups – the evolution of ultrasociality is beginning to be understood.

Ultrasociality is an example of a well-established pattern in the evolution of life on earth. Evolutionary history can be seen as a series of abrupt changes from simpler to more complex levels of organization.[1,2,3,4] Keller[5] writes: "The major transitions in evolutionary units are from individual genes to networks of genes, from gene networks to bacterialike cells, from bacterialike cells to eukaryotic cells with organelles, from cells to multicellular organisms, and from solitary organisms to societies." Higher-level selection processes have been central to the evolution of complexity.[6] This applies to social as well as biological evolution. The process by which high-level entities evolve is uneven and marked by dead ends, overlapping categories, and alternative pathways.

• • •

Terms used to describe social animals are ambiguous and conflicting. Inconsistent uses of "eusociality," "ultrasociality," and "superorganism" present a problem in both evolutionary biology and the emerging field of evolutionary social theory. But if we focus on the strikingly similar group-level characteristics of agricultural ants, humans, and termites, it is apparent that these three organisms are socially, ecologically, and economically similar and require a common characterization. Social animals are usually called *eusocial* or *ultrasocial* but the use of these terms varies considerably, even by the same authors. Donald Campbell sometimes classifies ants, humans, and termites as ultrasocial but other times refers to ultrasociality as large-scale cooperation among unrelated individuals, thus excluding ants and termites.[7,8] Richerson and Boyd[9] use the term ultrasocial to describe humans after agriculture, but do not include social insects in their definition. Turchin[10] also defines ultrasociality as large-scale cooperation among unrelated human individuals and focuses on cooperation in warfare as a driving force in the evolution of large groups.

Adding to the inconsistency in defining social complexity are the many different uses of the word "eusociality." Eusociality applies to cooperative groups but usually includes the presence of a sharp division between sterile and reproductive castes. However, E. O. Wilson defines eusocial groups as those composed of several generations, and containing individuals performing altruistic acts associated with a division of labor.[11] By this definition eusociality encompasses such diverse social groups as human hunter-gatherers, human industrial civilizations, ants, termites, African wild dogs, naked mole rats, thrips, and other social animals. But the term eusociality, so defined, misses the sharp break in social evolution that came with managed food production. Recognizing the similarities among large-scale, food-producing, highly social species facilitates understanding of the origins and drivers of the evolution of social complexity. Campbell's 1982 definition of ultrasociality recognizes the importance of complex division of labor and very large permanent settlements with elaborate material infrastructures:

> Ultrasociality refers to the most social of animal organizations, with full time division of labor, specialists who gather no food but are fed by others, effective sharing of information about sources of food and danger, self-sacrificial effort in collective defense. This level has been achieved by ants, termites and humans in several scattered archaic city-states.[12]

Following Campbell, *the term ultrasociality will refer here to large-scale human, ant, and termite societies that actively manage food production.* This calls attention to the economic drivers of ultrasociality once agriculture began to take hold – the competitive advantage of economies of scale, an elaborate division of labor, and extremely large colony size. The term eusociality will refer to small-scale societies with cooperative raising of young, food sharing, and a simple division of labor. These characteristics imply a lack of large-scale management of food production in eusocial groups.

• • •

Leaf-cutter ants, and fungus-growing termites (ultrasocial archetypes) each began tens of millions of years ago as eusocial species. They each had within-group cooperation, simple division of labor, and cooperative raising of young. Human hunter-gatherers had complex social relationships including nonkin-based cooperation. But these early eusocial forms did not dominate ecosystems and their community populations were in the dozens or hundreds, not hundreds of thousands. Other animal societies have ambiguous intermediate and derivative social characteristics that may not fit neatly into the eusocial or ultrasocial group. Are bees ultrasocial or eusocial? They do not have true agriculture (they do not actively manage the production of their plant food sources), but they are able to use a wide variety of pollen sources to manufacture the food they live on. Because of this they have relatively large colonies and a simple division of labor. But their colony size and occupational complexity do not match that of leaf-cutter ants, fungus-growing termites, or post-agricultural humans.

By the definition of ultrasociality used here, fungus-growing ants, fungus-growing termites, and complex human societies with agriculture would be ultrasocial but not eusocial. Human hunter-gatherer bands are not ultrasocial since they lack agriculture, a complex division of labor, and large-scale permanent settlements. Like preagricultural ants and termites, humans were a minor player on planet earth until they began to control the process of producing their own food. Human populations ranged between 2 million and tens of thousands until the population exploded to 200 million within a few thousand years after agriculture began. Agriculture expanded the division of labor, increased the economic interdependence between people, and required the planning and management of the complex requirements of food production.

The division of labor in humans is not phenotypic (morphological) as in ants and termites. But occupational differentiation in humans is made possible to some extent by genotype-phenotype plasticity. Human brain plasticity allows for a remarkable degree of differentiation in terms of the ability of individuals to adapt to different cultures and behavioral patterns.[13,14] Occupational differences in humans are not genetically determined, but brain development plasticity gives humans the flexibility to adapt to a variety of occupations. With agriculture, the extent of the detailed division of labor became so great that individuals were locked into very narrow roles in society. This created an interdependence that molded the group into an interlocking economic unit, but it also promoted a loss of individual autonomy and flexibility. The key point is that human and insect societies that manage large-scale food production are fundamentally different from the small-scale foraging societies from which they evolved.

A word frequently used to describe complex societies is "superorganism," implying that these societies function as if they were a single organism. The Merriam-Webster dictionary defines a superorganism as "an organized society (as of a social insect) that functions as an organic whole." The word superorganism was coined by the ant biologist William Morton Wheeler in 1911 in an essay entitled "The Ant Colony as an Organism." When Wheeler was awarded an honorary Ph.D. from Harvard University he was congratulated for showing that insects, "like human beings, can create civilizations without the use of reason."[15] More recently Hölldobler and Wilson[16] use the term superorganism to describe the "beauty, elegance, and strangeness" of ant and termite societies.

• • •

All existing species of agricultural (fungus-growing) ants and termites apparently arose from a single common ancestor for each line.[17,18] Old World termite agriculture arose between 24 and 34 million years ago, and New World ant agriculture appeared about 50 million years ago. Aanen and Boomsma write of the agricultural transition in fungus-growing ants and termites: "No secondary reversals to the ancestral life style are known in either group, which suggests that the transitions to farming were as drastically innovative and irreversible as when humans made this step about 10,000 years ago."[19] These two independently evolved insect agricultural systems and human agricultural systems are examples of *mutualistic symbiosis*, that is, reciprocally beneficial relationships between genetically distant species. Ants and termites have practiced agriculture for tens of millions of years and have evolved a much more stable system based on symbiosis between one species of ant or termite and one species of fungus.

Fungus-growing termites evolved in the Cretaceous period (from about 120–166 million years ago). They existed for at least 50 million years without dominating ecosystems. They are uncommon in the early fossil record, representing about 1 percent of arthropods.[20] Recent discoveries in fossilized amber from Myanmar indicate that these early termites (*Krishnatermes yoddha)* were eusocial with three castes, queens, workers, and soldiers. Engel et al. ask: "If eusociality indeed imparts such adaptive superiority, why did it take 50 million years to become ecologically dominant?"[21] Termites apparently (the record is sparse) became ecologically dominant only after the adoption of agriculture some 30 million years ago. Agricultural termites today not only dominate ecosystems,[22,23] they have an elaborate division of labor and technologically impressive architecture and city-states.

The termites considered to be the most advanced belong to the fungus-growing subfamily *Macrotermitinae* in Tropical Africa and Southeast Asia. They construct elaborate mounds that can reach several meters above the ground and extend just as far underground. Hölldobler and Wilson describe a termite mound:[24]

> They construct tremendous nests that have been called castles of clay. The excrement of these insects is built into fungus combs,

Figure 2.1 A termite city in Tanzania

which occupy special gardens in the center of the nests. The combs resemble sponges, with numerous convoluted ridges and tunnels. The basidiomycete fungus sprouts round white spherules out from the substratum, but these are not especially favored as food bodies. Instead, the termites consume everything in the comb: substratum, mycelia, spherules, and all. In a special royal chamber built from cementlike material reside, well protected, the gigantic queen and her "king" surrounded by different stages of workers and soldiers ... In contrast to ant societies and those of other social hymenopterans (such as bees and wasps) that are female societies (males live only to inseminate the reproductive females and then die), termite societies consist of females and males.

A recently discovered complex of termite mounds in northeast Brazil covers 230,000 square kilometers, an area about the size of Great Britain.[25] Some of the mounds are thought to be 4,000 years old.

Macrotermitinae developed agriculture some 30 million years ago in East Africa. They dominate local ecosystems and it is estimated that more than 90 percent of dry wood in East African and Asian Savannahs are reprocessed by these termites.[26] Termite queens have the longest lifespan of any insect, sometimes living fifty years. They construct mounds as high as 9 meters (29 feet) consisting of carefully engineered tunnels, pinnacles, chimneys, and chambers.

The first known ants are found in amber deposits from the Cretaceous some 100 million years ago. Cretaceous ants in the genus *Gerontoformica* exhibit simple caste division and are considered to be eusocial.[27] They did not dominate local ecosystems. Barden and Grimaldi write: "Ants are rare in the cretaceous, constituting less than 1% of all individual insects from various deposits."[28] Like termites, ants existed as eusocial organisms for at least 50 million years before they became dominant in the mid-Eocene, when they comprised between 5% and 12% of the individual insect population.

Ant species vary greatly in terms of social complexity and colony size. According to Barden and Grimaldi:[29]

> Social hierarchy is plastic in some ants with small colonies (generally <100 individuals), such as Harpegnathos, where workers retain the ability to reproduce and are morphologically very similar to founding queens (Peeters et al. 2000). The characteristics of these ants contrast with highly social taxa living in huge colonies (>100,000 individuals), such as *Atta* leaf-cutter ants and *Eciton* army ants, in which dimorphism between reproductives and workers is profound.

Attine, or leaf-cutter ants, found in the tropical and subtropical parts of the Americas, are one of the most advanced kinds of ants in terms of social complexity. Nest size can reach 26–67 square meters with tunnels that connect to a harvesting area of more than 1 hectare.[30] "Lower" attine ants are agricultural ants that cultivate a variety of fungus types. The more recently evolved "higher" attine ants grow only one species of fungus.[31,32] As an evolutionary strategy monoculture is a more stable kind of agriculture than raising a variety of crops. It is a kind of mutualism and it is easier to maintain an evolutionary stable state with only two players.[33]

Leaf-cutter ants intensively monitor the fungus gardens by (1) hatching a variety of microbes for disease suppression; (2) maintaining reservoirs of genetically variable cultivars; (3) sharing domesticated fungal cultivars with distantly related ant colonies; (4) producing antibodies to protect the fungus from bacteria; and (5) maintaining a sophisticated waste management system accounting for about 10 percent of the work done by an attine ant colony.[34]

Figure 2.2 Ants tending their aphid livestock

A recent study by Mueller et al.[35] found that leaf-cutter ants are unique in that they use freshly cut leaves to grow their fungi. This ability to use living leaves was a "quantum leap" in evolution because it opened up a new ecosystem for exploitation. According to one of the study's coauthors, Scott Solomon, "Once you can use fresh leaves, it gives you access to so much more food. If you can grow and raise your own food on any leaf that's growing out there, then the sky's the limit."[36] Furthermore, the ability of the leaf-cutter's fungus to digest fresh leaves seems to be due to the way the fungus crop is managed rather than to some unique property of the fungus. Leaf-cutter ants exhibit a more complex division of labor than that found in other fungus-growing ants. These economic drivers allow leaf-cutter colonies to grow to millions of individuals.

Flannery[37] makes a case that ants evolved from hunter-gatherer ancestors in a way similar to humans:

> The progress of ants from this relatively primitive state to the complexity of the most finely tuned superorganisms leaves no doubt that the progress of human evolution has largely

followed a path taken by the ants tens of millions of years earlier. Beginning as simple hunter-gatherers, some ants have learned to herd and milk bugs, just as we milk cattle and sheep. There are ants that take slaves, ants that lay their eggs in the nests of foreign ants (much like cuckoos do among birds), leaving the upbringing of their young to others, and there are even ants that have discovered agriculture. These agricultural ants represent the highest level of ant civilization, yet it is not plants that they cultivate, but mushrooms.

Humans, ants and termites all made the transition from hunting and gathering to agriculture, a major evolutionary transition that radically changed the evolutionary trajectory of those organisms.[38] The adoption of agriculture led each of these ultrasocial animals to dominate the earth's ecosystems. With ultrasociality also came a degree of subjugation of individuals to meet the requirements of food production, not seen in other evolutionary lines. Domination of ecosystems and the subjugation of individuals for the benefit of the group superorganism are key characteristics of ultrasocial species.

Compared to social insects, our transition to ultrasociality is in its infancy, but when we look at the results of the ant, termite, and human transitions, the similarities are too striking to ignore. The human transition to ultrasociality explains some basic puzzles of human social evolution:

- Why did *Homo sapiens* exist for 300,000 years while the total human world population never exceeded 1 million, then suddenly jump to 200 million within a few thousand years after the adoption of agriculture?
- Why, for 300,000 years, did humans live in small egalitarian bands having only a few "occupations" with most people in these societies able to do any task (except for those based on age and gender), then suddenly switch to societies having hundreds of largely hereditary, hierarchical, caste-based specialized occupations?
- Why did human groups live sustainably for 300,000 years within the confines of local ecosystems then suddenly become characterized by the domination and rapacious exploitation of nature?

• • •

How did ultrasociality evolve? Contemporary theoretical concepts in evolutionary biology – including group selection, epigenetics, and social evolution – can help to understand the transition to ultrasociality. Twentieth-century biology was dominated by a gene-centric view of evolution and natural selection. Today, biologists and social scientists are applying the basic principles of Darwinian evolution – selection, variation, and inheritance – at multiple levels. Concepts of group selection can be successfully applied to understand how and why differentiated social structure and social complexity evolved. The recognition that Darwinian natural selection need not be gene based opens the door for a rigorous analysis of the common factors in the transformative evolution of humans and social insects that came with agriculture.

Twentieth-century biology was dominated by a gene-centric view of evolution and natural selection. This view was developed by evolutionary biologists in the 1930s and 1940s, and popularized by Richard Dawkins in *The Selfish Gene*.[39] The Modern Synthesis in evolutionary thought took the position that the only inherited variations are genetic.[40] There were several reasons why the gene-centric view came to be dominant. First, the selfish gene fits nicely within the dominant paradigm of competition and selfish individualism. It is the biological equivalent of the concept of "economic man," the rugged individual independent of human society, that still dominates political economy. Secondly, it was a reaction to some bad twentieth-century science promoting the inheritance of acquired characteristics – most notably the work of the Stalinist biologist T. D. Lysenko in the former Soviet Union. Thirdly, the mathematical formulation of the selfish gene model, and its derivative kin selection (inclusive fitness), was so precise and elegant that it blinded researchers to empirical evidence contradicting it.[41] The upshot was that environmental and social influences were usually downplayed in discussions about the mechanisms of inheritance.

Natural selection above the level of the individual was a quite acceptable idea to Darwin, Wallace, and Spencer, all of whom believed in the differential survival of groups. In *The Descent of Man* Darwin wrote:[42]

> It must not be forgotten that although a high standard of morality gives but a slight or no advantage to each individual man and his children over other men of the same tribe, yet that an increase in the number of well-endowed men and advancement in the standard of morality will certainly give an immense

advantage to one tribe over another. There can be no doubt that a tribe including many members who, from possessing in a high degree the spirit of patriotism, fidelity, obedience, courage, and sympathy, were always ready to aid one another, and to sacrifice themselves for the common good, would be victorious over most other tribes; and this would be natural selection. At all times throughout the world tribes have supplanted other tribes; and as morality is one important element in their success, the standard of morality and the number of well-endowed men will thus everywhere tend to rise and increase.

Group selection has had a hostile reception partly due to V. C. Wynne-Edwards' book *Animal Dispersion in Relation to Social Behavior*, which received such strong criticism from biologists that theories of group selection were discredited for several decades.[43] Wynne-Edwards argued that animal populations evolve to avoid overexploiting resources "for the good of the group." His version of group selection asserted that altruism usually trumps selfish behavior and opened the door for criticisms based on more sophisticated models of natural selection. One was *kin selection*, based on the work of William Hamilton[44] showing how apparent altruism is genetically based because altruists are protecting their own genes by helping close relatives survive (*inclusive fitness*). An extension of this idea was *reciprocal altruism*, the view that apparent altruism was based on the expectation that favors would be returned.[45] In the 1960s and 1970s the new field of sociobiology initially opposed the idea of group selection, arguing that social behavior is entirely the result of gene-level mechanisms.[46,47] Wilson[48] writes of his initial enthusiastic acceptance of inclusive fitness theory:

> At first I found the theory of inclusive fitness, winnowed down to a few cases of kin selection that might be studied in nature, enchanting. In 1965, a year after Hamilton's article, I defended the theory at a meeting of the Royal Entomological Society of London. Hamilton himself was at my side that evening.

By the year 2000 inclusive fitness theory had become so entrenched that other explanations, even those based on careful experimental studies, were dismissed. But eventually scientific opinion became more critical of the selfish gene–based explanation of the evolution of pro-social behavior.[49] E. O. Wilson writes:[50]

Looking back today, it is apparent that by the 1990s two seismic flaws had already appeared and begun to widen. Extensions of the theory itself were growing increasingly abstract, hence remote from the empirical work that continued to flourish elsewhere in sociobiology. At the same time the empirical research devoted to the theory remained limited to a small number of measurable phenomena. Writings on the theory mostly in the social insects were repetitive. They offered more and more about proportionately fewer topics. The grand patterns of ecology, phylogeny, division of labor, neurobiology, communication, and social physiology remained virtually untouched by the asseverations of the inclusive theorists.

While the critics of Wynne-Edwards's version of group selection were correct in asserting the importance of within-group competition, their criticisms do not apply to later, more sophisticated, concepts of group selection. E. O. Wilson is now an enthusiastic proponent of group selection.[51]

Inclusive Fitness and Genetic Relatedness in Ants and Termites

Close genetic relatedness in social insect colonies is the usual explanation for altruism and self-sacrifice for the good of the group in these societies. Ants are "haploid/diploid," referring to the number of copies of chromosomes in the genome of an organism. Diploid organisms have two copies of each chromosome and haploid organisms have only one copy. Ants are haploid/diploid with males having only one set of chromosomes and females two, so that siblings with the same father and mother are 75 percent related. Ants share all their father's chromosomes and half of their mother's. By helping their sisters, ants are insuring the survival of 75 percent of their genetic material. This is called inclusive fitness. But further examination shows that this explanation is problematic. Leaf-cutter ant queens mate with multiple males, so their offspring are less related than human siblings with the same parents. Boomsma et al. (1999) used DNA analysis to look at the relatedness of leaf-cutter ants. They found that leaf-cutter ants have a relatedness value of .33, lower than the .5 for siblings with the same parents, and much lower than the .75 ratio assumed in the inclusive fitness haploid/diploid models. Furthermore, unlike ants and like humans, termites are diploid. Termite workers with the same parents are no more related to each other than are human siblings.

J. Boomsma, E. Fjerdingstad, J. Frydenberg, Multiple paternity, relatedness and genetic diversity in *Acromyrmex* leaf-cutter ants. *Proceedings of the Royal Society, B*, (1999) 266, 249–254.

Evidence for group selection comes from artificial selection experiments and empirical analysis of animals, plants, communities, and ecosystems.[52] Group selection experiments have been done on beetles (various cases), domestic rats (group selection through male cooperation in mating), plants (leaf area), and chickens (interaction between egg production and aggression). Biologist Michael Wade's experiments with red flour beetles (*Tribolium castaneum*) found significant evidence for group selection including altered rates of cannibalism related to group composition.[53] Experimenters have found differences in egg production between isolated chickens and those in groups. Group selection mediates the trade-off between productivity and aggression, which is important if chickens are to be housed in multiple groups. Groups composed of the most productive individual chickens had lower rates of egg laying compared to groups that were chosen for their group productivity. Selection of the most productive groups realized a 160 percent increase in group yield or group–average egg production versus unselected controls, and likewise less aggression. The economic value of this result was not only more egg production but also reduced hen mortality and less need for beak trimming.[54] Group selection can also occur among communities through interactions between individuals or populations of multiple species.[55,56] Other remarkable cases of nonkin altruistic behavior have been documented, for example, the recent discovery of cooperative brood raising by two different species of spiders.[57]

Darwin saw that the essence of evolution is variation, inheritance, and selection. Today scholars are applying Darwinian natural selection on multiple levels. In their book *Evolution in Four Dimensions*, Jablonka and Lamb[58] summarize new findings and theories in evolutionary biology, expanding the role of natural selection in evolution. They describe four dimensions of variation and selection in evolution – genetic, epigenetic, behavioral, and symbolic.

- *Genetic evolution* is central to our understanding of how the natural world is modified through time. Genes are the fundamental units of information transfer in living organisms. Evolutionary changes are the result of changes in gene frequencies in response to variations in environmental conditions. The molecular basis of genetics is DNA and its replication, but this is not the only source of material for natural selection.

- *Epigenetic evolution* encompasses non-DNA cellular transmission of traits. The idea is that development can influence the transmission of genetic information. Environmental factors such as temperature can switch genes on and off and affect how cells read genes. Inheritance is still based on genes but how genes are expressed in phenotypes – the physical characteristics of an organism – is determined not only by changes in the DNA sequence but also by non-DNA influences. An example of this non-DNA influence is the effect of ambient temperature on the sex ratio of crocodile hatchlings. Temperatures below 31.7° C produce more females and temperatures higher than that produce more males. Another example is the effect of zebra finch mother bird songs on the size and behavior of the hatchlings.[59] Mothers sing a specific kind of song to embryos (in the egg) when ambient temperatures exceed 26°C and this song alters future nestlings' begging behavior and growth, and adults' reproductive success and temperature preferences. The advantage of this in terms of natural selection is that when they leave the nest they seek microhabitats that best suit their phenotype. Through their songs mothers signal information about ambient environmental conditions and this is reflected in the physical characteristics of offspring. Variation in genetic expression is an evolved characteristic of evolutionary systems. Epigenetic processes play an important role in ultrasocial species, for example in the regulation of phenotypic variation in social insect colonies.[60,61,62] Epigenetics may be the enabler of the complex division of labor in social insect societies.
- *Social learning and behavioral inheritance* is a third kind of evolution described by Jablonka and Lamb. This sort of evolution is most familiar to social scientists, although many would not use the term "evolution" to describe it. Jablonka and Lamb[63] write:

> We see culture as *a system of socially transmitted patterns of behavior, preferences, and products of animal activities that characterize a group of social animals.* The transmitted behaviors can be skills, practices, habits, beliefs and so on . . . cultural evolution can be defined as *change, through time, in the nature and frequency of socially transmitted preferences, patterns, or products of behavior in a population.*

Economists have made significant contributions to understanding this kind of social evolution. An important figure in early study of social evolution was Thorstein Veblen, who at the turn of the twentieth century wrote eloquently about the transmission of social norms. Recently, economist Geoffrey Hodgson and his colleagues have applied "generalized Darwinism" to the study of social evolution.[64,65] The basic idea is that drivers of genetic natural selection – variation, inheritance, and selection of favorable traits – also drive social evolution. Hodgson's conception of social evolution is that *replicators* (behaviors such as repeated habits and routines) exist above the level of genes and are mediated by *interactors* in a kind of gene-culture coevolution.[66,67,68] Hodgson's replicator-interactor model is a model of epigenetics for social behavior.[69] Such behavior is not restricted to humans. Social learning in a variety of nonhuman animals is now a legitimate field of study and has been extensively documented.[70,71]

- *Symbolic thought* is the fourth dimension of evolution that Jablonka and Lamb[72] consider to be distinctly human: "Rationality, linguistic ability, artistic ability, and religiosity are all facets of symbolic thought and communication." Symbolic systems are networks of mental relationships that influence human behavior. It may be that the capacity for abstract thought in *Homo sapiens* is the result of our degree of sociality. A remarkable finding from neuroscience is that most of the neurons in the human brain develop after birth. The way they are configured depends in part on how a child is socialized. There is evidence that humans have "social brains" that develop after birth to encode one's culture. Brain plasticity is another way that variability is introduced into evolutionary mix. The field of neuroscience and human brain is one of intense and revolutionary research and new findings will certainly change our perspective on "human nature."

The more researchers learn about the intricate mechanisms of natural selection the more blurred the divisions between genetics, epigenetics, and social learning become. It would be premature to say that the expansion of evolutionary theory has won the day and that non–gene-based evolution is widely accepted by biologists. But recent advances in evolutionary theory and growing empirical evidence have opened the door for nongenetic factors to have a major role in natural selection.

• • •

E. O. Wilson identified the important questions about the evolution of complex social life:[73]

> I will propose that scientific advances, especially those made during the last two decades, are now sufficient for us to address in a coherent manner the questions of where we came from and what we are. To do so, however, we need answers to two even more fundamental questions the query has raised. The first is why advanced social life exists at all, and has occurred rarely in the history of life. The second is the identity of the driving forces that brought it into existence.

Attempts to answer these questions have fallen short of the mark. Most explanations of social complexity fail to address the unprecedented and abrupt change that happened to human societies and the human relationship with the natural world that came with agriculture. This abrupt and radical change in human social evolution requires a group-level explanation as to the advantages of agriculture. Most discussions of human social evolution focus on individual characteristics, ignoring the question of how and why differentiated social structure and social complexity evolved with the adoption of agriculture. This change in social organization is not primarily an individual-level phenomenon but a product of the fundamental change in the material basis of the human economy. For humans and other ultrasocial animals, the evolution of complexity was propelled by their ability to produce surplus food. Basic economic laws drove the evolution of ultrasociality in ants, humans, and termites.

Over the past several decades, new theories of natural selection beyond the level of the gene have improved our understanding of ultrasociality. D. S. Wilson and Eliot Sober argue for the importance of group selection in understanding how ultrasocial superorganisms evolve.[74] They point out that most modern theorists have ignored all non-gene level explanations of adaptations. Further, they assert that groups are subject to natural selection as they possess the properties of variation, inheritance, and selection that drive evolution by natural selection. Despite the frequently visceral resistance to group selection,[75,76] there is a growing interest in applying natural selection more broadly to include human social evolution. Social scientists and biologists have acknowledged the importance of the coevolution of genes and culture.[77,78] The group selection approach has been fruitfully applied to the evolution of cooperation,[79] the evolution of state societies,[80] and the role of warfare in early agricultural societies.[81,82] Campbell provides guidance as to how group selection works in human societies:[83]

> Non-linear, multiple-social-parent transmission, with a majority amplifying effect, pushes face-to-face groups to internal unanimity in the absence of selection. This provides the raw material of within group homogeneity and group-to-group heterogeneity prerequisite for group selection. Such selection would come through differential group success, differential growth, conquest with cultural imposition, voluntary attraction of converts, imitation, etc.

• • •

A generalized form of Darwinism – multilevel selection theory or MLS – argues that the principles of Darwinian evolution operate at different levels. It postulates that a trait such as altruism may decrease individual fitness but enhance the competitiveness of groups that practice it. Groups having many altruists have a competitive advantage over groups that have few, and altruistic individuals in the former get reproduced.[84] Individuals in the group benefit because if the group does not survive, neither will the individuals in that group. In some versions of MLS natural selection still operates at the individual level, but is also influenced by the characteristics of the group: "traits that can be easily measured in individuals but require group selection to evolve because they are locally disadvantageous."[85] This is fully consistent with traditional gene–based natural selection.

Formulations of MLS become more complicated when selection at the group level is limited not to a single trait but to a cluster of characteristics present in a group. According to Okasha:[86] "Emergent characters are often complex, adaptive features of collectives [groups of individuals taken together], which it is hard to imagine evolving except by selection at the collective level." Okasha accepts that natural selection can operate on clusters of characteristics but argues that it applies only to the later stages of an evolutionary transition (after the collective units have formed and are replicating). In the early transitional stages, cooperation must spread among the members of the group so that they will eventually give up their individuality and form discrete collectives.

MLS theory limits the notion of "fitness" to successful collectives producing more offspring collectives. Regarding the transition to ultrasociality it does not fully capture the importance of food production for the expansion of a group. For ant, human, and termite societies that develop large-scale agriculture, fitness is not simply that more new colonies form by outcompeting others, it is that any single colony can grow to an enormous size by reorganizing the production structure of the group. MLS theory focuses on the advantages to an individual of being in a cooperative group. Selfish individuals outcompete altruistic individuals within a group, but altruistic groups outcompete selfish groups. E. O. Wilson points to the limits of MLS theory in explaining the process through which ant colonies are selected:

> Group selection occurs, in the sense that success or failure of the colony depends upon how well the collectivity of the queen and her robotic offspring does in competition with solitary individuals and other colonies. Group selection is a useful idea in identifying precisely the units of selection when queens (and their colonies about them) are competing with other queens. But multilevel selection, in which colonial evolution is regarded as the interests of the individual worker pitted against the interests of its colony, may no longer be a useful concept on which to build models of genetic evolution in social insects.[87]

MLS theory does not explain how the group becomes the unit of selection regardless of the effect on the fitness of individuals within the group. Nor does it explain how "individually" passes from the individual members of the group to the group itself. Researchers are developing models that explain the life histories of ant colonies, which, like ordinary organisms, have their own birth, growth, and death stages at the superorganism level.[88]

• • •

E. O. Wilson describes how ants became ultrasocial through a series of steps: (1) formation of groups; (2) acquisition of preadaptations that form the ingredients that reinforce eusociality; (3) the appearance of mutations that reinforce group persistence; (4) emergent group traits that are reinforced through natural selection; and (5) group selection that drives the evolution of superorganisms. The point in the evolution of insect colonies where they move to the level of a superorganism "comes very early … in particular when an anatomically distinct worker caste first appears, hence when a colony can most meaningfully be called a superorganism."[89] The key ingredient for becoming a social insect superorganism is an anatomically distinct worker class. The worker class is reinforced in a positive feedback process by the increased efficiency in producing food arising from the division of labor.[90,91]

Entomologist Barbara Thorne described a similar collection of preadaptations leading to social complexity for termites: "A suite of ecological and life-history traits of termites and their ancestors may have predisposed them toward eusocial evolution. These characteristics include familial associations in cloistered, food-rich habitats; slow development; overlap of generations; monogamy; iteroparity; high-risk dispersal for individuals; opportunities for nest inheritance by offspring remaining in their natal nest; and advantages of group defense."[92]

How Does "Individuality" Pass from the Members of the Group to the Group Itself?

Group fitness is usually viewed as the average of lower-level individual fitness. Why would individuals cooperate if it made them, on the average, worse off? But as the transition to ultrasociality progresses, group fitness becomes decoupled from the fitness of individuals in the group. Group level mechanisms come into play to enforce the acquiescence of individuals to their roles supporting the new group entity. These mechanisms range from the policing of reproduction in ant colonies to the caste system in human societies.

As Michod and Nedelcu (2003) discuss, a basic problem in explaining major evolutionary transitions is to understand how a group of individuals becomes organized into a new higher-order entity with heritable fitness characteristics.

> During an evolutionary transition, for example, from single cells to multicellular organisms, the new higher-level evolutionary unit (multicellular organism) gains its emergent properties by virtue of the interactions among lower-level units (cells). We see the formation of cooperative interactions among lower-level units as a necessary step in evolutionary transitions; only cooperation transfers fitness from lower levels (costs to group members) to

higher levels (benefits to the group). As cooperation creates new levels of fitness, it creates the opportunity for conflict between levels as deleterious mutants arise and spread within the group. Fundamental to the emergence of a new higher-level unit is the mediation of conflict among lower-level units in favor of the higher-level unit. The acquisition of heritable variation in fitness at the new level, via conflict mediation, requires the reorganization of the basic components of fitness (survival and reproduction) and life-properties (such as immortality and totipotency) as well as the co-option of lower-level processes for new functions at the higher level. The way in which the conflicts associated with the transition in individuality have been mediated, and fitness and general life-traits have been re-organized, can influence the potential for further evolution (i.e., evolvability) of the newly emerged evolutionary individual.

Richard Michod and Aurora. Nedelcu, on the reorganization of fitness during evolutionary transitions in individuality. *Integrated Computational Biology*, 43, (2003), 64–73.

• • •

The usual explanations for human ultrasociality include language, the campfire, abstract thought, and cooperation with nonkin. But all these human characteristics existed for hundreds of thousands of years before the Holocene. They all fail to answer the basic question: What changed 10,000 years ago? As with any evolutionary change there must have been fundamental conditions – the evolutionary material to work with – that made possible a transition from one state to another. Agriculture arose several times in different places around the world at about the same time, so some fundamental drivers, in combination with some universal human qualities, must have been at work. Some sort of "evolvability"[93] must have been present in all preagriculture human populations. Furthermore, the evolution of similar complex societies among those who adopted agriculture led to strikingly similar cultural configurations. In broad outline, the same complex cultural patterns and institutions evolved independently in the Indus Valley, the Far East, and the Middle East. This suggests that some common underlying forces drove the evolution of complex human societies – the transformation of hunter-gatherers into agriculturalists – that transcended human intentionality and the specific characteristics of preagricultural cultures. The social institutions that arose with complex agriculture were broadly identical. There must exist some common factors that drove the evolution of ant, termite, and human agriculture.

The population size of all living organisms is limited by the available food supply. This makes agriculture a uniquely powerful evolutionary force. Once a group acquires the ability to produce its own food it is no longer dependent upon direct flows of food from nature. It can augment those flows by actively redirecting solar energy from wild plants to crop production and actively managing the inputs needed to produce the food it consumes. This sets in motion an efficiency-in-production arms race among competing agricultural groups. Economic drivers kick in and successful agricultural groups take advantage of their greater complexity, greater division of labor, and larger size, all of which drive the expansion of the new economic system.

• • •

With the adoption of agriculture, evolutionary forces reorganized the human traits of cooperation and altruism to create a society with striking resemblances to those of advanced eusocial insects. This change made civilization possible, but it also altered human relationships in profound ways. Social and individual life in small-scale egalitarian social groups was radically changed with the move to large-scale highly stratified agricultural theocracies where work was harder, more regimented and more repetitious, and requiring less of the creative and executive capabilities of the human brain. Individual freedom (self-actualization) was more limited, and the orientation of the individual to the nonhuman world was reduced to exploitation for economic gain. During the Upper Pleistocene, humans became compassionate and empathetic, employed a simple division of labor, and lived and cooperated with nonkin. But the ability to cooperate and share with unrelated individuals was co-opted with agriculture and became a kind of mechanistic coordination. The requirements of surplus production demanded subjugation to authority with limited room for individual agency compared to hunter-gatherer social organization. In the human transition to agriculture, the ability to cooperate that arose before agriculture paved the way for a radically different kind of cooperation, more properly called coordination, that was harnessed to facilitate the complex organization of food production. This involved the "co-option of lower-level processes for new functions at the higher level."[94]

The natural selection of the most economically efficient food-producing groups drove the evolution of ultrasociality. Mueller et al.[95] list the defining features of agriculture in humans and social insects: (1) habitual planting; (2) cultivation; (3) harvesting; and (4) nutritional dependency on the crop (obligate in ants and termites and effectively obligate in humans). The production of crops is a physical process characterized by economic drivers giving a common structure and dynamic to all ultrasocial agricultural societies. Selection pressures favored groups with the ability to take advantage of these economic efficiencies. As the group became a cohesive whole organized around surplus food production, economic life was restructured in similar ways in very dissimilar species.

● ● ●

Human hunter-gatherers lived off the flows of nature – from the solar energy directly captured by living plants and indirectly present in the flow of animals feeding on those plants. They had limited control over these subsistence flows. If hunter-gatherers, like any large carnivores, took too many animals or harvested too many wild plants, immediate shortages would have resulted, and this negative feedback tended to keep human populations in ecological balance. Human hunter-gatherer culture evolved over a period of several million years. By comparison, the transition to agriculture was a sudden, sharp, and decisive break. It created a new dynamic with profound consequences. This is not to deny that human sociality as it emerged in early hunter-gatherer cultures was also a major evolutionary transition. The gradual evolution of human culture, language, cognitive ability, and capacity for abstract thought in Africa paved the way for ultrasociality. But with the shift to ultrasociality, economic activity changed fundamentally from production for livelihood to production for surplus.

With the adoption of agriculture, human society and the relationship between humans and the natural world changed dramatically. Biologists note that population explosions are common as new species move into new territories with exploitable resources. Populations rise and fall regularly, sometimes dramatically, as resources wax and wane. Ultrasocial species actively produce and expand their food supply rather than wait for nature to provide it. Agricultural societies are uniquely characterized by positive feedbacks favoring growth. The active harnessing of the inputs to food production, together with the ability to store surplus food, reconfigured early agricultural groups into an integrated unit designed for economic production. A greater division of labor increased productive efficiency, and this increased efficiency made possible more economic growth and a still greater division of labor. The new mode of production gave them a decisive evolutionary advantage over larger groups.

Members of agricultural societies became economically inter-dependent and a large proportion of the day-to-day lives of individuals was spent in specialized production activities. Individual autonomy was suppressed for the benefit of the ultrasocial agricultural group. Biologists have documented that in ultrasocial ant societies, compared to non-ultrasocial ants, individuals have less flexibility in the tasks they perform, they have a limited repertoire of tasks compared to all those present in the group, and like humans after agriculture, they apparently experience a loss of individual intelligence.[96] Although less extreme than with social insects, a loss of individual autonomy is seen in human societies after the adoption of agriculture. With the advent of large-scale agriculture, individuals were designated to more nar-rowly defined occupational roles. People were born into distinct and rigid castes that determined their life trajectories and occupations. The subjugation of human individuals is, of course, mediated by culture and, unlike insects, humans often resist this subjugation. Ant and termite classes are based on different phenotypes, while the human division into castes and occupational classes is based on culture, customs, and social institutions. In human agricultural societies rigid social hierarchies were firmly established, and there was a general decline in the well-being of the average person.[97,98,99,100]

The loss of autonomy after agriculture raises the question of individual choice in human affairs. Why would people accept the significant costs of poorer nutrition, shorter life spans, and the diseases that came with sedentary existence and dense settlements? The adop-tion of agriculture was not a choice, but rather a gradual, cumulative process, perhaps imperceptible within the lifetime of a single individ-ual. There were likely marginal payoffs that propelled society toward further embracing agriculture. Yet, certainly, humans could not have anticipated where agriculture would lead them – to hierarchical dom-ination by an elite class, regimentation of productive life, ecological degradation, patriarchy, slavery, and poor health. Once in place, the growth in population facilitated by agriculture can only be supported by intensifying food production. Humans did not consciously choose agriculture. This again underscores the difficulty in understanding transitions themselves rather than just comparing their before and after characteristics.

The question of whether human cultural change is the result of conscious choice or the blind unfolding of natural laws is really two questions. The first is whether human agents act purposefully in pursuing chosen ends. The answer to this must certainly be "yes." But the more interesting question is whether or not the cumulative outcome of individually chosen activities can be explained as the result of human design. For some of the most important cultural transitions in human history (agriculture, civilization, and market capitalism), the answer is no. Choices small in scale and time – even choices that are perfectly rational from the point of view of an individual acting at a point in time – can lead inexorably to outcomes that are not only unanticipated but also actually detrimental to the individual. The economist Alfred Kahn[101] calls this "the tyranny of small decisions." The transition to agriculture took place through a series of incremental decisions made by innumerable individuals over thousands of years.

Two million years of evolution made the genus *Homo* cooperative, caring, intelligent, introspective, and creative. These human characteristics were co-opted by an odd and rare confluence of economics and higher-level evolutionary forces, creating an ultrasocial system characterized by the exploitation of nature and individuals comprising the system. This system should be understood as a unified whole molded by the impersonal forces of group selection.

Production for livelihood was replaced by the imperative of surplus production and expansion. The evolutionary imperative to survive and reproduce passed from the individual to the supergroup. Clearly this ultrasocial transition has not been an unqualified success when evaluated in the context of individual well-being or the biophysical impact of humans on planet earth. The good news is that for almost all our existence as a species, we lived in societies that were egalitarian and environmentally sustainable.

3 OUR HUNTER-GATHERER HERITAGE AND THE EVOLUTION OF HUMAN NATURE

Anatomically modern humans, *Homo sapiens*, have inhabited the earth for 300 millennia.[1,2] For almost all of this time all people lived as hunter-gatherers in communities that were egalitarian and environmentally sustainable. Upper Pleistocene hunter-gatherers had complex social lives, art, music, and abundant leisure time. Surely we have something to learn from hunter-gatherers in our attempts to address the greatest challenges our species face today – staggering inequality that threatens social stability, and the relentless exploitation of the natural world that is undermining the life support systems of the planet.

The dominant view of hunter-gatherers before the 1960s was embedded in Western notions of inevitable progress through human ingenuity and technological advances. In this view, civilization and the material comfort enjoyed by the world's most fortunate have resulted from a long struggle to conquer nature. Modern life is a struggle with scarcity – a battle to reconcile means and ends through science, technology, and the power of global markets. The life of the hunter-gatherer then, without modern technology and science, must have been, in the words of Thomas Hobbes, "nasty, brutish and short." As Marshall Sahlins puts it, "Having equipped the hunter with bourgeois impulses and Paleolithic tools, we judge his situation to be hopeless in advance."[3] The anthropologist Robert Braidwood summed up the pre-1960s view of hunter-gatherers: "A man who spends his whole life following animals just to kill them to eat, or moving from one berry patch to another, is really living like an animal himself."[4]

The Hobbesian view of hunter-gatherers was overturned as anthropologists doing field work among existing hunter-gatherers began to publish reports on the state of actual hunter-gatherer societies. In stark contrast to the prevailing view, they found that in spite of having simple technologies, hunter-gatherers were for the most part healthy, happy, and prosperous.[5,6,7] Hunter-gatherer societies – the !Kung of Southern Africa, the Aborigines of Australia, the Hadza of East Africa, and the Inuit of northern Canada – were found to be generally well-fed, egalitarian, socially and intellectually complex, and with an abundance of leisure time. In a classic essay Sahlins described hunter-gatherers as "the original affluent society"[8] – a view that has held up reasonably well.[9] The affluence of these societies was particularly remarkable in that the reason for their survival into modern times is their location in some of the most inhospitable parts of the planet. The lives of hunter-gatherers in late Pleistocene Europe must have been at least as affluent given the abundance of game and the variety of plant species available to them, and the absence of genocide against them that came with civilization. Agriculture did not become dominant by out-competing hunting and gathering in the sense of offering them a better life. Agriculturalists won out by out-breeding hunter-gatherers and by systematically exterminating them. In spite of this, as late as the year 1500, one-third of the habitable part of the planet was occupied exclusively by hunter-gatherers.[10]

Favorable opinions of hunter-gatherers were held by many of the earlier explorers who first encountered "primitive" cultures. Alfred Russel Wallace wrote:

> Now it is very remarkable, that among people in a very low stage of civilization, we find some approach to such a perfect social state. I have lived with communities of savages in South America and in the East, who have no laws or law courts but the public opinion of the village freely expressed. Each man scrupulously respects the rights of his fellow, and any infraction of those rights rarely or never takes place. In such a community, all are nearly equal. There are none of those wide distinctions, of education and ignorance, wealth and poverty, master and servant, which are the product of our civilization; there is none of that wide-spread division of labour, which, while it increases wealth, produces also conflicting interests; there is not that

severe competition and struggle for existence, or for wealth, which the dense population of civilized countries inevitably creates. All incitements to great crimes are thus wanting, and petty ones are repressed, partly by the influence of public opinion, but chiefly by that natural sense of justice and of his neighbour's right, which seems to be, in some degree, inherent in every race of man.[11]

After the publication of *The Original Affluent Society*, there was a predictable reaction against the positive portrait of hunter-gatherers.[12,13,14] Much of the negative characterization of hunter-gatherers lumps together preagricultural hunter-gatherers, small-scale agriculturalists, and contemporary marginalized peoples who hunt using modern weapons and engage in trade with a dominant culture.[15,16,17] Recent evidence confirms the basic insights of Lee, Marshall, and Sahlins. Hunter-gatherer societies were egalitarian,[18,19,20] generally peaceable,[21,22,23] and until the twentieth century at least, they were generally healthier than agriculturalists.[24] The myth of linear steady progress clouds our understanding of human biological and cultural evolution and distorts our understanding of our hunter-gatherer heritage.

• • •

Great confusion exists about what characterizes hunting and gathering societies.[25] For example, Kelly[26] refers to "sedentary hunter-gatherers" as practicing horticulture and having settled communities and domestic animals. Pinker, in a TED talk[27] on the human propensity to violence presents evidence of "hunter-gatherer" violence based on seven cultures: the Jivaro and two Yanomani groups; horticulturalists from the Amazon; four agricultural cultures from the New Guinea highlands; and the Murngin Aborigines from northern Australia (these examples are from Keely's 1996 book). The only group that might remotely be considered hunter-gatherers are the Murngin, but the data for them was collected in 1975, decades after they had been absorbed by Western commercial society. Agriculturalists, including simple horticulturalists and pastoralists, are not hunter-gatherers. Agriculture did not appear until about 10,000 years ago. Most of the world's remaining contemporary hunter-gatherers have been in contact with agriculturalists for centuries.

A good definition of hunter-gatherers is given by Panter-Brick et al.:[28]

Hunter-gatherers rely upon a mode of subsistence characterized by the absence of direct human control over the reproduction of exploited species, and little or no control over other aspects of population ecology such as the behavior and distribution of food resources.

A further elaboration is given by Woodburn who distinguishes between *immediate-return* and *delayed-return* hunter-gatherers. Immediate-return hunter-gatherers have the following characteristics:[29]

People obtain a direct and immediate return from their labour. They go out hunting or gathering and eat the food obtained the same day or casually over the days that follow. Food is neither elaborately processed or stored. They use relatively simple, easily acquired, replaceable tools and weapons made with real skill but not involving a great deal of labor.

Delayed-return hunter-gatherers have more complex technologies and "capital" in the form of nets, boats, traps, and other material artifacts. Producing food may take place over long time periods of months or even years. Some storage is present and wild crops are selectively tended. Neither delayed-return nor immediate-return hunter-gatherers practice agriculture or animal husbandry.

Figure 3.1 A contemporary group of San Bushmen in Namibia

Hunting and gathering societies are defined by their mode of subsistence – the economic system and social relations of production supporting the physical processes through which food is obtained. Hunter-gatherers did not actively manage (or minimally managed) the game they hunted or the plants they used. Hunter-gatherer societies varied considerably depending on the specific ecosystems they occupied and the technologies required to exploit those ecosystems. In contrast to hunter-gatherers, agricultural societies control the production of food and the entire chain of inputs necessary to produce, harvest, and distribute that food. The transition to agriculture was a slow evolutionary process taking thousands of years. As with any evolutionary process there are intermediate steps, derivatives of original patterns, and dead ends. As humans went from hunting and gathering to control of the process of producing food, there were societies that exhibited intermediate forms. For example, because of the abundance of salmon and the ability to preserve and store them, the Northwest Coast Indians were non-agriculturalists that had settled communities, inherited property rights, and the beginnings of social hierarchy. Some groups that adopted agriculture did not evolve into large state societies, as in the highlands of New Guinea. This does not mean that the differences between agriculture and hunting and gathering are unimportant or that these differences are exaggerated.

• • •

The transition from hunting and gathering to agriculture was the most profound change in the history of *Homo sapiens*. It is only with agriculture that human societies came to match the complexity of social insect societies. Yet this change is almost always ignored in discussions of the physical, psychological, and social evolution of our species, and even the transition to ultrasociality. E. O. Wilson, one of the world's most foremost authorities on the evolution of social complexity, recognizes the great change that came with agriculture but misses its importance in the evolution of human ultrasociality. Instead he attributes the origin of human social complexity to the "nest" of the campfire, arguing that campsites were the equivalent of social insect nests.[30] But the human use of fire goes back at least 500,000 years to our *Homo erectus* ancestors,[31] long before the complex division of labor and ecosystem domination of the last 10,000 years. Likewise, in otherwise excellent books about the evolution of human ultrasociality and our propensity for cooperation and altruism on a large scale, the importance of agriculture is given short shrift or is not mentioned at all.[32,33,34] Nowak and Highfield[35] recognize the importance of agriculture and the parallels between insect and human eusocial evolution but they do not pursue the idea.

In spite of the wealth of information about human biological and social evolution, there is still a lack of appreciation of the importance of the hunting and gathering way of life. Reasons for this include the following misconceptions:

- The still widespread belief that progress is a natural law and that agriculture freed us from savagery and starvation. What can civilized people learn from savages?
- Any sympathy for the hunter-gatherer lifestyle is dismissed as a fantasy for the noble savage and a longing for the garden of Eden. We can't go back so why talk about hunting and gathering?
- The belief that hunter-gatherers ravaged the natural world just like we do. To be human is to be rapacious and acquisitive. They behave just like us so what can we learn from them?
- The belief that hunter-gatherers lived like us in hierarchical societies with chiefs and subjects. What can they teach us about power and inequality?
- The focus of social science research is for the most part on the individual, not on how the material basis of society drives the configuration of institutions and social values. Since the structure of the human brain has not changed since the late Pleistocene, our basic individual behavior patterns must be the same.

• • •

Becoming human did not happen suddenly. There is no magic moment when the finger of Michelangelo's God reached down and created us. But the belief is widespread that some sort of "divine intervention" caused a sudden breakthrough in human physical and social evolution some 70,000 years ago. According to Harari:[36]

> The appearance of new ways of thinking and communicating, between 70,000 and 30,000 years ago, constitutes the Cognitive Revolution ... The most commonly believed theory argues that accidental genetic mutation changed the inner wirings of the brains of Sapiens, enabling them to think in unprecedented ways and to communication using an altogether new type of language.

We continually grasp at any straw that makes us feel unique. But recent evidence is undermining the "suddenly we became human" view of evolution. Neanderthals in Spain painted cave walls and decorated seashells some 115,000 years ago.[37] Evidence from South Africa indicates that humans developed sophisticated techniques for cooking plant starches 120,000 years ago.[38] Fire use goes back 500,000 years at least and possibly over 1,000,000 years. *Homo erectus* used shells for tool production and ornamentation at least 430,000 years ago.[39] These findings suggest that the human capacity for sophisticated abstract thought and art has a long lineage.

Human physical and cultural evolution is a mosaic, not a straight line of ever-increasing complexity. The evolutionary success of Pleistocene humans depended on honing the valuable traits of variety, flexibility, and adaptability. Over the past 2 million years many interconnected waves of humans moved out of Africa, and back again, driven by changing climates and the opening and closing of new migration corridors. Sophisticated technology was present in *Homo erectus* cultures beginning some 1.8 million years ago. The Acheulean technology, notably the fine-crafted pressure-flaked hand-axe, was the dominant technology for most of human history, lasting more than 1.5 million years.[40] The Acheulean culture covered half the inhabitable world. With this technology *Homo erectus* spread from Africa to the Middle East, Europe, and Asia between 1.5 million and 800,000 years ago. The earliest known Acheulean site is from Kenya dating to around 1.8 mya. The culture was present in South Asia by 1.5 mya.[41] Acheulean tools have been found in Spain dating about 900,000 years ago.[42] Researchers in Java, Indonesia found geometric engravings on shell and holes in them associated with *Homo erectus*, indicating that they were used as necklaces some 540,000 years ago.[43] Acheulean culture stone huts dated at 400,000 years ago have been found near Nice, France and others dated at 500,000 years ago in Japan.[44] A *Homo erectus* find from Dmanisi, Georgia has been dated at 1.8 mya, throwing many current ideas about our evolutionary history into confusion.[45]

Something to keep in mind when considering human evolution is that the hominid fossil record is very sketchy and new finds, together with breakthroughs in DNA analysis, are continually altering our understanding. For example, a redating of a *Homo sapiens* skull from Morocco pushed the time of emergence of our species back an astonishing 100,000 years. We now know that *Homo erectus* evolved into *Homo sapiens* by at least 300,000 years ago. Until about 40,000 years ago, our species had at least three known subspecies, *Homo sapiens sapiens*, *Homo sapiens neanderthalensis*, and *Homo sapiens denisovan*. "Modern" humans are hybrids of a variety of earlier *Homo sapiens*.[46] It is believed that the common ancestors of the three lineages (and according to DNA evidence, a fourth *Homo sapiens* not yet found) lived between 765,000 and 550,000 years ago. This lineage split between 445,000 and 473,000 years ago with one branch leading to modern humans and the other to the Neanderthals and Denisovans.[47] The common ancestor of Neanderthals and Denisovans spread across Europe and Asia by around 400,000 years ago. Those in Asia, ranging from Siberia to Indonesia, become Denisovans and those in Europe became Neanderthals. These humans bred with each other and with *Homo sapiens sapiens*. A wave of early modern humans moved into Europe sometime earlier than 270,000 years ago and bred with Neanderthals.[48] Modern Europeans and Asians have about 2 percent Neanderthal ancestry.[49] Denisovan DNA is found in contemporary populations in Oceania and native populations in Australia. About 6 percent of the genome of contemporary Papuans come from Denisovans.[50] The discovery of a first-generation Neanderthal-Denisovan hybrid suggests that interbreeding among our recent human ancestors was fairly common.[51] A 180,000-year-old fossil from Israel provides further evidence that *Homo sapiens* left Africa for western Asia earlier than previously thought.[52,53]

A remarkable early man site near Johannesburg, South Africa called Rising Star, contains a rich assemblage of fossils from a new species named *Homo naledi*, a hominid with a mixture of primitive traits (small brain, very long arms) and modern traits (long legs and modern teeth).[54] When first discovered it was thought that the species lived more than 2 million years ago and was an intermediate form between *Australopithecus* and *Homo habilis*. However, when a reliable date was established it turned out to be between 236,000 and 335,000 years ago, contemporary with early *Homo sapiens*.

These discoveries lend support to a picture of human evolution that is multiregional rather than unilinear. The out-of-Africa hypothesis of human evolution as a more or less steady, straight-line unfolding in space and time is being replaced by a much more comprehensive and complicated picture of multiregional specialization and recombination. Wolpoff, Hawks, and Caspari write:[55]

> Multiregional evolution is a model to account for the pattern of human evolution in the Pleistocene. The underlying hypothesis is that a worldwide network of genetic exchanges, between evolving human populations that continually divide and reticulate, provides a frame of population interconnections that allows both species-wide evolutionary change and local distinctions and differentiation. Multiregional does not mean independent multiple origins, ancient divergence of modern populations, simultaneous appearance of adaptive characters in different regions, or parallel evolution. A valid understanding of multiregional evolution would go a long way toward reducing the modern human origins controversy.

Human evolution is not a steady, inevitable march to increasing perfection driven by competition among individuals. It is not a straight line of simple to complex forms culminating in "modern man." It is not even a bush with many branches leading in different directions. It is more like a river delta with major and minor streams – some dry up and stop, others merge to form major channels, and some diverge and merge again. For all of human history the genus *Homo* has been characterized by a rich tapestry of technologies, physical types, and diverse cultures adapted to specific local environments. This branching and recombining of cultures and technologies made us human and may have played a major role in the ability of humans to survive and even thrive in the rapidly changing environment of the Pleistocene.[56] The concept of "species" is ambiguous through time. It is also ambiguous over space. Several different kinds of humans lived at the same places at the same time, and some of them were capable of interbreeding and producing fertile offspring.

Related to this is new research about the importance of hybrids in evolution. Hybrids were once thought to be accidents or anomalies that were invariably dead ends like mules – an infertile offspring of a female horse and a male donkey. In fact, fertile hybrids are common in nature and apparently help pass advantageous traits to their descendants. For example, there is evidence that jaguar(s) interbred with lions in the distant past and retained two genes from them that control the growth of the optic nerve. These genes were advantages and they replaced the jaguar optic nerve genes. Other lion genes were lost because they were not adaptive in a jungle environment, but those that were adaptively advantageous were retained.[57] Hybrids played a key role in the rapid speciation and proliferation of cichlids, a small fish that dominates Lake Victoria.[58] Horizontal gene transfer is another once heretical idea that is gaining traction in evolutionary theory. Genes do not just move vertically from parents to offspring but sometimes can be transferred laterally from one species to another. Lynn Margulis[59] revolutionized views of evolution with her work on the evolution of cells with nuclei as products of the symbiotic mergers of different kinds of bacteria. None of this contradicts Darwinian natural selection. It is not surprising that any mechanism that adds more variation – possibilities and opportunities for increasing fitness – will be harnessed by the process of evolution.

The mosaic picture of evolution also calls into question the belief that "more modern" *Homo sapiens sapiens* outcompeted Neanderthals and drove them to extinction. This story combines the myths that we evolved from "killer apes" and that we "won the competitive battle" because we are superior. But as mentioned, there is evidence that a group of *Homo sapiens sapiens* migrated 230,000 years ago out of Africa into Europe where Neanderthals already lived, some 90,000 years before they disappeared. There is evidence of *Homo sapiens sapiens* DNA from a Neanderthal fossil dated 124,000 years ago. Evidence from Qafzeh cave in Israel indicates that *Homo sapiens sapiens* lived there 100,000 years ago, but were replaced by Neanderthals about 75,000 years ago when the climate changed in their favor as glaciation made the area cooler and drier.[60] It is thought that some modern humans have Neanderthal traits, such as red hair and immunity against Eurasian pathogens.[61]

The evolution of the human brain and human intelligence is also a mosaic, not a straight line of ever-increasing size. Textbooks typically have a diagram showing a steady increase in hominid brain size from Australopithecus to Homo sapiens. But this is grossly misleading. The average size of the modern human brain (circa 2018) is 1350cc, considerably smaller than either Upper Pleistocene *Homo sapiens sapiens* or *Homo sapiens neanderthalensis*. The brain of Homo sapiens has not steadily and smoothly increased over time. One of the oldest Homo sapiens fossils is from Hero, Ethiopia dated at about 160,000 years ago. The cranial capacity was 1450 cc, "at the high end of the modern range".[62,63,64] Average cranial capacity in the Upper Paleolithic was 1500–1600cc for Cro-Magnons and even larger for Neanderthals.[65] In fact, some populations of *Homo erectus* had cranial capacities well within the modern range. For example, a *Homo erectus* cranium found in Ethiopia and dated at 600,000 years ago had a brain size of about 1300cc, close to the 1350cc average brain size of modern *Homo sapiens*.[66]

$$\bullet \ \bullet \ \bullet$$

Our knowledge of human social evolution during the Pleistocene is of course indirect. But some clues can be found not only in the archaeological record but also in the physical structure of the human brain. Many mammals – elephants, whales, the great apes, and humans for example – are highly social mammals with a variety of behavioral characteristics that evolved to facilitate social interaction. Two features of the human brain are particularly important to sociality and gene-culture co-evolution: brain plasticity and the existence of specific neurons that may facilitate social interaction. Neurons are a type of cell that processes information and transmits it to and from the brain by electrical and chemical signaling. A remarkable finding from neuroscience is that most of the neurons in the human brain develop after birth. Furthermore, the way they are configured depends in part on how a child is socialized. It is another way that variability can be introduced into the evolutionary mix. Wexler[67] writes about the evolutionary advantages of brain plasticity:

> There is an evolutionary advantage for life forms that reproduce sexually because mixing of genetic material from parents produces variety in their offspring. Thus, different individuals have different characteristics, which increases the likelihood that some members of the group will be able to function and reproduce even when the environment in which the group lives changes. In an analogous manner, the distinctive postnatal shaping of each individual's brain function through interaction with other people, and through his or her own mix of sensory inputs, creates an endless variety of individuals with different functional characteristics. This broadens the range of adaptive and problem-solving capabilities will beyond the variability achieved by sexual reproduction.

Another remarkable feature of the human brain is the presence in the human brain of *Von Economo* neurons that apparently evolved to enable people to make rapid decisions in social contexts. These neurons are located in cortical areas positioned at the interface between emotional and cognitive processing.[68] Allman et al. (2005) speculate that *Von Economo* neurons are designed for quick signaling of appropriate responses in the context of social ambiguity. The ability to quickly respond in social situations would be particularly important in species with fission-fusion with complex social networks and social uncertainties at reunions. Von Economo neurons are also found in smaller numbers in great apes, elephants, and whales and dolphins, other highly intelligent species with complex social systems. Among hunter-gatherers fusing and splitting was seasonal, with small bands being the group type for most of the year but coming together to form larger groups when resource availability permits. In this kind of social organization groups are continually changing in composition. Allman et al.[69] suggest that Von Economo neurons help humans to adjust quickly to social situations:

> We hypothesize that VENs and associated circuitry enable us to reduce complex social and cultural dimensions of decision-making into a single dimension that facilitates the rapid execution of decisions. Other animals are not encumbered by such elaborate social and cultural contingencies to their decision-making and thus do not require such a system for rapid intuitive choice.

In humans, most of these neurons are formed after birth and develop according to environmental influences, again pointing to the blurred line between heredity and socialization. The latest neurological evidence suggests that human behavior is highly dependent on social conditioning and that critical neurological pathways enhancing intimacy and trust must be established in infancy for healthy emotional development. These are characteristics that make us human and they evolved deep in our hunter-gatherer past.

Hunter-Gatherers and Sustainability: The Myth of Human-Caused Pleistocene Extinctions

The dominant view is that the current human assault on the natural world is due to "human nature." Humans evolved to be greedy, acquisitive and competitive and there is nothing we can do to change this. It is not surprising that this view is held by supporters of unchecked exploitation globalization. But it is surprising that many environmentalists take the same position. During a lecture about the failure of modern society to address environmental problems Jorgen Randers of the Club of Rome blamed human nature:[70]

> What went wrong? Randers asked to the audience to propose reasons. He got more than a dozen, from the financial system to greed. But he said that none of these is the real reason. It is not a fault of the government, it is not a fault of corporations, it is not a fault of banks. It is, simply, the fault of people. According to Randers, people are simply unable to postpone their immediate satisfaction for a better future.

Population ecologist William Rees also blames our current predicament on human nature:

> Humans may pride themselves as being the best evidence for intelligent life on Earth, but an alien observer would record that the (un)sustainability conundrum has the global community floundering in a swamp of cognitive dissonance and collective denial. . .Indeed, our alien friend might go so far as to ask why our reasonably intelligent species seems unable to recognize the crisis for what it is and respond accordingly. To begin answering this question, we need to look beyond conventional explanations–scientific uncertainty, societal inertia, lack of political will, resistance by vested interests, and so on–to what may well be the root cause of the conundrum: human nature itself.

> http://www.postcarbon.org/publications/human-nature-of-unsustainability

If the evil-human-nature view is true, we are left with nothing but despair and handwringing over our inevitable fate. But if it is "human nature" to ravage the natural world how did *Homo sapiens*, living in an innumerable variety of cultures and local environments, live sustainably on planet earth for 300,000 years? Studies using genome sequencing indicate that the San (Khoisan) people inhabited Southern Africa continuously for over 150,000 years. The San were the largest population of *Homo sapiens* on the planet for most of human history (Kim et al. 2014). The *Homo erectus* Acheulean hand-axe tradition flourished for 1.5 million years. The Neanderthal Mousterian culture, with regional variations, lasted 300,000 years. Even after agriculture many small-scale human societies lived in harmony with nature with stable populations and sustainable resource use. Humans are capable of almost any type of behavior depending on underlying institutional structures and the behavioral patterns arising from the requirements of particular economic systems. Blaming human nature for the current assault on the natural world is a defeatist position. If human cultures have always been unsustainable and characterized by overshoot and collapse nothing can be done. It's an apolitical easy way out that blames all humans as individuals, regardless of cultural context, and precludes a deeper analysis of the way specific cultures and economic systems encourage or discourage rapacious exploitative behavior.

• • •

Central to the human-nature-and-sustainability debate is the widespread belief in the Pleistocene overkill hypothesis – the idea that megafaunal extinctions from North America, Europe, and Australia were caused by a sudden blitzkrieg of extinctions perpetuated by hunter-gatherers. The tone of this view is illustrated by the title of a paper by the late Paul Martin, the chief proponent of the overkill hypothesis: "40,000 years of extinction on the 'planet of doom.'"[71] This view is accepted uncritically by many thoughtful popular commentators and most ecologists. Grayson and Meltzer[72] argue that the hunter-gatherer overkill hypothesis is not supported by evidence and that it represents a convenient "evil human nature" worldview supported both by environmentalists who want to protect nature and developers who profit from its exploitation.[73] Overkill is a convenient story that can be used to blame the environmental destructiveness of the Anthropocene on ethical shortcomings of the human species. The overkill hypothesis is used to support the notion that humans are uniquely predatory species – highly evolved killer apes that always outcompete and destroy all others. This view appeals to conservationists who use the "original sin" idea to argue for redemption through conservation. Martin used the idea to promote the "rewilding" of the planet to make amends for human-caused extinctions. George Monbiot[74] makes a similar argument. On the other side, the overkill hypothesis is also used by ecomodernists who argue that human domination of nature is natural, and therefore good.

The demise of megafauna has yet to be fully explained, but scientific opinion has swung against the overkill hypothesis. Many studies are flawed because of the lack of precise dates about extinctions, human presence, and climate.[75] But the most careful and detailed megafauna extinction studies point to climate change and the resulting ecosystem disruption as the culprit.[76] Cooper et al.[77] present forensic DNA evidence about Pleistocene Holarctic (North America and Europe) megafaunal turnover. They find that rapid climate, particularly rapid warming events, were responsible for megafauna extinctions whether humans were present or not. The results are summarized in the *New Scientist*:[78]

> Cooper and colleagues have simultaneously produced an unprecedentedly accurate map and timeline of changes in megafauna populations around Eurasia and North America, and precisely matched that timeline up with ancient climate records. It punches a hole in a key argument of the prosecution. This states that climate cannot have caused megafauna extinctions because it has changed so much over the past 60,000 years. There were lots of warm and cool periods – interglacial and glacial epochs, respectively. If climate change is the real megafauna killer, why did the animals survive those events only to die when humans turned up in their region? The new data show that they did not survive. Megafauna extinctions were actually relatively common during the past 60,000 years whether humans were around or not.

Late Pleistocene extinction events clustered in periods of warming including a period 37,000–32,000 years ago and at the end of the Pleistocene, 14,000–11,000 years ago. Cooper et al.[79] conclude: "Our results lend strong empirical support to the hypothesis that environmental changes associated with rapid climatic shifts were important factors in the extinction of many megafaunal lineages." Humans may have had a role in some megafaunal extinctions. But applying the coup de grâce after a climate-change–induced depopulation event is not the same as causing the extinctions. Mammoths coexisted with humans in Siberia for at least 30,000 years, and only became extinct after the last ice age.[80] The big climate event triggering environmental changes in the last few million years is the Holocene beginning about 12,000 years ago. The earth's climate has been comparatively warm and stable since then. Previous warm periods have been spikes, not the prolonged warming of the Holocene.

Striking changes in the earth's biota occurred only after humans began to practice agriculture. Lyons et al.[81] looked at DNA evidence showing the structure of biotic communities, based on the number of aggregated pairs of species, over the last 300 million years.[82] They found that percentage of aggregated pairs was stable for the entire 300-million-year-long period until it changed abruptly some 6,000 years ago. "This dominance of aggregated pairs persisted with little change for more than 300 million years on different continents and across diverse taxa, until about 6,000 years ago, when the sharp transition to the segregated co-occurrence pattern began."[83] Lyons et al.[84] conclude that the rapid expansion in the human population some 6,000 years ago explains why species co-occurrence patterns changed so rapidly:

> Aggregated pairs dominated from the Carboniferous period (307 million years ago) to the early Holocene epoch (11,700 years before present), when there was a pronounced shift to more segregated pairs, a trend that continues in modern assemblages. The shift began during the Holocene and coincided with increasing human population size and the spread of agriculture in North America. Before the shift, an average of 64% of significant pairs were aggregated; after the shift, the average dropped to 37%. The organization of modern and late Holocene plant and animal assemblages differs fundamentally from that of assemblages over the past 300 million years that predate the large-scale impacts of humans. Our results suggest that the rules governing the assembly of communities have recently been changed by human activity.

DNA analysis is exonerating hunter-gatherers from driving specific animals to extinction: "Ancient DNA analyses exclude humans as the driving force behind late Pleistocene musk ox (Ovibos moschatus) population dynamics."[85] Hill, Hill, and Widga[86] studied body size and mortality rates for North American Bison between 37,000 and 250 years ago and conclude "Overall, it appears that the changes in body size were a reaction to environmental conditions rather than the result of human predation pressure."

An example used to support Paul Martin's "blitzkrieg" hypothesis is that of the extinction of the world's largest known bird, the elephant bird of Madagascar. It was long believed that the birds became extinct around 1000 CE relatively soon after the arrival of humans on the island. But recent evidence indicates that humans arrived in Madagascar more than 9,000 years ago, meaning that humans and elephant birds coexisted for 9,000 years.[87,88]

> Our research provides evidence of human activity in Madagascar more than 6,000 years earlier than previously suspected—which demonstrates that a radically different extinction theory is required to understand the huge biodiversity loss that has occurred on the island. Humans seem to have coexisted with elephant birds and other now-extinct species for over 9,000 years, apparently with limited negative impact on biodiversity for most of this period, which offers new insights for conservation today," said Dr. James Hansford from the Zoological Society of London's Institute of Zoology ... It also seems likely that the introduction of farming and wide scale deforestation between 1,000 and 1,500 years ago quickly offset the equilibrium between human activities and the local wildlife. More evidence may help settle the now reopened question of Madagascar's extinct megafauna. [89]

Another argument for human hunter-gatherer caused massive environmental change is the use of fire. Mooney et al.[90] in a study based on 223 samples of sedimentary charcoal records over the last 70,000 years in Australia, found no evidence that human occupation affected biomass burning in Australia until 200 years ago. Aborigines redirected fires in local ecosystems but apparently did not significantly change the fire regimes that long preceded human arrival. They write: "There is no distinct change in the fire regime corresponding to the arrival of humans in Australia at 50ka (+ or – 10k) years ago. And no correlation between archaeological evidence of increased human activity during the past 40ka and the history of biomass burning."

Before agriculture humans lived directly off the flows from nature, not stocks of fertile soil and the other inputs required for food production. When a hunter-gatherer band overshot the carrying capacity of their local ecosystem (which they undoubtedly sometimes did) the results were immediate and obvious. They behaved sustainably not because they were more moral, but because their survival depended on it. Historically observed hunter-gatherers had a wide variety of rules and customs to protect against overexploitation of nature. The Australian Aborigines, for example, had an elaborate religious and kinship system, having at its center a personal and spiritual relationship to the land. Berndt and Berndt[91] write:

> In some areas of the Daly river, the Aborigines were careful about exhausting certain yam beds and always left a residue well scattered for the next season's crop ... Their intimate knowledge of the growth of various creatures, as well as of the increase of vegetable and other plants and trees, led many of them to realize that conservation was essential even in times of plenty. They could not afford to be careless.

There is no reason to believe there was an absence of rules regulating exploitation of nature in the Pleistocene. Also, with a lack of markets, an abundance of food for the taking, and a stable population, there was simply no reason to overexploit the environment, and lots of incentives not to.

Much of the discussion of overkill shows little understanding of the difference between hunter-gatherers and agriculturalists. The Maori may have exterminated the giant flightless birds of New Zealand, but they were agriculturalists, not hunter-gatherers. The early inhabitants of the Amazon Basin and the South Pacific may have created widescale landscape disturbance, but they were also agriculturalists. Despite the lack of evidence, the overkill hypothesis and the evil-human-nature arguments survive for a variety of reasons. The unfortunate consequence is that it puts the blame on individual behavior, not the ultrasocial economic system we live under.

Hunter-Gatherers and Equality: Hierarchical Human Societies Are Not "Natural"

Sociality, caring for others, and cooperation with nonkin are central characteristics of the human species.[92] These traits not only made it possible for humans to flourish and survive the extreme environmental changes of the Pleistocene, but they also fostered sustainable use of environmental resources and equalitarian social arrangements.[93,94] In hunter-gatherer bands, these traits worked both for the benefit of the group and for individuals within the group. Small-scale human societies have developed myriad forms of social organization to minimize group conflicts and to ensure that one individual or one small group of individuals cannot dominate. Woodburn[95] writes of immediate-return (simple technology and material culture) hunter-gatherers:

> Without seeking permission, obtaining instruction, or being recognized as qualified (except by sex) individuals in these societies can set about obtaining their own requirements as they think fit. They need considerable knowledge and skill but this is freely available to all who are of the appropriate sex and is not, in general, transmitted by formal (or even informal) instruction: rather it is learnt by participation and emulation. In most, but not all, of these societies neither kinship status nor age is used as a qualification to obtain access to particular hunting and gathering skills or equipment.

Cooperation among Insect Hunter-Gatherers

Cooperative hunting is well known in the animal kingdom. Chimpanzees, wolves, lions, killer whales, and other mammals, employ complex strategies and division of effort to hunt their prey. It is not well known that insects also cooperatively hunt. A kind of pseudoscorpion, *Paratemnoides nidificator*, live in packs of several dozen and cooperatively hunt prey much larger than themselves including large ants, beetles, and spiders. Moreover, they share their kills evenly among the members of the group – even with those who do not participate in the hunt.

Eberton Tizo-Pedroso and Kleber Del-Klaro, 2018. Capture of large prey and feeding priority in the cooperative pseudoscorpion *Paratemnoides nidificator*. *Acta Ethologica* 21, 109–117.

The status of women in hunter-gatherer societies was generally equal to men's. Leacock[96] suggests that "autonomy" is a better word than "equality" to describe gender relationships in these societies: "They held decision-making power over their own lives and activities the same way that men did over theirs." She argues that individual autonomy was necessary to support the hunter-gatherer way of life.

> The fact that consensus, freely arrive at, within and among multifamily units was both essential to everyday living and possibly has implications that we do not usually confront. Individual autonomy was a necessity, and autonomy as a

valued principle persists to a striking degree among the descendants of hunter/gatherers. It was linked to a way of life that
called for great individual initiative and decisiveness along with
the ability to be extremely sensitive to the feelings of lodge-
mates. I suggest that personal autonomy was concomitant with
the direct dependence of each individual on the group as a
whole. Decision making in this context calls for concepts other
than ours of leader and led, dominant and deferent, not matter
how loosely these terms are seen to apply.[97]

The success of hunter-gatherer bands depended on both autonomy and
cooperation. Living off flows from nature required freely available
knowledge about the hundreds of plants and animals they depended
on, as well as flexibility and decentralized decision-making.

Hunter-gatherer egalitarianism (sharing) is sometimes explained
by "risk reduction reciprocity," that is, hunters share their kill and
gatherers share their plant food because of the uncertainty inherent in
hunting and gathering. A hunter shares his kill because he is likely to be
unsuccessful in the future and will need food from another hunter. But
Hawkes et al.[98] found that this explanation does not explain sharing
among the Hadza of Tanzania. Among the Hadza the successful hunter
does not control the distribution of the meat. They write:

> These data and analyses do not support the proposition that the
> shares households receive from the kills of others are contingent
> on reciprocal shares from kills made by the hunter in those
> households. At least 90% (usually more) of the meat of large
> prey goes outside the hunter's household. In our sample of
> household shares, the men who supplied more meat to others
> did not get more meat from them. Poorer or less hard working
> hunters were no more likely to be excluded from the kills of
> others, or to get smaller shares ... Moreover, the men who were
> more skilled hunters spent more time at it, magnifying the
> disproportionate contribution they made to the diets of their
> neighbors. To the extent our sample is representative, the meat
> hunters supplied to others was not repaid by meat from them.
> The proposition that hunters share meat so they will get meat
> repayments later is, on these grounds, implausible. Risk reduc-
> tion reciprocity does not explain the persistence of widespread
> meat sharing among the Hadza.

Boehm[99] describes hunter-gatherers as having an ethos of "reverse dominance hierarchy." He argues that egalitarianism in these societies is deliberately shaped by members of these societies rather than arising from material conditions. Woodburn[100] recognizes the importance of sanctions on accumulation but cites other reasons as to why hunter-gatherers are aggressively egalitarian: access to food and other resources, mobility and flexibility, and access to means of coercion. Capital in hunter-gatherer societies is simple and immediately accessible. And because capital in immediate-return hunter-gatherer societies is intangible since it is comprised of knowledge and freely available information about resource availability, it is not a physical thing that can be controlled and manipulated. The two features of modern society that drive inequality, private property and hereditary wealth, were largely absent in immediate-return hunter-gatherer societies.

New evidence for egalitarianism among hunter-gatherers is provided by DNA analysis of the structure of hunter-gatherer groups. Dyble et al.[101] found that human hunter-gatherer bands, in contrast to other great ape social groups, have "fluid social networks where family units are relatively autonomous, with couples and their children moving often between bands, living with the kin of either the husband or the wife." They present an agent-based model showing that if men and women are equally likely to decide the group of residence after marriage (with the husband's family or the wife's family) the result will be the observed relatively low within-group relatedness. By contrast, DNA analysis of early agricultural communities (about 4,000 years ago) in the Lech River valley in Bavaria found evidence of patrilocality, and social differentiation based on gender and class.[102] One of the most striking findings was an absence of adult daughters from the local communities, and the presence of foreign women of unknown origin. In this society women traveled far from home to marry while men stayed home and kept wealth in their families.[103]

Borgerhoff Mulder et al.,[104] in a study of wealth inequality in twenty-one small-scale societies, found a strong ethos of equality among hunter-gatherer bands, and more economic stratification among agriculturalists. They attribute this to the intergenerational transmission of wealth. Carneiro[105] argues that power leads to surplus production, not the reverse. But the argument about which came first, power or surplus, is probably fruitless. Surplus made the intergenerational transfer of wealth, and the means of producing it, possible, and this encouraged those in power to coerce even more surplus production. In any case, it was agriculture and surplus production that gave rise to hierarchical societies and eventually large-scale repressive states. As Lee puts it: "[T]he development of inequality is first and foremost a consequence of food production. Foragers directly appropriate from nature; farmers and herders by contrast depend far more on *improvements* upon nature and the *husbandry* of resources."[106]

An aspect of equality is sympathy and compassion for others that may be less fortunate. Such traits were present in the Pleistocene. Spikins et al.[107] discovered that Neanderthals cared for severely injured individuals including a male aged 35–50 at the time of his death, whose degenerative disease would have made it impossible to care for himself long before his death. A Neanderthal individual found at Shanidar I cave in Iraq showed extensive debilitating injuries including the loss of an arm, serious wounds to his right leg, and loss of hearing.[108] Spikins observes: "Our findings suggest Neanderthals didn't think in terms of whether others might repay their efforts, they just responded to their feelings about seeing their loved ones suffering."[109] Evidence from the Sima de los Huesos site in Spain, dated at 400,000 years ago, indicates that a child with craniosynostosis, an individual with deafness, and an elderly man who would have had trouble walking, were taken care of for several years.[110,111] Even earlier evidence for long-term care of severely injured individuals comes from a *Homo erectus* site dated at 1.6 million years ago.[112] Despite evidence to the contrary, the belief in the moral superiority of modern humans continues to mar our appreciation of the humanity of our Pleistocene ancestors.

• • •

Hunter-gatherers were subject to the same foibles as all humans: aggression, jealousy, and avarice. Groups of hunter-gatherers had a significant impact on the natural environment, as any large species does.[113,114] Such societies, however, were in ecological and social harmony to a degree unmatched in industrial societies. This is informative in itself, since humans have lived as hunter-gatherers for almost all of the time our species has been on this planet. Also informative is the relationship between social egalitarianism and environmental sustainability. The same features that promoted an egalitarian social structure – sharing, collective decision-making, and a knowledge-based economy – also promoted environmental harmony. Hunter-gatherers did not deliberately cultivate a higher ethical consciousness; their patterns of behavior were embedded in the material conditions of their economies.

The evolved biological and social characteristics of Upper Pleistocene hunter-gatherers can be considered a baseline for what it means to be human. The sudden and profound changes in human society that occurred some 10,000 years ago should be seen in the context of what came before. To dismiss 97 percent of human history by saying "so what, we can't go back," is to ignore the rich possibilities of human existence and to resign ourselves to the narrow possibilities offered to us by commercial society. Lee[115] summarizes the relevance of hunter-gatherers to understanding the modern world:

> The contemporary industrial world exists in highly structured societies at immensely high densities and enjoys luxuries of technology that foragers could hardly imagine. Yet that world is sharply divided into have and have nots, and after only a few millennia of stewardship by agricultural and industrial civilizations the environments of large portions of the planet lie in ruins. Therefore the hunter-gatherers may well be able to teach us something, not only about past ways of life but about long-term human futures as well. If technological society is to survive it may have to learn the keys to longevity from fellow humans whose way of life has lasted at least one hundred times longer than industrial commercial "civilization."

Our long history as hunter-gatherers tells us that (1) it is not "human nature" to be greedy and exploitative and (2) hierarchical and repressive societies are not "natural" to the human condition. Pogo was wrong. The enemy is not "us" but rather the peculiar economic system we stumbled into 10,000 years ago.

4 THE AGRICULTURAL TRANSITION AND HOW IT CHANGED OUR SPECIES

The origin of agriculture is hotly debated. Price and Bar-Yosef summarize, "There is as yet no single accepted theory for the origins of agriculture, rather, there is a series of ideas and suggestions that do not quite resolve the questions."[1] This chapter does not provide a definitive explanation for every instance of the adoption of agriculture, which varied from place to place and time to time[2]. It offers instead, in broad outline, a plausible story of the general drivers of the transition from hunting and gathering to settled agriculture, and the social and environmental consequences of that change. Agriculture gave our species the ability to control and expand the supply of food, a tremendous evolutionary advantage judged by the sudden surge in total population, the unprecedented size of communities, and ecosystem domination. Domestication of plants was not due to a sudden cognitive breakthrough. People had extensive knowledge of wild plants long before the adoption of agriculture.[3,4] Kent Flannery[5] observed, "We know of no human group on Earth so primitive that they are ignorant of the connection between plants and the seeds from which they grow." There must have been some experimentation with managing plants during our lengthy hunter-gatherer history. But understanding, observing, and collecting wild plants is one thing, domestication is another. If hunter-gatherers had the knowledge to manage plants, presumably for hundreds of thousands of years, what took them so long to adopt agriculture?

One argument is that population pressure drove the adoption of agriculture.[6, 7] But others have pointed out that there is little evidence of population pressure in the areas where agriculture first appeared.[8] However, the Holocene warming may be indirectly related to population pressures in some areas. McCorriston and Hole[9] note that one effect of the Holocene warming in the Levant was to prolong summer aridity and that this would have negatively changed the availability of edible plants and affected the distribution of human groups. The drier climate also put more pressure on the availability of water and may have concentrated human and animal populations in areas with adequate water. Even incipient agriculture may have resulted in a more sedentary life, which in turn would have increased fertility rates. This may have created a positive feedback path, reinforcing the need for more agriculture as pressure on wild food sources and hunting increased.

Complicating speculations about the origin of agriculture is the fact that its adoption made the average individual worse off.[10,11] This brings up an obvious question: "If hunting and gathering was so good and agriculture was so bad for humans why did they choose to adopt it?" The answer is that humans did not "choose" to adopt agriculture. Agriculture came about because of the convergence of seemingly unrelated phenomena that resulted in the evolution of a complex and expansionary system. This system arose because of the unprecedented climate stability of the Holocene, and the preadaptation of human sociality and the ability to cooperate with unrelated others. Once agriculture began to take hold, natural section operating on diverse groups, driven by the economic requirements of surplus food production, favored those groups that could best take advantage of economies of scale and size, and a complex division of labor. The success of groups that could most efficiently organize the requirements of food production transformed the human population into a unified, interdependent economic machine. This took time. Even after climate stability permitted it, the social institutions necessary for large-scale agriculture took thousands of years to develop.[12, 13]

• • •

Our Upper Pleistocene hunter-gatherer ancestors had an intimate knowledge about the plants and animals they depended on for survival, yet agriculture appeared late in human history – quite suddenly and independently in at least three areas of the world. A growing body of evidence suggests that the unique climate stability of the Holocene made agriculture possible and that climate instability made it impossible

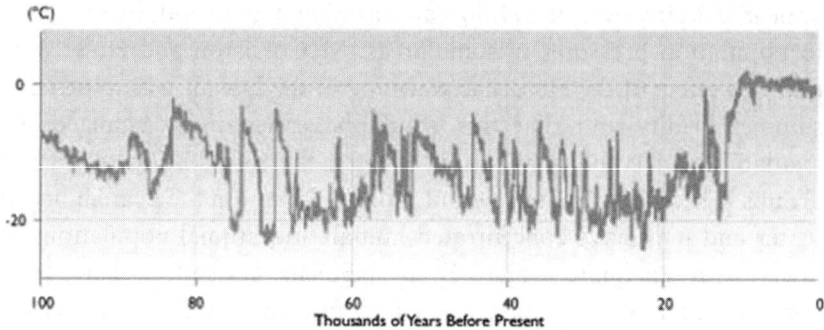

This record of temperature change (departures from present conditions) has been reconstructed from a Greenland ice core. The record demonstrates the high variability of the climate over the past 100 000 years. It also suggests that the climate of the past 10 000 years or so, which was the time during which human civilization developed, has been unusually stable. There is concern that the rapid warming caused by the increasing concentrations of greenhouse gases due to human activities could destabilize this state.

Figure 4.1 Holocene climate stability as shown in fluctuations in Greenland ice surface temperatures over the past 100,000 years

before then.[14,15,16] The Holocene climate has been uniquely warm and stable. During the Pleistocene there were four episodes when the earth's climate was as warm as today's, but these were brief compared to the Holocene. The pre-Holocene climate was extremely unstable as shown in Figure 4.1, showing temperature fluctuations in Greenland relative to the mean for the past 100,000 years using oxygen isotope ratios ($^{18}O/^{16}O$) as a proxy.[17] Prior to the Holocene, changes in average world temperatures temperature as great as 8°C occurred over time spans as short as two centuries.[18]

Unpredictable year-to-year climate fluctuations before the Holocene made any incipient attempt at agriculture impossible to sustain. An example is the Natufian culture that started down the path to agriculture but abandoned it during the Younger Dryas abrupt cooling event that occurred between 12,800 and 11,500 years ago. Another factor inhibiting agriculture might have been that plant productivity in the Late Pleistocene was low because of reduced CO_2 levels (about 190 ppm compared to 250 ppm at the beginning of the Holocene).[19,20,21] It is estimated that the total amount of stored organic land carbon was 33–60 percent lower in the Late Pleistocene compared to the Holocene.

• • •

Given what we know about the climate history of the Pleistocene and Holocene, the structure of hunter-gatherer societies, and how natural selection operates on groups, a plausible scenario of the human agricultural transition can be sketched out.[22] During the Pleistocene, mobile hunter-gatherers moved through places where wild grains thrived, and these grains provided a significant portion of their diets. As the climate warmed and became more stable, wild grains became more reliable and more important as a food source. As the weather became more predictable, people began to sow wild seeds to enhance grain growth, and they began to store the grain they collected. Surplus production and storage of annual grains was a good subsistence strategy since there was variability in climate and harvests from year to year. People cultivated more crops than they thought they needed and in most years there was a surplus of food. This enhanced and storable food supply led to larger and more concentrated populations. As they sowed plants, they also selected for desirable characteristics. Perhaps a portion of the population began to stay behind in the seasonal migrations in order to manage the wild crops. Selective planting and harvesting of crop varieties eventually led to managed agriculture, and populations more and more dependent on intensive food management. In turn, wild grains became domesticated and were eventually dependent on human intervention for their survival.

This plausible story fits with what we know of the agricultural transition in the Levant (which includes parts of modern Palestine, Syria, Israel, and Jordan) beginning around 10,000–12,500 years ago.[23] The transition to settled agriculture in the Levant is not a universal story. Agriculture arose several times after the beginning of the Holocene in different climates and with different plant ancestors. Nevertheless, the transition in the Levant, from the earlier hunter-gatherer Kebaran to the preagricultural Natufian to the later fully agriculturalist Pre-Pottery Neolithic, is well documented and it is consistent with the story outlined here. A key feature of the Holocene warming in the Near East was that it created conditions favorable to the development of annual grains. The climate of the Levant became more stable and seasonal differences became greater. The preagricultural Natufians began to rely more heavily on annual wild grains like wheat and barley.[24,25] Annuals have an advantage in places with distinct seasons, especially where there are hot, dry summers and strong seasonal rainfall variation. Annual grains store their reproductive ability in seeds that can wait (sometimes years) for enough rain to germinate. Grains can also be stored, and so a greater reliance on them meant a greater incentive to produce a surplus.[26] Evidence exists for food storage at about 11,000 BP.

An important mutation of wild wheat was non-shattering, a characteristic that allowed seeds to remain on the plant longer and not quickly fall to the ground. This mutation would have been noticed by those seed gatherers who were harvesting wild stands of early wheat varieties. The time period for harvesting wild wheat was short – three days to a week before shattering occurs depending on weather conditions. After seeds shatter, they must be harvested from the ground, which is more time consuming. Using a sickle would have been a particularly good technology for non-shattering seeds and evidence suggests that the preagricultural Natufians intensively harvested wild cereals using sickles.[27] In this way variations in wheat characteristics, combined with human intervention, created a selection bias for non-shattering seeds and other noticeable and desirable traits. During the initial domestication of grains, wild varieties would have been supplemented with plants benefitting from human intervention.[28] With cultivation there gradually developed a system of centrally controlled active management of food production, including a greater division of labor within the group.[29,30 31] Active management required complex and integrated tasks based on the characteristics of the crops and the groups managing the crops.

As the climate improved and stabilized during the Holocene, wild grains such as *Triticum monococcum*, a wheat-like grass, became more plentiful. There is evidence of heavy wear of teeth among the Natufians, presumably due to consuming coarsely ground cereals.[32] Hunting did not cease as the use of wild grains increased, but there was likely a shift in hunting strategies and in the relative importance of hunting in the diet. Hunting may have become less reliable because climate change altered the range and concentrations of wild animals.[33] Human population increases would have put more pressure on wild animal populations.

Belfer-Cohen and Bar-Yosef[34] argue that the stress of the sudden cooler and drier period of the Younger Dryas pushed the adoption of agriculture. But others point out that there is no evidence for more intensive resource use or food stress in the late (preagricultural) Natufians.[35] In fact, Natufian population densities and settlement patterns fell back to pre-Natufian levels during the Younger Dryas. It may be that the abrupt cooling interrupted rather than encouraged the transition to agriculture.

From Forest to Savanna: A Major Ant Evolutionary Transition

A climate transition in Africa from dense tropical rainforests to drier open savannas is thought to have triggered major physical and cultural changes in hominids. Although attine agriculture most likely originated in South American rainforests, the major transition from lower to higher (more specialized and intensive) agriculture, seems to have been triggered by a climate change to a drier, more open environment.

M. Branstetter et al. Dry habitats were crucibles of domestication in the evolution of agriculture in ants. *Proceedings of the Royal Society, B*, 284, (2017).

The Natufians were followed by the fully agricultural cultures of the Neolithic, referred to as Pre-Pottery Neolithic A (PPN-A). PPN-A sites are much larger than the Natufian sites, with storage bins for grains, ceremonial structures, and a rich lithic industry. The best known PPN-A settlement is Jericho (about 10,000 BP), one of the world's first towns, with a population of about 2,000–3,000 people. The Jericho site shows the first known domesticated cereals: emmer wheat and two-row hulled barley.[36] Storage technology is found abundantly in the Pre-Pottery Neolithic. Makarewicz[37] writes, "The Pre-Pottery Neolithic A marks a major shift in human approaches to subsistence from plant gathering to the consistent practice of plant cultivation, where wild plant resources were augmented by a more predictable food source in the form of managed plants, particularly cereals and legumes." Eventually the point was reached where the human population in the Levant could not survive without the grains, and the grains could not survive without human intervention.

• • •

The active management of crops fundamentally altered human economic organization. Like ant and termite agriculturalists, humans began to actively engage in the primary production of their food supply. Economic life was no longer a matter of living off the day-to-day flows from nature. It now involved a direct intervention into how, how much, and where food grows. Many species use social organization to get food, as in cooperative hunting, but directly creating the food supply is categorically different. With agriculture, the economic drivers of surplus production took center stage.

First of all, actively producing food requires a complex and interdependent division of labor. The division of labor is both a characteristic of ultrasocial systems and a preadaptation that enabled ultrasociality. Managing the planting, germination, growth, and reproduction of plants is much more complex than simply gathering them when they are ripe. It requires many distinct tasks whose timing and coordination must be carefully regulated. The crops must also be protected from animals, insects, and other humans at all stages of growth. Surplus production and storage gave insurance against a poor harvest. The reward was a large and steady food supply for the group as a whole, but the social repercussions were enormous.

The division of labor and economies of scale are intimately connected. It should be acknowledged that the division of labor is common in the animal world and is not by itself a distinguishing characteristic of ultrasociality. A division of labor based on care of the young is common among animals. It spontaneously appears in normally solitary queen ants when the queens are forced to associate, and similarly in normally solitary bees. Solitary sweat bees alternately dig nesting holes and guard the nest. When two are put together, one will specialize in excavation and the other will guard the nest entrance, resulting in efficiency gains in both tasks. According to Holbrook et al.:[38] "Paired individuals performed more per capita guarding, and pairs collectively excavated deeper nests than single bees – potential early advantages of social nesting in halictine bees." Even in a simple society of two individuals there is an advantage to a larger scale (from one to two), permitting a division of labor. The spontaneous appearance of the division of labor in these simple cases is remarkable and may hold keys to its development in ultrasocial societies. But the extent of the division of labor in ultrasocial species is unique in its complexity and interdependence.

A second feature of emergent agricultural society was an impetus to expand because of the advantages of larger group size.

More food allows expansion, and expansion captures the efficiencies of a greater division of labor and economies of scale. Also, complex agriculture requires many tasks that do not directly contribute to food production itself, for example, defense and administration. Those who directly produce food must provide for those not actively engaged in agricultural production. Another consequence of agriculture was an increase in reproductive rates caused by sedentary life. This also provided one of the most important resources for successful agriculture, a large supply of laborers. Those engaged in the direct production of food must produce enough to feed nonproductive individuals. Greater population creates a greater need for agricultural output, and greater agricultural output requires a larger population.

Warfare has been suggested as a key to the development of state societies.[39] Turchin[40,41] points to increasing returns to scale in warfare as a major driver of ultrasociality. Agriculture increased the payoff for aggression, which, in turn, necessitated more food production to feed the expanding military. Groups with more soldiers eliminated or absorbed smaller groups.

Finally, the ecological consequences of annual grain agriculture may have also encouraged expansion. Annual grains had a greater capacity for seed production, and the rewards of active management were greater, but they also had a greater potential for ecological damage such as soil erosion and soil fertility depletion.[42] Expansion into new territories was one way to offset the ecological problems caused by grain agriculture, even though in the long run it exacerbated ecological problems through deforestation of previously forested areas, soil erosion and nutrient depletion, and increased soil salinity.

• • •

The Consequences of Agriculture I: The Decline in Human Health

The consequences of agriculture were devastating for the average person. Agriculture led directly to a 10,000-year-long decline in physical health. According to Larsen:[43] "Although agriculture provided the economic basis for the rise of states and development of civilizations, the change in diet and acquisition of food resulted in a decline in quality of life for most human populations in the last 10,000 years." The archeological record substantiates Larson's claim. After agriculture, humans became shorter and less robust and people suffered from more debilitating diseases, from leprosy to arthritis to tooth decay, than their hunter-gatherer counterparts.[44,45] It is only in the last 100 years or so that longevity once again reached that of the Upper Pleistocene. The average human life span in 1900 was about thirty years, and for Upper Pleistocene hunter-gatherers it was probably about thirty-three years.[46] Only in the last century or so has the health of the majority of humanity improved dramatically compared to the Upper Pleistocene. It remains to be seen whether or not these improvements can be maintained. Care must be taken not to see the achievements of the very recent past as representative of the health consequences of the agricultural transition.

Favorable opinions about hunter-gatherers are frequently dismissed with something like "Hunter-gatherer life may not have been so bad but they rarely lived past age thirty." But do we really live longer than our hunter-gatherer ancestors? Over the past 160 years average life expectancy has increased by almost three months per year. Average worldwide life expectancy now stands at sixty-six years. Surely, living a long life is an unequivocally successful achievement of modern civilization. It turns out that such an assessment is not as clear-cut as most of us believe. Gurven and Kaplan,[47] after an extensive survey of the mortality literature in dozens of societies, conclude that life spans, as opposed to life expectancy, have not changed much over the course of human history. Almost all the recent increase in life expectancy can be attributed to a decrease in infant mortality. There is surprisingly little difference in expected life spans once a person survives childhood. They write:

> Our conclusion is that there is a characteristic life span for our species, in which mortality decreases sharply from infancy through childhood, followed by a period in which mortality rates remain essentially constant to about age 40 years, after which mortality rises steady in Gompertz fashion. The modal age of adult death is about seven decades, before which time humans remain vigorous producers, and after which senescence rapidly occurs and people die.

They found little difference between the life spans of those in developed economies, forager-horticulturalists, and extant hunter-gatherers.

The Consequences of Agriculture II: The Shrinking Human Brain

A major physical consequence of ultrasociality is that the human brain has been shrinking rapidly since agriculture. This fact is well documented and is independent of race, gender, and geographical location.[48,49,50,51,52,53,54] For example, Henneberg[55] writes of the decline in cranial capacity in Europe and North Africa during the Holocene:

> For both males and females the decrease through time is smooth, statistically significant and inversely exponential. A decrease of 157 cc (9.9% of the larger value) in males and of 261 cc (17.4%) in females is a considerable one, of the order of magnitude comparable to the difference between averages for *H. erectus* and *H. sapiens sapiens*.

Liu et al.[56] compared the cranial capacities of people living in Beiquen village in China 7,000 years ago compared to modern populations from the same area. The range was 1278–1747 cc 7,000 years ago with a mean of 1514. For females the range was 1148–1538 cc with a mean of 1368. The cranial capacities of modern humans ranged from 1219–1716 cc for males with a mean of 1471 cc, a decline of 2.9%. For females the modern range was 1062–1500 with a mean of 1289 cc, a decline of 5.7%.

Table 4.1 Mean human cranial capacity (cubic centimeters) before and after agriculture

Source	Location	Preagriculture	Present Day	% Shrinkage
Henneberg (1988)	Europe and North Africa	1,593 (male) 1,502 (female) (Mesolithic)	1,436 (male) 1,241 (female)	9.9 17.4
Liu et al. (2014)	China	1,514.3 (male) 1,367.7 (female) (7,000 kyr BP)	1,471 (male) 1,289 (female)	2.9 5.7
Ruff et al. (1997)	Worldwide	1,517 (males and females) (21–35 kyr BP)	1,349	11.1

If our bodies had shrunk at the same rate as our brains the average human would be 4' 6" and weigh 64 pounds (http://superscholar.org/shrinking-brain). According to Hawks,[57] the decrease in brain size during the last 10,000 years is nearly thirty-six times the rate of *increase* during the previous 800,000 years. There is no evidence that we are just as smart, or even smarter as some suggest, because our brains have become streamlined to be more efficient. There is no evidence that the human brain became more complex as it shrank. As with humans, increasing social complexity in ants is also associated with a loss of brain size. Riveros et al.[58] tested the association between brain size and sociality across eighteen species of fungus-growing ants and found that increased colony size was associated with decreased relative brain size.[59,60] With agriculture, ant and human brain size decreased dramatically.

The Consequences of Agriculture III: The Regimentation and Simplification of Everyday Life

A basic feature of ultrasocial systems is the subjugation of the individual for the evolutionary success of the group superorganism. Agriculture led to the loss of individuality as autonomy and intelligence were sacrificed for the benefit of surplus production. An important commonality in human and ant division of labor in ultrasocial agricultural systems is that *individual* behavioral complexity and flexibility are in general not as great compared to those societies relying on hunting and gathering. Subjugation can be understood partly as a byproduct of the division of labor in agricultural societies. The behavior of individuals, in the context of an elaborate division of labor, is simpler in ultrasocial societies even as the society grows more complex. In humans and social insects, increasing social complexity is not associated with increasing individual behavioral complexity.[61] Adam Smith recognized the danger for humans of labor specialization and the mental toll on individuals who endlessly perform the same tasks:[62]

> The man whose whole life is spent in performing a few simple operations, of which the effects are perhaps always the same, or very nearly the same, has no occasion to exert his understanding or to exercise his invention in finding out expedients for removing difficulties which never occur. He naturally loses, therefore, the habit of such exertion, and generally becomes as stupid and ignorant as it is possible for a human creature to become.

Commenting directly on Smith's observation, Mark Moffett, in reference to ants, writes:[63] "This deficiency can be observed for large ant societies as well, in which specialized workers are incapable of accomplishing much without the cooperation of nestmates." Likewise, Anderson and McShea[64] found that "individuals of highly social ant species are less complex than individuals from simple ant species." They found that individual ants in more complex ant societies with a high degree of division of labor exhibit "low individual competence" and "low individual complexity."

In both ultrasocial human and insect societies, there is a loss of *totipotency*, defined as "the potential, throughout life, to express the full behavioural repertoire of the population (even if never actually expressed)."[65] *Totipotency* is meant to capture the range of behavior in a society (e.g., occupations) compared to the range of behaviors available to a particular individual. It has been noted that workers in complex insect societies tend to be less totipotent.[66] Studies of social insects and colonial marine invertebrates (reef shrimp) show a negative correlation between colony size and totipotency.[67] In humans, the loss of totipotency is more complex. It is expressed in the extreme specialization that characterizes ultrasocial social organization, but it is also expressed by the fact that for the majority of humans, agricultural life became narrowly focused around a single economic purpose.

Interestingly, Adam Smith[68] also discussed the loss of individuality in complex societies as compared to what he called "barbarous" societies:

> Though in a rude society there is a good deal of variety in the occupations of every individual, there is not a great deal in those of the whole society. Every man does, or is capable of doing, almost every thing which any other man does, or is capable of doing. Every man has a considerable degree of knowledge, ingenuity, and invention: but scarce any man has a great degree. The degree, however, which is commonly possessed, is generally sufficient for conducting the whole simple business of the society. In a civilized state, on the contrary, though there is little variety in the occupations of the greater part of individuals, there is an almost infinite variety in those of the whole society.

Likewise Karl Marx observed: "the vitality of primitive communities was incomparably greater than that of Semitic, Greek, Roman, etc. societies and, a fortiori, that of modern capitalist societies."[69]

Intelligence, both social and collective, may be related to group size. Dunbar suggests that cognitive constraints imply a consistent group size for effective human communities:[70] "There is a species-specific upper limit to group size that is set by purely cognitive constraints." Effective group size is limited by the maximum number of individuals with whom a person (or animal) can maintain social relationships by personal contact. For humans this maximum number is somewhere around 150–200 individuals. Naroll (1956) presented evidence for a "critical threshold at a maximum settlement size of 500, beyond which social cohesion can be maintained only if there is an appropriate number of authoritarian officials."[71] The size of the neocortex increases with group size – but only up to a point. Dunbar's argument does not contradict the evidence that human brain size, and by implication cognitive ability, decreased after agriculture.

The Consequences of Agriculture IV: The Emergence of Inequality

Agriculture led directly to the emergence of hierarchical societies. Surplus production was perhaps initially a reasonable response to the favorable climate of the Holocene in the Near East. But once agriculture took hold, the expansion of surplus production became necessary to accommodate population growth, the increase in the proportion of non-productive individuals, and the unpredictable seasonal variation in harvests. Because of the premium placed on maximizing output, it was important to carefully control production and collectively manage the efforts of individual laborers. During key periods such as planting and harvesting, work was necessarily intensive and repetitive. The regimentation of work, the productive benefits of a complex division of labor, and economies of scale and size, promoted the success of agriculture but also increased the bureaucracy needed to manage the complex system. Managers were needed to regulate the timing of planting and harvesting, to monitor and distribute the surplus, and to deal with the associated ecological problems such as soil erosion and the negative effects of irrigation. In this new, complex social environment, relying on stored surpluses to carry societies over during periods of low production made maximizing surplus production in any given year all the more critical.

The need to control food surpluses and manage complex food production moved society toward social hierarchy and inherited property rights. The need for efficiency and control promoted a rigid and interdependent configuration of production and distribution. Under competitive pressure from other groups, the survival of a society depended on the successful management of food production. But those managers at the top were in a position to ensure that they benefited the most from increasing agriculture intensification and expansion. The fact that most individuals had no other options to secure the material necessities of their lives other than to take their designated place in the food-producing economy, put them at the mercy of those at the top of the social hierarchy.

Antecedents to hierarchical organization exist in nonagricultural societies, and these examples give credence to the idea that stored surplus led to the emergence of hierarchy. Delayed-return hunter-gatherer societies have some durable artifacts, such as nets and boats, and other valuable assets that can be assigned property rights, and these societies show some evidence of social stratification. An example of an incipient hierarchical culture without agriculture is that of the original inhabitants of the northwest coast of North America. A village on Keatley Creek in northwest Canada was occupied between 2,500 and 1,100 years ago by hunter-gatherers who lived on the abundant seasonal salmon runs. The village consisted of more than 115 pit houses and other structures with log and earth roofs. The peak population of the village was about 1,500 people. Evidence indicates disparities in living standards, which may have originated in unequal access to prime fishing grounds.[72,73]

• • •

The transition to agriculture was a transition to ultrasociality. Two major consequences of this transition, common to humans and the social insects that adopted agriculture, are the subjugation of individuals to the needs of the superorganism and the domination of ecosystems. A third, unique to humans, is the emergence of rigid, hierarchical social systems, dominant castes that are able to exploit humans and nature for their own benefit.

Ultrasociality: Social Complexity and Individual Simplicity

Individual simplicity may be an advantage in collective decision-making. In fact, the standard economic model of extreme rationality may apply more to ant colonies than to humans. For example, several experiments show that humans are susceptible to the fallacy of irrelevant alternatives. A choice between alternative A (a fully paid ten-day vacation to Paris) and B (a fully paid ten-day vacation to Rome) should not be influenced by the inclusion of an irrelevant unrelated choice C (a paid vacation to your least favorite nearby city). Humans are consistently susceptible to this fallacy,[74] but ants are not. Edwards and Pratt,[75] in an experiment involving the choice of an ant colony between nesting sites, showed that the colonies are not influenced by irrelevant alternatives. They surmise: "We suggest that immunity from irrationality in this case may result from the ants' decentralized decision mechanism. A colony's choice does not depend on the site comparison by individuals, but instead self-organizes from the interactions of multiple ants, most of which are aware of only a single site." In some species of ants, the colony can solve very complex problems of economic organization, and in fact it may outperform humans.[76] Collectively, ants have developed complex strategies to manage agricultural production. Like humans, they have developed a number of herbicides to control weed molds that attack the fungus they rely on, they have elaborate manuring regimes that maximize harvests, and they share cultivars between distantly related ant colonies.[77]

The social insects demonstrate that collective intelligence can be quite impressive without a corresponding level of individual intelligence. Off-loading of tasks in complex human societies is one explanation given for the decline in human brain size after the Pleistocene.[78] People may not have to be as smart to stay alive.[79] Cognitive scientist David Geary refers to this as the "idiocracy theory" after the 2006 film *Idiocracy*.[80] Geary, and Bailey and Mithen,[81,82] among others, argue that the complex material culture that came with agriculture allowed humans to off-load some cognitive requirements, allowing the energy-expensive human brain to decrease in size. Off-loading individual intelligence to the "environment," "technology," or the "social brain" is not necessarily a good thing from the point of view of an individual human. Social intelligence may have increased, but individual intelligence has declined.[83]

According to Mithen,[84] even the social brain may have deteriorated with agriculture and civilization:

> This development [sociality and social intelligence] has nothing to do with *Homo habilis* or handaxes, bipedalism or brain size. It is the origin of farming at, or soon after, 10,000 years ago. It

is only with the economic basis that farming provides that writing, mathematics, and digital technology could be invented, and it is these that effectively define the nature of our cognition today. The brain is important, of course, but it now plays a mere supporting role to a cognitive system that is primarily located in materials entirely outside the body – books, computers, paintings, digital stores of data and so forth. There are, of course, our capacities for empathy, mind reading and social interaction that no digital computer is ever likely to replace. But I doubt if these today are very different to those of our early human ancestors living several million years ago (Mithen 1996). Indeed, if anything, I suspect they have deteriorated through lack of use as we have become dependent on material items as the source of information.

A basic categorical mistake is to conflate the collective accomplishments of civilization with the understandings and intelligence of the average human. Scientific understanding of the origins of the universe and our species, the works of Shakespeare and Mozart, space exploration, and so on, are equated with individual human intelligence even though most people on the planet are unfamiliar and little affected by these achievements.

There is an important distinction between the "social brain," or "social intelligence," or "collective intelligence." According to the "social brain" hypothesis, human intelligence evolved to facilitate within-group cooperation, empathy, and mind-reading.[85,86] Collective intelligence, on the other hand, refers to the ability of groups to solve complex problems far beyond the capabilities of any individual within the group. Collective intelligence can increase while individual intelligence declines.

Do smaller brains really mean we are dumber? In general, the answer is "yes." The shrinking brain implies that humans have become less intelligent over the past few thousand years.[87] The relationship between human brain size and intelligence is controversial. But in a meta-analysis of the relationship between in vitro brain volume and intelligence, McDaniel concluded:[88] "For all ages and sex groups, it is clear that brain volume is positively correlated with intelligence." Until fairly recently the positive relationship between brain size and general mental ability (GMA) was taken for granted.[89] In the second half of the twentieth century, as a reaction to the racist ideas of the eugenics movement and the revulsion toward Nazi genocide, the subject of brain size and intelligence was more or less taboo. The subject was rekindled in the 1970s by Van Valen[90] and others. In general, recent studies have shown a significant correlation between brain size and GMA. Rushton and Ankey[91] surveyed twenty-eight studies using imaging techniques and these studies showed correlations ranging from 0.04 to 0.69, with a weighted (by sample size) mean of 0.38). In most of these studies, brain size accounts for less than half the variation in GMA. Nevertheless, the correlation is highly significant. It is sometimes argued that although the human brain has shrunk, it has become more efficient and that we have actually become more intelligent. In fact, recent research has shown just the opposite. The higher cognitive regions of the brain – the specialized regions of the cerebral cortex – are preferentially larger in individuals with larger brains.[92,93]

In view of the past abuses of brain size/intelligence data, it must be emphasized that the evidence suggests only that there has been a significant decline in average human cranial capacity during the last few thousand years, since the widespread adoption of agriculture. But this decline (again, about 10 percent) is larger than differences among contemporary humans based on race or gender. This decline in brain size is consistent with arguments that humans have become less intelligent because the survival advantages of being smarter were greatly reduced after agriculture. Crabtree writes:[94]

> I would wager that if an average citizen from Athens of 1000 BC were to appear suddenly among us, he or she would be among the brightest and most intellectually alive of our colleagues and companions, with a good memory, a broad range of ideas, and a clear-sighted view of important issues. Furthermore, I would guess that her or she would be among the most emotionally stable of our friends and colleagues. I would also make this wager for the ancient inhabitants of Africa, Asia, India or the Americas, of perhaps 2,000–6,000 years ago. The basis for my wager comes from new developments in genetics, anthropology, and neurobiology that make a clear prediction that our intellectual life and emotional abilities are genetically surprisingly fragile.

Why has brain size decreased? The human brain is an expensive organ in terms of its energy requirements. It represents about 3 percent of our body weight yet requires about 30 percent of the calories our bodies burn. If large brains are not required for survival because we have become domesticated in large groups supported by collective (group level) intelligence, it is no surprise that evolution economized on brain size and intelligence by shrinking them. But is this good for individual humans?

Agriculture involves not only managing plants but also domesticating animals. Like *Homo sapiens*, other animals have been domesticated with similar results. Compared to their wild ancestors, the brains of domestic sheep have shrunk by 24 percent over the last 10,000 years. Domestic pigs have brains 30 percent smaller than their wild ancestors.[95] As in humans, the parts of the brain that became smaller in domesticated pigs, sheep, and dogs, are those associated with the limbic system – responsible for "higher-order" functions like reason and socialization. Zeder et al. write: "With physical protection and nutrition more secure, the domesticated animal can be less intently alert to its immediate surroundings than its cousins in the wild."[96] This also applies to contemporary humans.

Agriculture and ultrasociality have had other physical effects on human populations. Hypotheses recently advanced by Brace and Ryan[97] suggest links between changes in human sexual dimorphism and changes in technology and subsistence practices. Their results indicate that present-day agriculturalists exhibit a greater degree of sexual dimorphism in stature than present-day hunter-gatherers.

Ultrasociality and Ecosystem Domination

Agriculture and the resulting transition to ultrasociality led directly to ecosystem domination. Ultrasociality evolved in only a handful of species, yet those species dominate the ecosystems within which they occur and indeed the entire planet.[98] Sanderson et al.[99] calculated that over 80 percent of the global terrestrial biosphere is under direct human influence. Astonishingly, the total dry weight human biomass (about 125 million metric tons) is over twelve times the weight of all other vertebrates combined.[100] Social insects also dominate their ecosystems to an amazing degree. Wilson estimates the total number of ants to be 10^{16}, or 10 thousand trillion.[101] If one ant weighs one-millionth of the weight of a human, the total weight of the world's ants is about the same as the total weight of all humans. In subtropical and tropical ecosystems, termites can make up as much as 95 percent of the soil insect biomass.[102,103] Ants, like humans, reengineer the ecosystems they dominate. Folgarait[104] discusses some of the major functional roles of ants in ecosystems, including soil modification through physical and chemical changes, changes in nutrient and energy fluxes, and changes in vegetation. Other species have coevolved to accommodate themselves to the presence of the numerically dominant ant and termite colonies. By contrast, the archeological and historical record of early agricultural societies is characterized by rapid expansion, followed by social disintegration.[105,106,107] Examples include the Akkadian empire, Old Kingdom Egypt, the Classic Maya, and the Harappan of the Indus valley. These civilizations disintegrated because of a variety of factors including the loss of soil fertility, erosion from reliance on annual plants, soil salinization, water mismanagement, and the inability to withstand prolonged droughts. Climate change in particular is increasingly accepted as a driver of past societal collapse and disruption.[108,109] Agriculture required the subjugation of nature for human economic benefit. The new relationship is starkly described in the book of Genesis:

> Every moving thing that lives shall be food for you; and as I gave you the green plants, I give you everything . . . The fear of you and the dread of you shall be upon every beast of the earth, and upon all the fishes of the sea; into your hand are they delivered.[110]

Social insects have had tens of millions of years of evolutionary trial and error to hone sustainable agricultural cultures. It is quite possible that the early history of ultrasocial ants and termites is also littered with unsuccessful experiments with agriculture, but today they dominate ecosystems through ways of living that are sustainable. Can humans learn something about sustainability from insect farmers? Aanen and Boomsma write:[111]

> The farming insect societies had tens of millions of years of natural selection to solve many of the challenges that are also well known to human farmers. They have conveyer-belt substrate processing, produce their own pesticides and antibiotics, and practice active waste management. Neither the ants nor the termites, however, have been able to overcome the fundamental laws of host–symbiont conflicts, which imply that only monoculture farming is evolutionarily stable. Our own farming practices evolved culturally by frequent exchange of crops, and learning and copying innovative practices. The problem is that, on the larger scale that we apply today, many of these practices are unlikely to be sustainable, even on an ecological time scale.

Ants and termites have practiced monoculture successfully for tens of millions of years, while the short history of human management of a few crops shows a pattern of recurring instability and disruption.[112] One reason social insects have achieved sustainable agriculture is that their agricultural practices have more successfully harnessed the benefits of mutualism – the advantages of cooperation between ants and termites and the fungus they raise and feed on. Our mutualism around annuals is more ecologically problematic due to soil erosion, pest control, and a number of other challenges. Cooperation between unrelated agents can have great benefits, but there is always tension between the benefits of cooperation and the benefits of defecting – the classic prisoner's dilemma. Social insects have largely overcome prisoner's-dilemma-type reproductive conflicts by developing mutualism because one-to-one cooperation is more stable (easier to enforce) than cooperation among several agents.

An Ant Perspective on Human Agriculture

Humans are one of a handful of other animals which have developed agriculture, though they only started practicing it relatively recently – roughly 15,000 years ago, no more than a brief moment compared with the 50 million years during which we've been cultivating fungi. In general, human agriculture is relatively primitive, similar to the techniques used by some of our less advanced cousins. Only recently have humans discovered the techniques required for the large-scale cultivation of pure monocultures, an advance which may be linked to the development of certain social structures in a handful of human super colonies.

In some cases, the plant partner in the mutualism appears to have lost the ability to propagate itself without the help of humans. There is even evidence that humans may select cultivars that perform best in their environment, although it's still unclear how they might accomplish this in the absence of true communication. While some researchers suggest that humans can communicate by modulating acoustic signals (imagine a more refined version of our stridulations), it's hard to imagine how such a system could be used for true communication or to coordinate behaviors on a large scale. How, for example, are messages retained over a long time period or integrated between different individuals?

In addition to the difficulties of communication, other biological limitations of humans may serve to explain some of the shortcomings of their agricultural practices. For example, while we can provide important liquid supplements to our fungi, individual humans appear unable to directly produce the nutrients needed by their crops, which are instead provided by the activity of specialized castes working in structures dedicated to this task. Studies have demonstrated that the fragrant anal paste produced by humans is a suitable substrate for plant growth; surprisingly, however, humans do not take advantage of this resource. Some researchers have suggested that humans may be unable to properly ensure the hygiene of crops grown in this manner and would thus be exposed to an unacceptable risk of parasitism, although others contend that the anal paste has in fact been used by some colonies. Clearly, further research is needed to understand this aspect of human agriculture.

Sedeer el-Showk
www.nature.com/scitable/blog/accumulating-glitches/ant_agriculture

• • •

Agriculture and ultrasociality changed the organization of human communities so that the focus became the production of agricultural surplus. This fundamentally changed the relationships among individuals within the community and the relationship of both the individual and the group to the biophysical world. Once in place, the economic factors driving efficiency in production gave a competitive advantage for those groups that could best capture them.

Sociality, caring for others, and cooperation with nonkin are defining characteristics of the human species. These traits not only made it possible for humans to flourish and survive the extreme environmental changes of the Pleistocene, but they also fostered sustainable use of environmental resources and equalitarian social arrangements. Before we became ultrasocial, these traits worked both for the benefit of the group and for individuals within the group. Small-scale human societies have developed myriad forms of social organization to minimize group conflicts and to ensure that one individual or one small group of individuals cannot dominate.[113,114] But sociality and cooperation took on a different character with ultrasociality. Coordination of agricultural production activities led to the subjugation of the individual to further the needs of the emerging superorganism. With agriculture, the almost unique ability of humans to cooperate with nonkin, was harnessed by the superorganism and restructured in a rigid and hierarchical way. Cooperation became coordination. Individuals had little choice about their role in the agricultural enterprise. The human social system was transformed into a self-organizing, self-referential entity whose "goal," indeed imperative, was to maximize agricultural output. Although the mechanisms of transformation were different than they were for social insects, the results were remarkably similar.

The emergence of ultrasociality led directly to a loss of autonomy at the individual level because autonomy interferes with the coordinated functioning of the group.[115] In evolutionary terms, adaptation at any given level in the multilevel selection hierarchy tends to be undermined by what happens at lower levels.[116] Suppression of autonomy at lower levels facilitating the smooth functioning at higher levels is called "downward causation." What is good for the higher level may not be good for entities at the lower level. For individual humans, cooperation was co-opted with agriculture, and human interactions were rigidly structured around narrowly defined productive roles. Cooperation became coordination of production. When food production became the organizing principle of society, the "good of the group" became "the good of the ultrasocial entity," not the good of the average member of the group.[117]

With agriculture the evolutionary leap to ultrasociality was made, and individual survival (and by extension to humans, individual well-being) became secondary to the survival of the superorganism as an evolutionary entity. The power of the superorganism over the individual becomes greater with increasing complexity. In an ultrasocial system, there is no reason why *specific individuals* should be more likely to survive and flourish. Like cells in a body or bees in a hive, the role of the individual is to serve the collective. In humans, sacrifice for the group is not expressed by suppressing reproduction. Rather, it is seen in the extreme interdependency that encompasses the individual and reduces the richness of individual life. When the group begins to take on a life of its own and actively begins to shape its environment, individuals and elements of the natural world come to be expendable. The surplus-generating superorganism becomes the entity driven by the imperative to survive and grow.

Part II

THE RISE AND CONSOLIDATION OF STATE/MARKET SOCIETIES

These meticulous, demanding, interlocked, and mandatory annual and daily routines, I would argue, belong at the center of any comprehensive account of the "civilizing process." They strap agriculturalists to a minutely choreographed routine of dance steps; they shape their physical bodies, they shape the architecture and layout of the domus; they insist, as it were, on a certain pattern of cooperation and coordination. In that sense, to pursue the metaphor, they are the background musical beat of the domus. Once Homo sapiens took that fateful step into agriculture, our species entered an austere monastery whose taskmaster consists merely of the demanding genetic clockwork of a few plants ...
> James Scott, 2017, *Against the Grain*, p. 91.

The ideas of the ruling class are in every epoch the ruling ideas.
> Karl Marx, 1846, *The German Ideology*, p. 46.

A key difference between humans and social insects is that human societies are characterized by hereditary social castes. Individual ants and termites do not inherit resources, privileged individual humans do. With the advent of large-scale state societies some 5,000 years ago, the lion's share of the economic surplus was commandeered by an elite class whose power was enforced by hierarchical religions, the police and military, and belief systems supporting domination and control of the everyday lives of individuals. The reorganization of human society that came with the agricultural revolution still controls and constrains our social evolution today. The human global economy has become a global, unified, interlocking system of resource extraction and surplus production. Integral to this system are institutions and belief systems supporting it. Today, neoliberalism is the dominant ideology supporting the ultrasocial system. Far from supporting individual freedom, it is a philosophy that defends sacrificing the well-being of individuals for the benefit of the global market. Fredrich Hayek, the leading figure of neoliberal philosophy, was influenced by theories of group selection and recognized that the market economy was a kind of superorganism. Neoliberals explicitly argue that the market is a supreme information processing system, far superior to human reason. They recognize the conflict between individual humans and the market superorganism, but their loyalties are with the market.

5 THE RISE OF STATE SOCIETIES

Human history after agriculture shows a gradual but uneven consolidation of small-scale societies into today's global integrated superorganism dedicated to the production of economic surplus. By our definition of ultrasocial societies, city-states with large populations, human agricultural societies took several millennia to evolve into ultrasociality. This was not a linear progression. It took 5,000 years of fits and starts, with short periods of consolidation punctuated by long periods of dispersion and decentralization. Ants and termites made this major evolutionary transition tens of millions of years ago. Humans made the same transition quite recently. Today, writ large, human society mirrors those of our agricultural ant and termite cohorts. Each individual member of these ultrasocial societies is a part of a highly integrated and highly differentiated surplus-producing super colony. Individuals cannot live outside the economic superstructure of the colony. But one critical feature separates humans from social insects – human societies are dominated by an elite few supported by ideological, legal, and religious institutions that allow them to expropriate the bulk of the produced surpluses for themselves. Throughout recorded history the expropriation of surplus by the elite has been orchestrated by the power of the state.

Against the backdrop of the 300,000-year-long evolution of *Homo sapiens*, the transition from hunting and gathering to complex, large-scale societies was quite rapid. It happened independently in a period of a few thousand years in at least three places – the Near East, China, and Mesoamerica. Yet viewed from the current epoch of rapid change, the evolution of state societies was quite slow. There is evidence of small permanent settlements and field agriculture beginning about 10,000–12,000 years ago, but full-fledged city-states did not appear until about 5,000 years ago. During that time, the growth in world population was explosive by Pleistocene standards – from about 2–4 million people 10,000 years ago to 18 million 5,000 years later – but that was nothing like the increase that occurred over the next few thousand years. By the beginning of the Common Era the human population had reached 200 million. By then the kinds of societies we are familiar with today were common, with large cities, autocratic rulers, bureaucracies, life-long hereditary occupations, taxes, and formal punishment structures for those who do not accept the discipline of the elite. Early states were fragile, prone to epidemics, environmental degradation, and political collapse.[1] The use of the word "domus" by Scott in the lead quote to this section is instructive. He uses it to describe the entire social and biological structures and substructures of agricultural society, including the birds, animals, insect parasites, and weeds that all benefited from human occupation. With agriculture, Scott argues, people, soils, cultivars, and landscapes were transformed into an integrated whole as the domus became an evolutionary force of its own.[2] The environment itself was domesticated. Agriculture and the resulting transformation of the economy into a fully integrated, surplus-producing enterprise locked us into an antihuman ultrasocial system whose consequences we are still trying to escape 10,000 years later.

The evolution of early agricultural societies in different parts of the world – from hunter-gatherers to large-scale state societies – is a remarkable example of parallel evolution – a term referring to the development of a similar trait in related, but distinct, species descending from the same ancestor. From similar hunter-gatherer ancestors, strikingly similar civilizations developed independently in several places in the world. Around 15,000 years ago all humans lived in small groups, hunting a wide variety of animals and gathering a diverse collection of plants. Most preagriculture hunter-gatherer human groups resembled the one depicted at the left in Figure 5.1. From simple societies having little division of labor except that based on age and gender and group populations of a few dozen people, similar complex cultural patterns and institutions evolved independently in the Near East, Indus Valley, the Far East, and the Americas.

Tikal

Angkor Wat

Rome

Figure 5.1 The parallel evolution of complex civilizations from similar hunter-gatherer groups

Ronald Wright[3] describes the result of the parallel evolution of agriculture in Europe and the Americas:

> What took place in the early 1500s was truly exceptional, something that had never happened before and never will again. Two cultural experiments, running in isolation for 15,000 years or more, at last came face to face. Amazingly, after all that time, each could recognize the other's institutions. When Cortés landed in Mexico he found roads, canals, cities, palaces, schools, law courts, markets, irrigation works, kings, priests, temples, peasants, artisans, armies, astronomers, merchants, sports, theatre, art, music, and books. High civilization, differing in detail but alike in essentials, had evolved independently on both sides of the earth.

The fact of the parallel social evolution of complex human state societies has some disturbing implications. It suggests that the forces driving the evolution of states and civilization transcend human intentionality and the specific characteristics of preagricultural cultures. From similar simple beginnings, the social institutions that arose with complex agriculture evolved independently to have broadly identical characteristics. This implies that major evolutionary transitions override the ability of cultures to decide their own fates. Even more disturbing, the economic structure of these civilizations, also in broad outline, resemble social insect societies. Common economic drivers and the physical requirements of the production process drove the evolution of the structure of ant, termite, and human civilizations. These patterns were the result of economic laws and natural selection, although for humans it is the natural selection of social institutions, not genes. The same patterns emerged in several human societies not in contact with each other. The historical record also shows an inevitable tendency toward consolidation of power and the capture of surplus by the elite. Central to this process is the importance of the state in maintaining the superorganism's growth and subjugation of its constituent parts to its own ends.

• • •

Economic drivers – economies of scale and scope, the complex division of labor, tapping into resource stocks like fertile soil, and redirecting flows of solar energy from nature – gave ultrasocial societies their common characteristics, huge populations dominating local ecosystems and a large variety of occupations. The details of these broad features take different forms in human and insect societies. Social insect colonies have had tens of millions of years to perfect the advantages of occupational differentiation and large size. The agricultural enterprises of social insects are sustainable.[4] Human ultrasocial societies, by contrast, have been plagued by instability. Unlike social insect societies human societies are characterized by the destabilizing existence of castes (hereditary control of economic surplus) and an overexploitation of the natural world. Inequality and ruthless exploitation are not "natural" for *Homo sapiens* – they did not exist for most of human history – and evidence indicates that they were slow to develop even after agriculture took hold. The mobility of hunter-gatherers, and their knowledge-based technologies, made the accumulation of possessions and material inequality impossible. Mobility and flexibility were efficient responses to the variable paths and timing of animal migrations and the shifting seasonality of plants growing in an unstable climate. When the climate became more stable with the Holocene, human societies in the Middle East became more sedentary even before agriculture took hold. Hunter-gatherers extensively used wild grains and there is even evidence of bread baking in northeast

Jordan some 14,000 years ago.[5] Domesticated crops did not suddenly result in very large-scale oppressive state societies. In the Near East it took thousands of years for these to develop.[6,7]

After the initial establishment of agriculture there was a period of several thousand years of small, settled communities – "stateless" societies that practiced a combination of agriculture and foraging. Scott argues that, in the Near East, along the Indus river, coastal China, and the Valley of Mexico, these early agricultural societies were based in riverine wetlands with alluvial floodplains making agriculture relatively easy and easily supplemented by a variety of fish, aquatic plants, and animals. Because of their economic flexibility, wetland societies were resistant to control from centralized authority. Scott writes:[8]

> They were based on what are now called "common property resources"—free-living plants, animals, and aquatic creatures to which the entire community had access. There was no single dominant resource that could be monopolized or controlled from the center, let alone taxed.

Early Neolithic societies may have been more egalitarian than later state societies, but their economic structure and supporting institutions laid the foundation for the repressive societies that came later. They depended on surplus production of a few grains and a complex division of labor compared to foraging societies without agriculture. These societies were ripe for a new social order based on control and exploitation. The first well-documented large-scale culture was Sumer in what is now Mesopotamia. It was settled around 7,000 years ago and was comprised of several villages, the largest of which was Eridu with about 5,000 inhabitants, thought to be the largest human settlement in the world at that time.[9] By 5,000 years ago in Sumer, much of the land was owned by family groups who controlled "temple estates," managed by the rulers in the name of the god worshipped by the population.[10] By that time Uruk had become a city of about 40,000 inhabitants. What triggered the next phase of rapid population growth and the emergence of centralized state societies? The answer to this question is far from certain but three likely candidates are climate change, warfare, and grain agriculture. These were likely interdependent and self-reinforcing.

• • •

Climate change may have triggered the formation of early states. The period 5,500–4,500 years ago was marked by increasing aridity and a sharp decline in sea level and water flow in the Euphrates.[11,12] The surrounding marshes shrank and provided less subsistence for the population. Increasing soil salinity reduced the amount of arable land. The increasing scarcity of alternatives to agriculture increased the dependence on grains. The negative consequences of a shrinking subsistence base promoted concentrations of populations and the concentration of political and economic power. Scott writes:[13]

> The shortage of irrigation water confined the population increasingly to well-watered places and eliminated or diminished many of the alternative form of subsistence, such as foraging and hunting ... Aridity proved the indispensable handmaiden of state making by delivering, as it were, an assembled population and concentrated cereal grains in an embryonic state space that could not, at that epoch, have been assembled by any other means.

Climate change may have also played an important role in the transition to state societies in the Nile Valley. The flow of the Nile river decreased significantly around 5,300 years ago resulting in an increased concentration of populations and more centralized control to manage increasingly scarce resources.[14] The increasingly arid climate concentrated the population in larger settlements and necessitated the intensification of agricultural production to offset the reduction in wetland resources. With the concentration of populations, greater dependence on storage of grains, and without the protection of the marshes, cities became a target of looting. Looting became another subsistence choice.

Warfare enhanced the consolidation of power in state societies. The existence of large stores of surplus food meant that there were now three ways to make a living – foraging, agriculture, and looting. Looting triggered an arms race for larger armies, increased top-down discipline, and military strategy and technology. Not only did warfare flourish with the development of large concentrated cities, it made living in larger cities more desirable because they had more resources to defend themselves. Human societies that were larger and better able to organize warfare, and develop war-making innovations, outcompeted others and expanded rapidly.[15,16] Eventually, warfare became prevalent as larger-scale state societies became the norm. By 1285, BCE Egypt was able to deploy an army of 20,000 people for one battle at Kadesh.[17] As Larsen puts it:[18] "The record strongly suggests that population size increases associated with food production provided conditions conducive to the rise of organized warfare and increased mortality due to violence."

The Horror of Ant Warfare

Ants are very efficient in organizing wars against other ants. They use suicide bombers, engage in chemical warfare, and employ sophisticated tactics in fighting their enemies. The endosomatic weapons of soldier ants evolved not to attack or defend against other species but rather to be used against other ants or termites. Ant armies are much more efficient than their human counterparts. In combat, army ants emphasize numbers and strategic placement, not the quality of individual soldiers. When a battalion of ants charge enemy lines the first ones in are the smallest, oldest, and most expendable. Attacks are coordinated so that the larger and more effective soldiers swarm in only after the enemy lines are breached and the target softened. Unlike humans, ants are pragmatic in warfare. Severely wounded soldiers are left to die.

In southern California, the territory of the Argentine ant Lake Hodges colony spreads over almost 50 square kilometers. To the north is the Very Large Colony, a single society whose territory stretches almost 1,000 kilometers from the Mexican border to California's Central Valley. The total population of this colony is estimated to be more than 1 trillion ants. Warfare between these two colonies results in the deaths of 30 million ants in a single year.

Mark Moffett (2010, 203–204) describes a battle between these two Argentine ant colonies:

> Trails of ants, converging in all directions, led troops over the remains of the dead. Scanning the action through my camera, I gave Melissa and David the blow-by-blow on dozens of fierce confrontations. Most started one-on-one, with a slow and meticulous approach followed by a trust-and-grab. Atop the corpses, pairs of workers pulled on each other, indefatigably, for minutes (and for all I know hours) on end. Here and there, a third or fourth worker joined in. I focused by camera on a group of three ants pulling on another that was already missing an antenna. As I watched, a hind limb tore free. The worker who wrenched it off stood for a moment as if surprised at her success, the leg hanging from her jaws, before dropping it and inspecting her adversary's stump.

Ponting[19] describes the importance of warfare to the development of the state in Sumer:

> Warfare was central to the emergence of the Sumerian city states. The earliest cylinder seals from 4000 BCE show battles and prisoners of war, and warfare became more intense as the cities developed. Armies were made up of conscripts who served as part of their obligation to the state and they fought with axes, adzes, spears and leather shields ... Cities were very vulnerable to the occupation of the land on which they depended for their food and sieges were brutal affairs. When a city was captured its walls were normally destroyed, the male population killed or enslaved and blinded, and the women and children enslaved.

The process of concentration of populations, enslavement of the general population for military service and massive construction projects, and a concentration of power in the hands of a few ruling families happened in Egypt, China, and the Indus Valley. The similar pattern of settlement, city sizes of about 50,000 people, and similar institutions including writing, court systems, religions reinforcing the oppressive social order, and organized warfare is a remarkable example of parallel evolution driven by similar environmental constraints and the requirements of surplus production.

Grain agriculture was conducive to taxes and state control. As Scott[20] points out, the subsistence base of the early state societies, from Mesopotamia, to the Indus Valley to China, was grain agriculture – wheat, barley, and millet. Later state societies added rice and maize. Grains have the unique and highly desirable characteristics of being highly nutritious, easily measured and controlled for taxation and confiscation, and providing the basis for a predictable agrarian calendar. Grains ripen at about the same time, making taxation and appropriation all the easier. Other crops such as legumes and tubers have some of these characteristics, but none have all the advantages of grains. Add to the mix the social evolution of institutions promoting and protecting inherited wealth, including religions whose authority was based on predicting the seasons of the agricultural cycle, and you have all the necessary ingredients for the hierarchical state/enterprise hybrids that have characterized human society for the past 5,000 years. Scott writes:[21]

The dense concentration of grains and manpower on the only soils capable of sustaining them in such numbers—alluvial or loess soils—maximized the possibilities of appropriation, stratification, and inequality. The state form colonizes this nucleus as its productive base, scales it up, intensifies it, and occasionally adds infrastructure—such as canals for transport and irrigation—in the interest of fattening and protecting the goose that lays the golden eggs ... one can think of these forms of intensification as elite niche construction: modifying the landscape and ecology so as to enrich the productivity of its habitat.

• • •

A striking characteristic of early state societies is their susceptibility to collapse.[22,23,24] These civilizations disintegrated because of a variety of factors, including the loss of soil fertility and soil erosion from reliance on annual plants, soil salinization, water mismanagement, and the inability to withstand prolonged droughts. Climate change in particular is increasingly accepted as a driver of past societal collapse and disruption.[25] A basic problem is that ultrasocial societies have a built-in drive to expand. The larger the surplus, the better the opportunities for food security, trade, and a larger population. But this makes them more and more vulnerable to endogenous and exogenous disturbances. Because of inertia from the interdependence between institutions, castes, and economic sectors, when destabilization begins it is difficult to change course before the point of no return is reached.

Tainter makes a strong case that collapse is driven by decreasing returns to complexity. He writes:[26]

> More complex societies are more costly to maintain than simpler ones, requiring greater support levels per capita. As societies increase in complexity, more networks are created among individuals, more hierarchical controls are created to regulate these networks, more information is processed, there is more centralization of information flow, there is increasing need to support specialists not directly involved in resource production, and the like. All this complexity is dependent on energy flow at a scale vastly greater than that characterizing small groups of self-sufficient foragers or agriculturalists. The result is that as a society evolves toward greater complexity,

the support costs levied on each individual will also rise, so that the population as a whole must allocate increasing portions of its energy budget to maintaining organizational institutions. This is an immutable fact of social evolution, and is not mitigated by type of energy source.

Social instability is an important difference between human and insect societies. Unlike insect societies, human groups are characterized by recurrent and sometimes calamitous within-group conflicts. Social inequality and the insatiable desire of the elite to confiscate economic surpluses, combined with a growth imperative supported by environmental exploitation, almost inevitably led to the disintegration of early state societies. As Scheidel documents, the longer state societies were stable, the more surplus they extracted from the laborers, the more socially unstable they became, and the more susceptible they were to exogenous shocks like climate change. In many of the societies Scheidel discusses, some members of the elite recognized the perils of overexploitation and tried to reform the system before it disintegrated into social chaos.[27] For example, during the Han empire in China between 140 BCE and 2 CE, eleven attempts were made to redistribute land to the peasants. Top government advisors recommended legal restrictions on land ownership and the number of slaves a person could have. Scheidel writes:[28]

> Unsurprisingly, these regulations—inasmuch as they were indeed attempted and not merely invented or embellished by later Han propaganda—proved unenforceable and were soon abandoned. The new regime failed in short order as the Han, backed by landlords, successfully staged a comeback.

Collapse was frequently due to environmental degradation. Compared to long-run stability of hunter-gatherer economic systems, agricultural systems led within a few thousand years to huge population increases and environmental disruption. One of the best-documented examples of this pattern comes from ancient Mesopotamia. Even before the rise of large city-states, villages were being abandoned as deforestation and soil erosion caused crop yields to decline.[29,30] The first large-scale state collapse was the empire of Akkadia in Mesopotamia. Weiss et al.[31,32] document in detail the pattern of rapid growth, environmental degradation, and abrupt collapse of this empire. The Akkadian Empire was at its peak from 2300 BCE to 2200 BCE. The period from about

2500 to 2200 was characterized by agricultural intensification and gradual environmental degradation from erosion and irrigation. Weiss et al. argue that collapse was triggered by an abruptly drier climate that led to the abandonment of the area for the next 300 years. At this time historical accounts record an influx of "barbarians" and the construction of fortifications to keep them at bay. During the Akkadian and Ur periods the negative effects of irrigation were apparent. There was a shift from the cultivation of wheat to more salt-tolerant barley. Around 3500 BCE, equal amounts of barley and wheat were grown, but by 2500 BCE wheat represented only 15 percent of the crop.[33] There was a steady decline in total grain production and during the period from 2100 BC to 1700 BC, it is estimated that the population in this area declined by nearly three-fifths. Ponting writes:[34]

> The artificial system that was the foundation of Sumerian civilization was very fragile and in the end brought about its downfall. The later history of the region reinforces the point that all human interventions tend to degrade ecosystems and shows how easy it is to tip the balance toward destruction. It also suggests that it is very difficult to redress the balance or reverse the process once it has started. Centuries later, when the city states of Sumer were no longer even a memory, the same processes were at work elsewhere in Mesopotamia. Between 1300 and 900 BCE there was an agricultural collapse in the central area following salinization as a result of too much irrigation.

How Ant Slaves Overthrow Their Masters

In the northeastern United States, a species of ant called *Protomognathus americanus* invades the homes of its neighbor ants of the genus *Temnothorax* and captures their brood to be raised as slaves. The slave ants do not reproduce, so there seems to be no evolutionary reason why they would rebel against their masters. Yet the slave ants will frequently stop feeding and caring for their masters and will sometimes revolt and tear their young charges apart. Some 60 percent of the brood cared for by slaves die, compared to only 20 percent in colonies without slaves. The evolutionary explanation is that by doing this they reduce the number of slave catchers, thereby protecting their nearby relatives from capture.

http://discovermagazine.com/2013/may/05-how-ant-slaves-overthrow-their-masters

Another well-documented example of environment-induced collapse is the Mayan civilization that flourished for several centuries in southern Mexico, Belize, Guatemala, and Honduras. This area of lowland tropical jungles had fairly large settlements by 450 BCE. The city of Tikal had emerged by 250 BCE. Mayan cities became increasingly complex and by 600 CE had large cities of up to 50,000 inhabitants, huge pyramids, elaborate courts and architecture, trade routes, and complex administrative and religious institutions. Mayan civilization began to disintegrate after 850 CE with increasing warfare between Mayan cities, population dispersal, and abandonment of the large ceremonial centers. The later years were characterized by soil erosion and deforestation. The decline of the Mayans coincided with a centuries-long drought between 850–925 CE. The drought explanation was once considered suspect because it was thought that the northern Maya cities did not suffer the kind of decline during the drought that the southern ones did. But a recent study using detailed information from Mayan stone calendars and new radiocarbon dating techniques found that the North was also severely impacted by the drought.[35] There was a 70 percent decline in stone calendar inscriptions after 850 CE and a sharp decline in the number of wooden structures. Following the Mesopotamian pattern, the severe drought was exacerbated by the environmental consequences of a large population and increasing agricultural intensification. All of this fed political instability and warfare between cities.

• • •

The overshoot and collapse pattern supports Tainter's[36] thesis of decreasing marginal returns to complexity because of the fragility of complex systems. Recurring themes are:

- Increasing scale leads to environmental degradation. The economic, political, and military advantages of larger-scale societies lead to agricultural intensification, over-irrigation and salinization, declines in soil fertility, eventual declines in agricultural output, and political/ social instability.
- Political and economic concentration leads to increasing social fragility. The pattern of early agricultural states seems to be long periods of relative autonomy punctuated by relatively short periods of unification and coercion. Thompson[37] writes: "[I]t is not only disintegration needs to be explained but rather also the occasional, temporary, and essentially aberrational successes at integration or unification."

- Complex societies are increasingly susceptible to *exogenous* environmental changes such as slight shifts in rainfall patterns, and/or periods of warming or cooling.

State collapse improved the lives of most people. The power of the state makes it possible to move surpluses from the masses to the elite through seizing the means of production (land) and imposing confiscatory taxes. Ester Boserup writes:[38] "it is impossible to prevent the members of the lower classes from finding other means of subsistence unless they are made personally unfree. When population becomes so dense that land can be controlled it becomes unnecessary to keep the lower classes in bondage; it is sufficient to deprive the working class of the right to be independent cultivators." In early state societies slavery was taken for granted. As Scott puts it:[39] "No slavery, no state." Finley writes:[40]

> The pre-Greek world – the world of the Sumerians, Babylonians, Egyptians, and Assyrians; and I cannot refrain from adding the Mycenaens – was, in a very profound sense, a world without free men, in the sense in which the west has come to understand the concept.

Did State Societies Select for Genes of Domination and Obedience?

Figure 5.2 Roman crucifixions after the Spartacus slave revolt

After the Spartacus slave revolt, in 71 BCE, some 6,000 slaves were killed and crucified along the roads to Rome. Michael Harner estimates the number of persons sacrificed in central Mexico in the fifteenth century to be as high as 250,000 per year. Did these mass killings suppress genes for rebellion and dissent? The systematic slaughter of rebels in ancient China, the Middle East, and Europe certainly repressed descent and may have skewed our genetic makeup toward passivity and acceptance of strong leaders.

On the other side, successful rulers were astoundingly successful in propagating their genes. Genghis Khan is estimated to have fathered thousands of children in Russia, India, and Central Asia. A recent study estimated that 1 out of every 200 individuals alive today is a direct descent of Genghis Khan.

Michael Harner. 1977. The enigma of Aztec sacrifice, *Natural History* 86(4), 46–51; Tatiana Zerjal et al. 2003. The genetic legacy of the Mongols. *The American Journal of Human Genetics*, 72 (3), 717–721

We are all taught to admire the Ancient Greeks for their philosophy, literature, and art. But the population of Athenian society was two-thirds slaves, and that of Sparta even higher. The classical state societies are considered to be pinnacles of human achievement. The periods when state societies were in decline are called "dark ages." But as Scott asks, "dark for whom?"

The histories of early state societies are ones of relatively short periods of consolidation and control followed by long periods of dispersal and decentralization. For most of human history after agriculture, powerful states were the exception rather than the rule. For example, after the fall of Ur III around 2800 BCE there was a thousand-year-long hiatus of "ruralization" and pastoralism – a respite from taxes, wars, disease, and bondage. Scott argues further that the period from the first appearance of states until their complete hegemony some 5,000 years later, was a "golden age of barbarians." Barbarians had the best of both worlds. They had the autonomy to pursue limited agriculture, foraging, and hunting, and they had the opportunity to take some of the spoils of the state through raiding and pillaging. The barbarians, according to Beckwith:[41]

> [w]ere in general much better fed and led easier, longer lives than the inhabitants of the large agricultural states. There was a constant drain of peoples escaping from China to the realms of the

eastern steppe, where they did not hesitate to proclaim the superiority of the nomad lifestyle. Similarly, many Greeks and Romans joined the Huns and other Central European peoples, where they lived better and were treated better than they had been back home.

• • •

By the beginning of the Common Era 2,000 years ago, the basic institutions that rule us today were in place – hierarchical states, organized religion to justify the power of the elites and the subjugation of the masses, social castes, and economies dominated by highly integrated state/market subsectors like the military, agriculture, and trade. Reliable population records did not exist until about 200 years ago. Nevertheless, it is possible through tax records, historical accounts, and partial censuses to have some idea of world and regional populations in the Common Era. Interestingly, the human population was relatively stable after the first state societies were established until about 1500–1600 CE. According to Ponting, the world population at the beginning of the Common Era was about 250 million and in the year 1500 CE about 350 million.[42] During that period the population of China increased from 50 million to about 75 million, and that of Europe from about 50 million to 60 million. Populations were periodically decimated by plagues and famine, and energy use was limited by the costs of feeding and caring for draft animals. With organic agriculture, and energy coming only from wood and grain for draft animals, societies were particularly susceptible to even small changes in climate. Within these state societies life for most people was far inferior to that of early agriculturalist or their hunter-gatherer ancestors. Ponting writes of the early state societies:[43]

> All but about 5 per cent of the people in the world were peasants, directly dependent on the land and living a life characterized by high infant mortality, low life expectancy and chronic undernourishment, and with the ever-present threat of famine and the outbreak of virulent epidemics. The food they ate was almost entirely vegetable in origin (especially in Asia, Africa and the Americas) and the dietary staples were the three major crops of the world—rice in Asia, maize in the Americas and wheat (supplemented by oats and rye) in Europe. Because of the overwhelming dependence of these societies on agriculture there were severe limits on the scale of other activities and the numbers of soldiers, priests and craftsmen that could be supported by the peasantry.

Societies in the first few thousand years after large-scale agriculture began lived in a precarious balance between population levels, agricultural output, seasonal weather, and longer-term climate change. Agricultural technology was simple, transportation was slow, and the amount of food that could be stored was limited. All agriculture was essentially local and crop failures in one area could not be offset by surpluses in other areas. Intensive cultivation of the same crops reduced soil fertility as did deforestation and irrigation. These problems were made worse by the confiscatory power of religious and political elites who expropriated food from the peasants. Marauding armies moved through the countryside looting, destroying crops, and killing farm animals. States were generally short-lived because they added another level of complexity and vulnerability to an already vulnerable system.

Peasants

Traditional peasant villages, although besieged by surrounding cities and state power, have existed semi-independently within state societies for millennia. Observers of traditional peasant communities are struck by the self-sufficiency of these societies. Georgescu-Roegen describes the peasant village as "a perfectly natural, atomic, social unit." Access to resources – gardens, wood, land, pastures, hunting grounds – was open to all by virtue of membership in the group that controlled them. Individuals could not be denied access to the means of subsistence. Without labor compulsion or an individual drive to accumulate, there was no incentive to produce more than was required by local standards of living. When these standards were met there was no reason to further increase the drudgery of agricultural work.

The fortunes of the peasantry ebbed and waned with the power of the state to force and extract surplus production. The changing fortunes of peasant communities depended critically on the power of the state. Once the basic needs of the village were met, there was no reason to produce more surplus. The logic of capitalist accumulation did not apply. Surplus production had to be coerced and the power to do so rose and fell with the ability of the elite to control the countryside.

Nicholas Georgescu-Roegen, N. 1972. The institutional aspects of peasant communities.

It is hard to appreciate the brutality of these early state societies because we have been indoctrinated since childhood about the glories of civilization – the grand architecture and religious monuments, "advanced" monotheistic religions, the wisdom of kings, art, literature, and record keeping. Our history books glorify state societies. But it should not be forgotten that even the achievements of writing and mathematics came about in order to document and quantify surpluses so they could be expropriated from the people who produced them. Pierre-Joseph Prudhon writes:[44]

> To be governed is to be at every operation, at every transaction, noted, registered, counted, taxed, stamped, measured, numbered, assessed, licensed, authorized, admonished, prevented, reformed, corrected, punished.

Writing began as an instrument of control. One of the earliest examples of writing is the cuneiform tablets of Sumer. Tablets from the city of Uruk some 5,000 years ago, reveal a massive effort to document and quantify the production and productive capacity of this early state society. These tablets quantify units of land, labor, and grain, into standard categories. Labor standards are specified for different kinds of work and for quantities of commodities like fish, oil, and textiles. Livestock, slaves, and workers are counted and measured in terms of gender and age. It was not until much later that writing came to represent human speech.[45] Algaze suggests that writing was resisted in areas not controlled by states because it was seen as an instrument of repression and subjugation.[46] A similar view was expressed by Lévi-Strauss:

> Writing appears to be necessary for the centralized stratified state to reproduce itself ... Writing is a strange thing ... The one phenomenon which has invariably accompanied it is the formation of cities and empires; the integration into a political system, that is to say, of a considerable number of individuals ... into a hierarchy of castes and classes ... It seems to favor rather the exploitation than the enlightenment of mankind.[47]

• • •

Scott points out that most of the world's population, prior to 1500–1600 CE, did not live in state societies. Most of the earth's population were what he calls "free barbarians," people living in the periphery of a state but not within it. They typically lived in areas hard to penetrate and hard to cultivate – dense forests, swamps, and marshes. They could be shifting cultivators, hunter-gatherers, or anything in between. Barbarians were the original "deplorables," eating meat instead of grains, living in hills, forests, and swamps instead of within city walls. Barbarians could not exist without the other world of state societies. The existence of the barbarian world provided a frontier that waxed and waned with the fortunes of the state. To be a barbarian was a viable alternative to being a peasant.

Do barbarians still exist with modern societies? In her pathbreaking book *White Trash: The 400-Year Untold History of Class in America*, Nancy Isenberg documents the continued existence of an underclass seemingly incapable of being assimilated into mainstream society. "Vagrants" have always plagued civilized countries, even the leading commercial successes like England. London's Bridewell Prison, explicitly built for reforming vagrants, was chartered in 1553. Isenberg writes:[48]

> The English had waged a war against the poor, especially vagrants and vagabonds, for generations. A series of laws in the fourteenth century led to a concerted campaign to root out this wretched "mother of all vice." By the sixteenth century, harsh laws and punishments were fixed in place. Public stocks were built in towns for runaway servants, along with whipping posts and cages variously placed around London. Hot branding irons and ear boring identified this underclass and set them apart as a criminal contingent.

> Slums enveloped London. As one observer remarked in 1608, the heavy concentrations of poor created a subterranean colony of dirty and disfigured "monsters" living in "caves." They were accused of breeding rapidly and infecting the city with a "plague" of poverty, thus figuratively designating unemployment a contagious disease.

Barbarians were enveloped by modern states but not absorbed.

The colonies of America and Australia were first and foremost a repository for that class of people who were not assimilated into proper British society. As John White put it in 1630 in *The Planter's Plea*: "Colonies ought to be Emunctories or Sinkes of States; to drayne away the filth." Conditions at the new world settlement at Jamestown clearly illustrated the continuation of the pattern of surplus extraction based on slave labor that began with the earliest state societies:[49]

> The leaders of Jamestown had borrowed directly from the Roman model of slavery: abandoned children and debtors were made slaves. When indentured adults sold their anticipated labor in return for passage to America, they instantly became debtors, which made their orphaned children a collateral asset. It was a world not unlike the one Shakespeare depicted in *The Merchant of Venice*, when Shylock demanded his pound of flesh. Virginia planters felt entitled to their flesh and blood in the forms of the innocent spouses and offspring of dead servants.

The massive accumulation and concentration of wealth that characterizes state societies could not have occurred without the apparatus of state control and coordination with the expropriating class. Throughout history a prime source of accumulation has been the expropriation of common property by the elite. The confiscation of common property has been one of the driving factors behind the existence of the barbarian/vagabond castes. Polanyi writes:[50]

> Enclosures have appropriately been called a revolution of the rich against the poor. The lords and nobles were upsetting the social order, breaking down ancient law and custom, sometimes by means of violence, often by pressure and intimidation. They were literally robbing the poor of their share in the common, tearing down the houses which, by the hitherto unbreakable force of custom, the poor had long regarded as theirs and their heirs'. The fabric of society was being disrupted; desolate villages and the ruins of human dwellings testified to the fierceness with which the revolution raged, endangering the defenses of the country, wasting its towns, decimating its population, turning its overburdened soil into dust, harassing its people and turning them from decent husbandmen into a mob of beggars and thieves.

• • •

The fossil fuel revolution supercharged the superorganism. After millennia of slow growth, punctuated by declines driven by disease and famine, the human population began its second major explosion, the current demographic transition. World population increased from under 700 million in the year 1700 to over 7 billion today.[51] The impetus for this transformation was the fossil fuel revolution, although economic life began to change before fossil fuels were important. Trade and transportation expanded and production began to be reorganized and rationalized. Guilds and merchants predate the industrial revolution and the "putting out" system was well established in rural areas before the industrial revolution took hold. But there were increasing inefficiencies and bottlenecks. Steffen et al. point out:[52]

> One feature stood out in the world that humanity left as it entered the Industrial Revolution; it was a world dominated by a growing energy bottleneck. The primary energy sources were tightly constrained in magnitude and location. They consisted of wind and water moving across the Earth's surface, and, on the biosphere, plants and animals. All of these energy sources are ultimately derived from the flow of energy from the Sun, which drives atmospheric circulation and the hydrological cycle and provides the fundamental energy source for photosynthesis. These processes have inescapable intrinsic inefficiencies; plants use less than 1% of the incoming solar radiation for photosynthesis and animals eating plants obtain only about 10% of the energy stored in the plants. These energy constraints provided a strong bottleneck for the growth of human numbers and activity.

As a massive influx of fossil fuel energy entered the human economy, economic life was transformed from being predominantly agricultural to one dominated by manufacture, trade and finance. Fossil fuels – a vast, accessible, and flexible energy source – moved humans to another level of ultrasociality. Landes lays out the transition in economic terms and brings the industrial revolution into focus:[53]

> By 1800 the United Kingdom was using perhaps 11 million tons of coal a year; by 1830, the amount had doubled; fifteen years later it had doubled again; and by 1870 it was crossing the 100-millionton mark. This last was equivalent to 850 million calories of energy, enough to feed a population of 850 million adult males for a year (actual population was then about 31 million).

With the industrial revolution, the level and variety of economic output expanded and production was reorganized beyond recognition in just a few centuries. The organization of work was altered as the rhythm of economic life came to be dictated, not by agricultural seasons but rather by the pace of the machine.

So much has been written about fossil fuels and the industrial revolution that they will not be discussed in detail here.[54,55] However, the energetic transformation of the productive process is relevant to the intensification of human ultrasociality. One barrel of oil contains the energy equivalent of 20,000 person-hours of work. Moreover, this energy is flexible, storable, and transportable. Fossil fuel energy has transformed every aspect of human society, from an individual's capacity to perform work to global population size. Cheap energy has also transformed the size and metabolism of population centers. In the year 1500 only three cities in the world had populations around 500,000: Beijing, China, Vijayanagar, India, and Cairo, Egypt. By 1900 dozens of cities had more than 1 million inhabitants, with London, the center of the early industrial revolution, having a population of 6 ½ million. As recently as 1950 only one city, New York, reached a population of 10 million. Today, more than twenty cities have populations larger than 20 million and three of them have more than 30 million.

The energetics of hunter-gatherer bands are little different from those of, say, a wolf pack or a chimpanzee group. The energetics of ultrasocial societies, however, point to a major evolutionary transition such that the metabolic characteristics of the entire society resemble those of an individual organism. Here again, there are parallels to the social insects. Larger group size may be more metabolically efficient because of economies of scale in energy use. Hou et al.[56] and Shik et al.[57] demonstrate this in their studies of ant colonies using Kleiber's Law. The rate at which an organism processes energy increases at a rate that is approximately equal to that organism's body mass to the power of 3/4. Larger colonies have lower rates of per capita energy use.[58] But there seems to be an upper limit on leaf-cutter ant colony size due to the fact that colonies will eventually reach a limit where the returns to increasing foraging territory are not profitable. Eric Chaisson[59] has calculated the energy rate density (ERD) – how much energy flows through each gram of a system per second – for a number of diverse systems. For example, a star has an ERD of 2 ergs per gram per second and a houseplant 3,000–6,000 ERD. He estimates that human hunter-gatherer societies have an ERD of 40,000 ERDs, while technological societies have ERDs of 2 million ergs per gram per second. Post–hunter-gatherer societies are qualitatively different. However, it takes energy to get energy, and sooner or later the human economy will reach the point where the energy returns to energy invested will be less than one.[60] Whether the transition to a declining growth economy will be relatively smooth or chaotic remains to be seen.

• • •

In the period since World War II, dubbed the Great Acceleration, the human presence on planet earth has undergone a transformation comparable to the magnitude of the agriculture revolution and the age of fossil fuels. In fact, the human impact on the natural world in that period is unique in human history. In the past seventy years the world population has tripled from 2.5 billion to 7.5 billion and is expected to reach 9–10 billion by 2050. World economic output has grown by fivefold and energy consumption has quadrupled – all as a consequence of the expansionary drive of the global market economy unleashed after the breakdown of the old world order after the wars and economic disruptions of the first half of the twentieth century.[61] Since World War II atmospheric CO_2 has increased by a staggering 100 ppm, from 300 ppm to over 415 ppm. The rapidity of this increase is 10–100 times greater than any recorded during the last half-million years.[62] The human imprint on the planet is now observable in worldwide geological indicators of ocean, atmospheric, and land changes.

An Ant Super Colony Takes Over the World

Argentine ants have formed colonies numbering in the billions and some of them constitute a single global super colony stretching across several continents. They are all genetically similar and will refuse to fight one another. One colony ranges for 6,000 kilometers across southern Europe, another extends for 900 kilometers across California, another colony lives in New Zealand, another in Australia, two more in Hawaii, and another on the west coast of Japan. Ants from any of these colonies can be introduced into any other of the colonies and be accepted as if they belong to that colony. These ants do show aggression toward ants from other

Argentine super colonies in South America and smaller colonies in California and Hawaii.

Wilgenberg et al. found that the eight tolerant populations were remarkably homogeneous in spite of their geographical separation and the fact that some of them were established over a century ago. Wilgenberg et al. write "Our genetic and chemical data support the behavioral data: the supercolonies that are mutually tolerant are also genetically and chemically very similar, whereas those that are aggressive are genetically and chemically more different."

Ellen van Wilgenburg, Candice Torres, and Neil Tsutsui. 2010. The global expansion of a single ant supercolony. *Evolutionary Applications* 3, 136–143

The recent effects on the earth's biota have been dire. The numbers of birds, fish, insects, and mammals have declined by half since the 1970s. Climate change is upsetting the balance within ecosystems as some species adapt faster than others, predator–prey synchronization is upset, and the rapidity of change makes adaptation impossible for many species. Perhaps the greatest threat to wildlife is the ongoing boom in land disturbance. Driven by Chinese mega-enterprises, vast areas of Southeast Asia, Africa, and South America are being transformed through road building and dam construction. China's belt and road initiative consists of 7,000 projects in seventy countries, with a projected spending of $7 trillion.[63] An estimated 12 million kilometers of roads have been built since 2000 with another 25 million kilometers projected to be built by 2050. Most of these roads will be in the tropics in areas where biodiversity is particularly great.

• • •

Human history since the adoption of agriculture shows some remarkable examples of parallel evolution. First of all, the three kinds of organisms that developed agriculture – ants, humans, and termites – differ from all others by their domination of the ecosystems they occupy, by their complex division of labor and array of occupations, and by the subjugation of individuals for the group "goal" of surplus production. Secondly, once agriculture took hold in societies that were able to rely on grains, human societies developed in remarkably similar ways. Cities, states, writing, accounting, bureaucracies, state-sponsored religions, caste systems, royal based on divine right, and extreme inequality appeared in every case. The key word describing these societies is exploitation – the ruthless extraction of productive resources from nature and the equally ruthless extraction of labor power from human beings. In broad terms the same economic drivers have the same impact on all ultrasocial systems. Humans are not ants, but the forces of natural selection have the same effect of channeling similar results when similar initial conditions are present.

With the transition from hunting and gathering to small-scale settled communities, and then to large-scale agricultural production and powerful states, human societies were transformed into highly integrated, self-reinforcing systems dedicated to surplus production. The emphasis on producing surplus was critical to the transformation of the human economy from small-scale societies living off direct flows from nature, to large-scale city-states organized to maximize economic production by exploiting humans and nature. In many (almost all) cases, this set these societies on the path to collapse, either from the over-exploitation of nature (water, soils, forests) or the overexploitation of the masses by the elite leading to social upheaval (wars, revolts, social disintegration). Usually, environmental and social collapses went hand in hand through positive feedback loops. Overexploitation of the environment led to shortages and social unrest, and overexploitation of people led to more environmental degradation.

The first challenge is to identify the forces driving human society in certain directions and to evaluate the effects of these drivers. The second, and much more formidable challenge is to blunt and redirect those forces in ways to make the ultrasocial system more responsive to the needs of individual humans.

Nature as a Resource to Be Exploited – resource exploitation for surplus production is a characteristic of human and social insect societies. But tens of millions of years of ant and termite evolution have produced systems to avoid recurrent instability. There are natural cycles of life, death, and reproduction of colonies to ensure their long-term survival. Human societies, on the other hand, if not aggressively and systematically checked by conscious intervention by carefully crafted human institutions, will bring about the disruption of the earth's basic biophysical processes and will likely bring the human enterprise to a halt.

Human Beings as a Resource to Be Exploited – humans have castes, social insects do not. The history of state societies is one of the actual or virtual enslavement of most people to produce the opulence enjoyed by a tiny minority. This again is a natural tendency in human social evolution and it too must be checked by human agency if we are to avoid social disintegration.

Is collapse inevitable? The word collapse is widely used to describe the fall of past civilizations, but the demise of most of these societies was not sudden or final. Remnant populations survived and they were usually able to migrate to other areas, sometimes without a dramatic decline in material well-being. But past societies collapsed *local* ecosystems and now humans are in danger collapsing *global* systems. Still, it would be foolish to predict the imminent collapse of global capitalism. Such predictions have been made many times before and yet the system rolls on, apparently unaffected by any of the potential calamities listed. Yet if we ask not "when" but "whether" the current world system will disintegrate, whether slowly or suddenly, the answer would seem to be a clear "yes." That answer comes not only from an examination of the current consensus on twenty-first-century scenarios on climate change, fossil fuel exhaustion, and the diffusion of weapons of mass destruction technology but also from a growing body of research on past societies that have exhibited the same general pattern as our own.

• • •

The common patterns in human history raise the question: "Do cultures have free will?" A dominant pattern of cultural evolution since the advent of agriculture is a tendency toward eventual social disintegration. Cultures seem to become locked into patterns of behavior that were successful in early stages of development but dysfunctional in later stages. Over time, cultures build up a complex superstructure of material capital, learned patterns of behavior, and ethical systems. "Sunk costs" include not only capital and technology but also social systems of beliefs justifying the established way of doing things. These social systems reinforce the power elites that invariably control complex societies. Those who have the most to lose by dramatic changes have the power to reward those who accept the status quo and punish those who do not. Those few cultures that were able to change course did so because they were apparently able to modify behavioral incentives to reward sustainable behavior. Two kinds of societies that were able to do this are egalitarian societies with small populations, such as the

Pacific island of Tikopia, that worked by bottom-up consensus and top-down hierarchical societies such as Tokugawa, Japan that could impose sustainability by decree.[64] Neither of these models is feasible in today's global market economy of competing nations.

These observations may seem overly pessimistic but the history of past societies – and the mounting evidence of our own unsustainability – strongly suggests that to survive collapse, piecemeal change will not be enough. It is better to face the future realistically from where we are rather than to pretend that limited measures within a business-as-usual framework will get us through the population and resource bottleneck of the current century. It may be possible to feed the projected human population of over 9 billion in the year 2050.[65] But we should not assume that technology will automatically solve the food production problem or the problems of destabilizing climate change, ocean acidification, and biodiversity loss. Will population growth continue unabated, or will the human global society collapse? Will the benefits of technology outpace the destabilizing effects of increased complexity, social instability, and environmental degradation? The human population is expected to peak at about 10 billion around the year 2100 and decline after that. If we are to survive the twenty-first century, more than a blind faith in individual initiative is required. We need collective policies to gain control of the market/state superorganism, whose growing domination of society is eliminating democratic human agency.

6 THE MODERN STATE/MARKET SUPERORGANISM

Markets could not exist without the state. The state and the market are parts of one integrated system "designed" for growth and surplus generation. The state is also essential to curbing the excesses of the market. Karl Polanyi writes:

> To allow the market mechanism to be sole director of the fate of human beings and their natural environment, indeed, even of the amount and use of purchasing power, would result in the demolition of society ... Robbed of the protective covering of cultural institutions, human beings would perish from the effects of social exposure; they would die as the victims of acute social dislocation through vice, perversion, crime, and starvation. Nature would be reduced to its elements, neighborhoods and landscapes defiled, rivers polluted, military safety jeopardized, the power to produce food and raw materials destroyed.[1]

Critical to the success of early states was the control of the population by institutions protecting the status quo – state-sponsored religions, hereditary rule, caste systems, the military, and police. Institutions and ideologies supporting the global superorganism emerged like antibodies to protect the system's ability to extract the resources it needs to grow and prosper. State religions indoctrinated belief in the divine right of rulers and submission to authority. The military has also been an essential part of the state, as a source of power and suppression, as a source of surplus extraction through looting neighboring states, and as a source of employment. A strong military was essential to protect the surplus and to seek out new opportunities for exploitation. These systems continue today – belief systems promoting economic expansion and resource exploitation, formal institutions coordinating economic activity, and state support for capital formation, large-scale investment projects, and confiscating common property for private gain. The details may differ, but the structure and functions of today's states are broadly similar to those that emerged thousands of years ago.

Since state societies began to organize surplus production and distribution, there has been a universal tendency for elites to form and to consolidate their power and control over economic surplus.[2] Robert Michaels dubbed this "the iron law of oligarchy."[3] But within the state/ market system, as observers from Adam Smith to Marx to Keynes have noted, there has always been a struggle between classes over the economic surplus. The benefits going to elites have waxed and waned as the relative power of the majority has increased or decreased. Events in the first half of the twentieth century, the devastation of two world wars, and the Great Depression, decimated the wealth and power of the elite and ushered in a period of remarkable economic growth and prosperity for the majority.[4] In recent decades, however, the relative power of elites has increased and entered a particularly virulent phase. For the past forty years or so almost all the benefits of surplus creation have gone to the top 1 percent and the costs have been borne by the rest of us and by the nonhuman world.

All ultrasocial systems function as single organisms. But human societies differ from those of social insects in that they function with centralized top-down control. Control in insect societies is diffused throughout the system in what Gordon calls "control without hierarchy."[5] Ant and termite colonies are held together by genes, the human economy is held together by social institutions and belief systems. Both systems arose through natural selection working on groups. To understand how the human ultrasocial economy works it is useful to focus on recurring general patterns such as the tendency toward increasing concentration of wealth over time, the development of ideologies supporting hierarchical control, and the capture of institutions to increase the wealth of the elite. The state, the market, and supporting ideologies function as a single entity. The dichotomy between "the government" and "the market" is a false one. Without strong central governments there would be no market economy. The real question is "whose interests does the state promote?"

• • •

Table 6.1 Government expenditures as percent of GDP for selected economies

Argentina	41	Australia	35
Austria	51	Belgium	53
Canada	42	China	24
France	56	India	27
Germany	45	Mexico	27
Norway	44	Sweden	51
Switzerland	34	United States	43

www.bing.com/search?q=gdp+and+government+spending&form=
EDGEAR&qs=AS&cvid=c505ea711f75406db1d4c1d6d2742705&
cc=US&setlang=en-US&PC=DCTS

The state dominates modern economies. In general, the richer the country the larger the government's role in the economy. The modern market economy could not exist without massive government control, spending, and resource allocation.

Government expenditure/GDP ratios are between 40 and 50 percent for most developed countries. The ratio is about the same in Canada, Germany, Norway, and the United States. The important difference between the United States and Scandinavian democratic socialist countries is not the size of government. It is how the government collects and spends its tax dollars – who benefits and who pays. It's a matter of where government money is directed, and which sections of the economy are supported by the state and which are not. Does government spending promote the public good or does it promote corporate interests and the ruling elite? The question is not how large the government should be but rather whose interests should it serve. In conservative ideology, government policies to protect the environment or to focus on the well-being of the average person interfere with individual rights. Policies that channel public funds to private gain and promote unsustainable resource exploitation take first place in government spending priorities. Economic models of behavior like "economic man" independent of social context, and "perfectly competitive firms" independent of government, perpetuate the false government/market dichotomy.

• • •

A prevailing myth is that the driving force behind the dynamics of contemporary capitalism is the independent entrepreneur. The free-wheeling innovator comes up with a new idea, forms a company, and creates thousands of new jobs. The only obstacle the entrepreneur faces is government bureaucracy and red tape that stifles private initiative. But as Mazzucoto[6,7] documents, the real driver of innovation is government research. She writes: "The real innovation engine in the global economy is not the entrepreneurial class blazing capitalist trails through the thicket of government red tape and taxation. No. The real engine of innovation is government."[8] One of Mazzucato's most telling examples for debunking the myth of the individual trail-blazing entrepreneur is the iPhone, an icon of corporate innovation. All of its core technologies – capacitive sensors, solid-state memory, the click wheel, GPS, Internet, cellular communications, Siri, microchips, touchscreen – came from research efforts and funding support of the US government and military. Taxpayer money and government-sponsored researchers developed the technology, while private corporations reaped the profits.

An oft-cited example of government ineptness is Solyndra – a California company manufacturing high-tech solar panels that received $537 million under the government's 2009 American Recovery and Reinvestment Act. Solyndra declared bankruptcy in 2011 and the company became a poster child for the conservative argument that the government "can't pick winners and losers" and shouldn't interfere with "natural" market forces. What most commentators fail to mention is that the other company to get such a large loan was Tesla ($465 million from the government, compared to $187 million from private funds).[9] The government had an option to buy several million shares of Tesla stock for about $5 per share, but did not exercise it. A few years later Tesla stock was worth over $300 per share. As the Tesla/Solyndra example shows, commentators have been quick to criticize public investments when things go wrong and slow to praise them when things go right. As Mariana Mazzucato argues, government investment should be seen as a portfolio with some investments working out and others not. She makes the case that the public should share the gains from its risk-taking, not just bear the losses.

• • •

The United States provides one of the best examples of the state/market superorganism employing an array of policies to promote the flourishing of economic growth and concentrated accumulation. Debates in the United States about the major social issues of our time – health, education, and welfare – focus on costs. Conservatives have shaped the debate by decrying "runaway government spending." How can the government afford to spend more money on health care by instituting affordable universal coverage? How can the government afford to provide a free college education for all? One answer is that the United States already spends more than enough money on health and education to achieve these objectives. Current subsidies go largely to corporations and those who can already afford health care and education rather than those who need them most. The degree of capture of governments by the elite varies from country to country. But every economically advanced country, from China to Sweden to the United States, is characterized by what might be called "niche construction by the 1%." Private–public arrangements have evolved to facilitate the capture of economic surplus by the elite castes. This process is particularly advanced in the United States. In every major sector of the economy, government spending is controlled by, and channeled to, those at the top.

Health care and education are two sectors of the US economy providing good examples to examine the question "who benefits and who pays from government spending." Health outcomes in the United States are near the bottom for developed economies. According to World Health Organization statistics, the United States ranks 37th in health indicators just ahead of Slovenia. Yet the United States spends 15 percent of its GDP on health care while most European countries spend 10 percent or less with much better outcomes. Total public and private per capita health care spending in the United States is nearly double that of European countries. Per capita government spending on health is about the same for the United States and other OECD countries. The difference is that government money in the United States goes disproportionately to private interests. According to a study on comparative health care by the Commonwealth Fund:[10]

> The U.S. ranked last on performance overall, and ranked last or near last on the Access, Administrative Efficiency, Equity, and Health Care Outcomes domains. The top-ranked countries overall were the U.K., Australia, and the Netherlands. Based on a broad range of indicators, the U.S. health system is an

outlier, spending far more but falling short of the performance achieved by other high-income countries. The results suggest the U.S. health care system should look at other countries' approaches if it wants to achieve an affordable high-performing health care system that serves all Americans.

Public research money drives the development of new drugs, but the economic benefits go to private corporations. An example is provided by Vallas, Kleinman, and Biscottii:[11]

> A new pharmaceutical that brings in more than $1 billion per year in revenue is a drug marketed by Genzyme. It is a drug for a rare disease that was initially developed by scientists at the National Institutes of Health. The firm set the price for a year's dosage at upward of $350,000. While legislation gives the government the right to sell such government-developed drugs at "reasonable" prices, policymakers have not exercised this right. The result is an extreme instance where the costs of developing this drug were socialized, while the profits were privatized. Moreover, some of the taxpayers who financed the development of the drug cannot obtain it for their family members because they cannot afford it.

The issue is not the level of government spending in the economy, but rather whose interests are supported by that spending. The US health care system, because of government support for private oligopolies, is one of the least competitive among advanced economies. Doctor's salaries are double the average salary in other high-income countries and per person spending on pharmaceuticals is $1,443 in the United States compared to $749 in other wealthy countries. Partly because of the complicated regulations designed in part to protect the private sector from competition, administrative costs are 8 percent compared to 3 percent in other advanced economies. From undecipherable billing procedures designed to inflate prices, to extravagantly paid administrators, the health care sector is a prime example of niche construction by an alliance of state and private interests. Steven Brill writes:[12]

> Over the past few decades, we've enriched the labs, drug companies, medical device makers, hospital administrators and purveyors of CT scans, MRIs, canes and wheelchairs. Meanwhile,

we've squeezed the doctors who don't own their own clinics, don't work as drug or device consultants or don't otherwise game a system that is so gameable. And of course, we've squeezed everyone outside the system who gets stuck with the bills. We've created a secure, prosperous island in an economy that is suffering under the weight of the riches those on the island extract.

Elizabeth Rosenthal has documented the economic "rationalization" of the health care industry over the last forty years or so.[13] In the 1980s the major players in health care began to respond aggressively to an obvious economic incentive; "if someone is paying you whatever you ask, why not ask for more?" The result is an out-of-control $3.6 billion industry where having a heart attack and a short hospital stay can cost $100,000 or more.[14] If the health care systems of other countries are a guide, the US health care system spends more than enough money per capita to provide universal coverage with far better outcomes than is currently the case.

The role of the state in the US educational system mirrors that of the health care system. The US government spends more per capita on education than any other OECD country, yet the results lag far behind other OECD countries. In 2014 the United States spent $12,300 per full-time-equivalent elementary and secondary student, behind Norway, Switzerland, and Austria. In that year the United States spent $29,000 per student for post-secondary education, the highest in the world.[15] Yet in 2014, the Pearson/Economist Intelligence Unit rated US education as 14th best in the world, just behind Russia. In 2015, the Programme for International Student Assessment rated US high school students 40th globally in Math and 24th in Science and Reading.[16]

Access to quality education is a form of hereditary wealth. Family background is the key factor in educational success. Only 11% of students from the bottom 20% income bracket earn college degrees, while 80% of children from the top 20% income bracket do so. The educational disadvantages of low-income students begin even before they start school. Eduardo Porter writes:[17]

Their story goes sour very early, and it gets worse as it goes along. On the day they start kindergarten, children from families of low socioeconomic status are already more than a year behind the children of college graduates in their grasp of both reading and math. And despite the efforts deployed by the American public education system, nine years later the achievement gap, on average, will have widened by somewhere from one-half to two-thirds. The challenges such children face compared to their more fortunate peers are enormous. Children from low socioeconomic backgrounds are seven times more likely to have been born to a teenage mother. Only half live with both parents, compared with 83 percent of the children of college graduates. The children of less educated parents suffer higher obesity rates, have more social and emotional problems and are more likely to report poor or fair health. And because they are much poorer, they are less likely to afford private preschool or the many enrichment opportunities — extra lessons, tutors, music and art, elite sports teams — that richer, better-educated parents lavish on their children. Even the best performers from disadvantaged backgrounds, who enter kindergarten reading as well as the smartest rich kids, fall behind over the course of their schooling.

And this gulf between the bottom and top quintiles pales in comparison to the gap between the bottom 99 percent and the elite. It is estimated that the excess educational investment that the 1 percent gives to their children over and above what the typical middle-class family can provide amounts to the equivalent of $5 million to $10 million per child.[18] This includes private schools, private tutors, summer programs abroad, and other resume-building activities.

An example of state-sponsored inequality in education is the reliance on local property taxes to fund public schools. This ensures that the bulk of government spending on primary and secondary education goes to the wealthiest communities. For example, one of the nation's poor districts, the Chicago Ridge School District in Illinois, spent $9,794 per child in 2013. Rondout District 72 in one of Chicago's wealthy suburbs, spent $28,639 per child.[19] Because of the relationship between income and public school funding, spending per pupil varies widely by state. New York has the highest per pupil spending at $23,091. Mississippi spends $8,771 per pupil.[20] Federal spending on public education accounts for only 8 percent of school budgets.

Public education has become a key battleground between the interests of "the market" and the well-being of ordinary people. The battle against public education is grounded in neoliberal ideology. According to Mirowski,[21] a major ambition of neoliberals is to sow doubt and division among the masses and this is easier with an uneducated population. A sophisticated philosophy with a long history supports this view. Neoliberals are quite clear about the need to have one version of their doctrine for themselves and another for everyone else. For the public, they warn of the inherent dangers of government involvement in the economy, but behind the scenes they promote interventionist policies to further the interests of the market. They portray the market as something natural and spontaneous, and at the same time actively shape it through legislation and the courts.[22] A major focus is to undermine public education and divert public funding to private schools through vouchers, charter schools, and religious education. If this results in a two-tier system, one for the elite and one for the masses, so be it.

• • •

Human and social insect societies are both under constant pressure from individuals whose actions threaten the stability and coherence of the group. For example, the coherence of societies of ants and termites depends on having one reproductive queen cared for by sterile workers. Uncontrolled reproduction can upset the division of labor in the colony and it can result in fewer offspring being closely related genetically. In these societies, workers prevent rogue females from reproducing by "policing" through intimidation, egg-eating, or isolating the offenders until they no longer produce eggs.[23] Policing works for the good of the colony by increasing its survival chances. Social insect societies are not divided into rulers and ruled. Class conflict is nonexistent.

Behavior in contemporary human societies is regulated by an elite caste or class. As Marx pointed out, the power of the elite in the human economy comes from the control of the way people make a living – control of the means of production. Hunter-gatherers, with their economies based on freely available knowledge, were not susceptible to coercion based on the control by specific individuals of the means to survive.

Figure 6.1 Ownership of the means of production[24]

  Policing in human society can work for the common good by maintaining civil order and reducing conflict. But it can also be more insidious as in the promotion of ideologies and belief systems that reinforce hierarchy and channel resources to those individuals in the dominant caste. Today's global economy could not exist without the direct coordination and integration of economic activity by the state. The state serves a critical role in mobilizing resources as economic inputs and creating new market outlets for the ever-growing economy. In contrast to egalitarian hunter-gatherer societies, state societies are characterized by anti-egalitarian, authoritarian institutions.

With large-scale agriculture, the human propensity to *cooperate* face-to-face with nonkin was harnessed to facilitate the impersonal *coordination* of economic production. Human society made a critical leap from small-scale cooperation to top-down coordination and coercion. Coordination of economic production is not cooperation.

Humans are not social insects and throughout human history people have resisted the state/market superorganism. From slave revolts in early states to twentieth-century revolutions and the rise of social democracies, people have attempted to curtail the system's excesses and create a better world for those oppressed by it. Such attempts have always been met with varying degrees of force and oppression to protect rule by the few. As the human ultrasocial experiment evolved into the global market economy, more sophisticated attempts were made to curb its power, and more counter forces came into play to deflect any measures to limit its scope. Today, human actions that interfere with the ability of the market to extract natural resources and to exploit human labor, come under attack from belief systems that reinforce the existing order. Conservative ideologies evolved to protect and reinforce the existing world order. In contrast to other free market ideologies, neoliberalism is explicit in recognizing the essential role of the state in protecting and promoting economic growth and in insuring that its benefits go to those at the top of the economic pyramid. Ironically, for all the talk about the sovereignty of the individual, at the core of neoliberal thought is the suppression of individual choice by limiting it to choices in markets.

• • •

Early states developed institutions, belief systems, and technologies to enshrine the power of those who controlled the economic surplus. This has been the pattern for millennia. The last seventy years or so of prosperity, relative peace, and lack of major disruptions have allowed those at the top to mold the institutions of democracy to serve their own interests. International rules and regulations, and trade agreements, have been put into place to override national sovereignty and majority rule. In the United States the legal system has been continually modified to promote and protect the interests of corporations over individuals. A single economic system and the ways of thought it generates now dominates the world's cultures and ecosystems. The homogenization of cultures, nature, and government policies is accelerating. We are well down the path toward a single world culture whose values derive from commerce and trade.

Recent studies provide some critical insights into the problem of power and public policy. These include (1) as long as the socioeconomic system is relatively stable, there is a natural tendency for wealth and power to be increasingly concentrated in the hands of a few; (2) a key to maintaining inequality is to limit access to ways individuals can make a living; (3) another key is the inheritance of wealth, including physical assets, money, and human capital; and (4) the gratification of the elite, not the opinions or needs of the majority, drive the policy agendas of governments.

Walter Scheidel[25] documents the evolution of inequality over the past 10,000 years and comes to the conclusion that increasing concentration of economic power is inevitable and continues to increase until broken by outside forces like wars, plagues, and revolutions. As wealth becomes more concentrated, so too does the ability of the elite to channel society's resources to themselves. The longer the periods of stability, the greater the concentration of wealth and power. This can be seen in the recent history of Western economies. The disruption of the established economic order with the Great Depression and World War II brought a period of increasing equality, followed by a return to the level of inequality present in the 1920s. In 1928, the top 1% accounted for 24% of all income. By 1970 this share had fallen to 9%. But by 2007 it had returned to 24% and has continued to increase since then.[26] The dramatic increase in wealth and income inequality is a worldwide phenomenon. And it may be worse than reported. Commonly used measures like the Gini coefficient are problematic because they only consider relative changes. So if incomes of the top 10% and bottom 10% increase by the same amount, the Gini coefficient does not change even though the absolute income gap grows. As the wealth of the elite increases, so too do the means of protecting that wealth. As much as $32 trillion in wealth may be stored away in tax havens – around one-sixth of the world's total private wealth.[27]

Elites control the distribution of surplus by limiting access to the means of acquiring it. Immediate–return hunters and gatherers lived by tapping into direct flows from the natural world. There was little or no long-term storage and no economic surplus to control. Everyone in a hunter-gatherer society had access to the means of production, which consisted of simple technology and a vast knowledge of the plants and animals they depended on. Early state societies limited access to acquiring economic surplus by rigid caste systems, religions asserting the divine right of rulers, and repressive taxation. Modern state/market systems limit access to top-quality education and careers, protect inherited wealth, and design taxation policies to favor capital over labor.

Inherited wealth is key to understanding the tendency toward inequality during the last 10,000 years. The beginnings of inequality can even be seen in preagricultural societies like the Northwest Coast Indians. Although they did not practice agriculture, because of the abundance of salmon and the ability to preserve and store them, they had settled communities, inherited property rights, and the beginnings of social hierarchy. The importance of inherited wealth in driving inequality has been thoroughly documented in recent books by Thomas Piketty, Walter Scheidel, and Robert Brill. Brill discusses the recent phenomenon of inequality being driven by meritocracy. Today's wealth accumulation by the elite is largely based on "labor" income and the explosion in wage differences between the lowest- and highest-paid workers. Exorbitant salaries are most prevalent in the financial and banking sectors, including the corporate lawyers who devise new ways of protecting the wealth of the elite and generating income from financial transactions. A relatively new phenomenon is the inheritance of human capital by children of the ultra-wealthy. Another aspect of inherited wealth is its persistence. In his book *The Son Also Rises*, Gregory Clark found that social mobility rates are far lower than commonly believed. Using historical records from societies as diverse as fourteenth-century England, the Qing Dynasty in China, and the United States he found that the advantages of family wealth persist for centuries.[28]

Ants Do Not Have Castes or Inherited Wealth

Ants are not plagued by instability caused by hereditary occupations or hereditary wealth. The colony, not specific individuals, inherits social insect wealth. Worker ants are not fertile so they have no offspring to pass the surplus to. With social insects, even at the level of the colony, nonrelatives inherit colony resources. Johns et al. conducted an experiment in which battles were staged between unrelated colonies of damp-wood termites (*Zootermopsis nevadensis*). During the battles kings and queens were killed and the surviving members of the two colonies merged into one colony. The survivors of each of the two colonies inherited the merged resources. They write (p. 17452): "[T]hese findings demonstrate how ecological factors could have promoted the evolution of eusociality by accelerating and enhancing direct fitness opportunities of helper offspring, rendering relatedness favoring kin selection less critical."

Phillip Johns, Kenneth. Howard, Nancy Breisch, Anahi Rivera, and Barbara Thorne. 2009. Non-relatives inherit colony resources in a primitive termite. *Proceedings of the National Academy of Sciences* 106, 17452–17456.

The concentration, growth, and persistence of wealth and power are accomplished through the power of the state to channel the economic surplus to the elite through public investment for private gain, and shifting the tax burden away from capital to labor. Much has been written about the efforts of corporations to capture public policy.[29] Martin Gilens and Benjamin Page empirically tested four hypotheses about the nature of policy making in the United States – majoritarian electoral democracy, interest group pluralism, economic elite domination, and biased pluralism.[30] They conclude: "average citizens' preferences continue to have essentially zero estimated impact upon policy change, while economic elites are still estimated to have a very large, positive, independent impact." These and similar findings illustrate the importance to progressive environmental and social change of focusing on gaining political power, and the limits to focusing on politically neutral education to change general public opinion.

• • •

Broadly speaking there are two conflicting functions of the state. The first is to facilitate the generation of economic surplus through the exploitation of people and nature. Without this top-down integration, human society most likely would not have become ultrasocial. The second, more recently emerging, function of the state to is mitigate the excesses of market exploitation by rules and regulations to protect individuals from the excesses of unregulated markets. The history of public policies has been a struggle between these very different world views. The state has been an essential part of human ultrasociality for 5,000 years. The real policy battleground is over whose interests the state serves.

7 NEOLIBERALISM
The Ideology of the Superorganism

The evolution of early small-scale agricultural communities into very large state societies was reinforced by a process of "downward causation."[1,2] Campbell writes:[3] "Where natural selection operates through life and death at a higher level of organization, the laws of the higher-level selective system determine in part the distribution of lower-level events and substances ... *All processes at the lower levels of a hierarchy are restrained by and act in conformity to the laws of higher levels.*" Higher-order organization calls forth adaptations at lower levels to reinforce the higher-order structure. As an ultrasocial system develops, individuals and subsystems come to be dominated by the requirements of the top rung in the hierarchy. With the emergence of human ultrasociality the needs of the economic superstructure began to mold human behavior, social organization, and the integration of the economic and social components of the system. The global economy acts as if it is a hierarchical superorganism whose interests take precedence over that of the individuals who compose it. The radically new economic dynamic that began with agriculture has been continually reinforced by human institutions and belief systems supporting the flourishing of the ultrasocial superorganism. Today, economic ideologies promoting deregulation, opposing social spending, and expanding the scope of the market are examples of downward causation in human social systems. *Free market ideologies, and the political expression of those ideologies, are the human social equivalent of genetic mechanisms of behavioral control that evolved in social insect societies.*

"Free Market" Ideologies

Libertarianism – the center of all policy decisions should be preserving individual choice. In practice this means freeing individuals from any interference by governments. Markets and individuals should be unregulated to the fullest extent possible.

Neoclassical Economics – the market is the preferred mechanism to allocate society's scarce resources toward their most efficient uses. The role of government should be limited to maintaining and expanding property rights and to correct "market failure" – cases where markets do not function efficiently because prices are distorted.

Neoliberal Economics – "the market" is an all-knowing, omniscient information processor that should be the arbiter of human affairs. Governments should play an active role in implementing policies that protect the market from any interference with its ability to generate economic surplus. Governments should actively promote laws, ideologies, and technologies to encourage economic growth and the expansion of the scope of markets.

The ideological center of market fundamentalism is what Phillip Mirowski calls the "Neoliberal Thought Collective" (NTC),[4] a well-formulated and well-financed movement with a long intellectual history. Neoliberalism is unique among conservative ideologies in that it recognizes that the global market economy is a highly evolved, impersonal superorganism with its own "rules," "needs," and "objectives." The core belief of the NTC is that the market is a near-perfect information processor superior to human agency in making fundamental decisions about the nature and direction of the economy, and indeed of all human society. In NTC ideology the only legitimate roles for public policy are to protect the market from misguided human interference – laws and regulations that interfere with its ability to harness and allocate available resources – to promote its expansion through trade agreements overriding national sovereignty, and to provide public financing for "private" projects, and growth-inducing technologies.

Neoliberalism is the dominant political ideology today supporting the drive for economic growth and the commodification of nature and human beings. It is associated with a school of political economy that took form in Austria in the 1930s and 1940s. Its history is closely linked with the Mont Pelerin Society founded in 1947 by a number of prominent conservative thinkers including Friedrich Hayek, Ludwig von Mises, and Milton Friedman.[5] The Mont Pelerin Society continues to be a powerful force and has spawned numerous offshoots and think tanks promoting neoliberalism. Neoliberalism is distinct from neoclassical economics, free market economics, and libertarianism. It differs from neoclassical economics, which acknowledges imperfections in market exchange (market failure) and the dangers of monopoly power. It differs from libertarianism, which seeks to limit the power of government including government promotion of corporate interests. It is not free market economics with its faith in the automatic working of spontaneous order with minimal government. The basic premise of neoliberalism is the supremacy of the market in human affairs. Not only should markets be the basic organizing principle of human society, governments should play an active role in promoting and expanding the scope of markets, and in protecting them from human management.

• • •

Neoliberal philosophy was most clearly articulated by Friedrich Hayek. He recognized that market capitalism was a kind of superorganism. He rejected the static equilibrium analysis of neoclassical theory and saw the market as a living dynamic system. He stressed the importance of the emergence of social rules and practices through cultural group selection. Hayek was explicit about the superiority of the market compared to human agency. He argued that true freedom means giving up our atavistic human proclivities (like altruism and a preference for fairness) that interfere with the spontaneous order of the market.[6] The human predisposition for equality and fairness is a primitive instinct that must be replaced by behaviors conducive to large-scale impersonal coordination. The market must be protected from human agency. Hayek is clear about sacrificing individual initiative to the collective will of the market:[7]

> It was men's submission to the impersonal forces of the market that in the past has made possible the growth of a civilization which without this could not have developed; it is by thus submitting that we are every day helping to build something that is greater than any one of us can fully comprehend ... The refusal to yield to forces which we neither understand nor can recognize as the conscious decisions of an intelligent being is the

product of an incomplete and therefore erroneous rationalism. It is incomplete because it fails to comprehend that the co-ordination of the multifarious individual efforts in a complex society must take account of facts that no individual can completely survey.

Redirecting policy decisions away from individual agency to the market is a primary objective of public choice economics.

The neoliberal icon Ayn Rand held a concept of the self that was based not on individual human freedom but on the interests of the market. According to Rand[8] there cannot be conflict among rational individuals. If two people are seeking the same job and one is more qualified, the less qualified person should step aside for the good of society (the market). Furthermore, it is ethical to cast aside those who do not contribute to economic output. In *Atlas Shrugged* the architect hero, John Galt, leads the country's capitalists on a crusade against the "looters" and "moochers" who make up most of the population: "We have granted you everything you demanded of us, we who had always been the givers, but have only now understood it … We have no demands to present you, no terms to bargain about, no compromise to reach. You have nothing to offer us. We do not need you."[9] Rhetoric by the followers of Hayek and Rand echoes the belief that a person's value as a human being is determined by his or her contribution to producing economic surplus. Dinesh D'Souza, formerly of the American Enterprise Institute writes:[10]

> The guy who is worth little has probably produced little of value. By the same token—perish the thought—the guy who's earning twice as much as you is most likely twice as good as you are.

In the neoliberal view, a person who does not produce economic value is a social parasite. The Nebraska attorney general compared welfare recipients to "scavenging raccoons."[11] North Dakota's workers' compensation insurer denied an injured worker a prosthetic left arm because it was "more elaborate" than needed for his job duties even though his quality of life would have been vastly improved.[12] To be of no use to the economic superorganism is to be condemned for merely existing.

Curbing attempts to make the market more responsive to human needs has long been a project of the NTC. Replace public education with private charter schools, oppose environmental regulations as restricting innovation, restrict workers' ability to organize, and fight every attempt to provide public services like affordable health care. The NTC has always had an uneasy relationship with democratic institutions. With democracy there is always the danger that "primitive" human emotions such as fairness and sharing will result in public policies to curb the market. "Freedom" means free to choose in unregulated markets. Hayek was clear that democratic countries could be unfree and totalitarian countries could be free. In recent decades this notion has taken an even more radical turn to undermine democratic institutions in the name of freedom. The watchword of neoliberalism is "freedom" – meaning free to choose in markets and freedom from the social constrictions of collectivism. Neoliberal freedom is not based on the autonomy of the individual but rather on the autonomy of the market. Mirowski puts it nicely:[13]

> [Neoliberalists] seek to paint all "coercion" as evil, but without admitting into consideration any backstory of the determinants of your intentions. Everyone is treated as expressing untethered context-free hankering, as if they were born yesterday into solitary confinement; this is the hidden heritage of entrepreneurialism of the self. This commandment cashes out as: no market can ever be coercive.

The essence of neoliberalism is to protect and promote the market superorganism. Neoliberals have an absolute faith in the market to solve any problem *and* they believe that the workings of the market must be actively protected from any attempts to interfere with it. This insight explains the seemingly contradictory policies originating in the NTC's many think tanks and policy forums. Like antibodies deployed to protect an organism from invading diseases, the NTC rushes to fend off any attempts to undermine the self-organized workings of the market. Trade agreements are written to defuse the power of national sovereignty, labor unions are restrained by repressive legislation, any attempt to regulate any product is thwarted, and environmental crises are denied and/or "solved" by more markets.[14]

Neoliberalism is not about promoting individual liberty or markets free of government involvement. It is all about protecting and promoting the market as an all-knowing superior force of nature. It is a kind of secular religion and like any other religion, it requires the submission of the individual to the spontaneous order of a greater power. For Hayek, the market is first and foremost the supreme information processor. This view explains Hayek's seemingly peculiar concept of "freedom" and his contention that "the chief aim of freedom is to provide both the opportunity and the inducement to ensure the maximum use of knowledge that an individual can accrue."[15] Freedom is the unconstrained ability of individuals to access and use the information processed and generated by the market to buy and sell economic goods.

• • •

Hayek recognized the conflict between evolved human propensities to cooperate and have compassion for others and the requirements of the market. He argued that merging human agency with the market superorganism requires giving up many of our evolved human characteristics that interfere with the spontaneous order of the market. The human predisposition for equality is a savage instinct that must be replaced by behaviors conducive to large-scale coordination. Hayek saw the conflict between evolved human emotions like altruism and a preference for fairness, and the impersonal rationality of the market. But he sided with the market superorganism and called for the suppression of individual human emotions that undermined its internal dynamic. Human destiny is to surrender our individuality and submit to the will of the market.

This view of human nature resonates with free market radicals. Steven Horowitz writing for the Cato Institute newsletter writes:[16]

> Hayek argues that our moral instincts were honed in millennia of living in small kin-based intimate orders, and thus notions of collective purpose, shared ends, altruism, and zero sum thinking, as well as the importance of good intentions, are deeply encoded in our minds. Unfortunately, these moral instincts are not appropriate for life in the autonomous world of the Great Society. In fact, the theme of *The Fatal Conceit* concerns the ways in which those moral instincts lead us astray when we try to apply them to the Great Society. So, he argues, the challenge of modernity is that we have to learn to live in "two sorts of worlds at once."

Horowitz, like Hayek, implicitly recognizes the break in human societies that came with agriculture – from community to selfishness, from cooperation to competition – but he sees this as a good thing. In the neoliberal view there is one world for family and friends, and another for the market. It is wrong for the government to impose standards of fairness, sharing, or equality on the amoral market. But this does not imply a weak government. It is the responsibility of the government to protect and promote the market against any attempt to undermine its omniscient unfolding. This line of thought takes a disturbing turn in Hayek's view of democracy. In a 1966 speech to the Mont Pelerin Society, Hayek argued: "Liberalism and democracy, although compatible, are not the same ... it is at least possible in principle that a democratic government may be totalitarian and that an authoritarian government may act on liberal principles." In a letter to the *Times of London* (July 11, 1978) in support of the Chilean dictator Pinochet, he writes: "More recently I have not been able to find a single person even in much maligned Chile who did not agree that personal freedom was much greater under Pinochet than it had been under Allende." Apparently, "personal freedom" did not apply to the thousands of people killed or tortured by the Pinochet regime. Freedom as self-actualization moves from the individual to the market superorganism. Hayekian neoliberalism is an instructive example of downward causation calling forth ideologies to serve the superorganism that is the market economy. It is the ideology of an ant colony – individuals are expendable for the good of the global market superorganism – the Hayekian Great Society.

• • •

Hayek was well-versed in evolutionary concepts and was strongly influenced by his London School of Economics colleague, the biologist Alexander Carr-Saunders, an early advocate of group selection.[17] Hayek invokes group selection to argue that the market economy is "natural" and therefore "good." He recognized that the market economy was a kind of superorganism that evolved spontaneously through natural selection operating on groups. According to Hayek,[18] "What may be called the natural *selection* of rules will operate on the basis of the greater or lesser efficiency of the resulting *order of the group*" (italics in original). Some groups have rules, and structures of rules, that are more "efficient" and "advantageous" in terms of competing with other groups. Such rules and orders are more conducive to the survival of the group in the struggle for existence. Groups with more efficient rules and orders tend to grow and multiply, while groups with less efficient rules and orders tend to disappear. According to Hayek the order of the market economy was far too complex to be the result of human design:

> The individual may have no idea what this overall order is that results from his observing such rules as those concerning kinship and intermarriage, or the succession of property, or which function this overall order serves. Yet all the individuals of the species which exist will behave in that manner because groups of individuals which have thus behaved have displaced those which did not do so.[19]

> The structures [i.e., orders] formed by traditional human practices are ... the result of a process of winnowing or sifting, directed by the differential advantages gained by groups from practices adopted for some unknown and perhaps purely accidental reasons.[20]

Hayek saw the market as an evolving, all-knowing information processor vastly superior to individual human judgment. As D. S. Wilson[21,22] points out, Hayek was ahead of his time in recognizing that human behavior, including our socially and genetically based behavioral tendencies, evolved in small-scale societies and that cultural evolution is not intentionally planned but rather based on Darwinian variation, retention, and selection acting on human groups. Hayek's ideology took a decidedly totalitarian turn with his view that a strong state was needed to enable the market to override interference from misguided human judgment.

Neoliberals recognize the conflict between "human nature" and the market, but they side with the market. Hayek never questioned the "goals" of the market superorganism. Like any other organism it has evolved to grow and expand within the limits of its "ecosystem," that is, human society and the natural world. The market economy has evolved into a unified and efficient system for organizing human activity to generate profits and surplus value. But evolution cannot see ahead. There is no way such a reactive, unplanned, and mechanical system can anticipate the disruptive effects on the environment of future climate change or the future disruptive consequences of extreme social inequality. The "fatal conceit" of Hayek is that he dismisses the fact that the interests of the superorganism may be fundamentally at odds with the interests of individual humans.

• • •

An underappreciated characteristic of neoliberalism is its wholehearted embrace of the state as an instrument to promote the interests of the market superorganism. According to Jamie Peck:[23]

> What is "neo" about Neoliberalism ... [is] the remaking and redeployment of the state as the core agency that actively fabricates the subjectivities, social relations and collective representations suited to making the fiction of markets real and consequential.

Neoliberals from Hayek on down have made it a primary task to seize and remake the state as an instrument of conservative policy. One function of public policy is to harness the power of the state to constrain and ultimately block any attempt by mortal humans to interfere with the "natural" workings of the market. The market, always vaguely defined, is a highly evolved entity that transcends space, time, and the characteristics of any specific human society. Generating and distributing surplus is a task too essential to be left to the whims of liberal democracy. Public policy must be decided by "the market," not by the thoughtful deliberation of human agents. As Bromley puts it:

> Suddenly, it seems that public policy is not what we thought it was. Democracy as public participation and reasoned discourse is somehow suspect – not to be trusted. It seems that the public's business cannot be properly conducted unless it adheres to the percepts of individualistic models of "rational choice" applied to collective action ... It is a quest for public policy in which applied micro-economics is deployed as the only way to impose "rationality" on an otherwise incoherent and quite untrustworthy political process.[24]

Far from "limiting government," the approach of the NTC is to capture basic government institutions with the goal of preventing any interference with the "spontaneous order" of the market. Influencing democratic elections through corporate donations is not enough. Voting rights can be effectively curtailed through gerrymandering and voter intimidation. And the judicial system can be captured through strategic interventions. One of the most important figures in the recent rise of the state as an instrument of neoliberal policy is the economist James Buchanan. Buchanan was instrumental in providing an intellectual foundation and a policy agenda to undermine representative democracy in order to protect the market from human agency. In the 1970s he found an ardent supporter in Charles Koch, who had been funding libertarian causes for years without much political success. The key insight Buchanan gave was the importance of focusing not on *who rules* but rather on *who makes the rules*.[25] He realized that the rules themselves could be changed. Buchanan's theory of public choice was grounded in the standard conservative view of human nature. People are motivated only by the emotions of greed and purely personal self-interest. As Buchanan bluntly puts it: "Each person seeks mastery over a world of slaves."[26] Politicians are no different. Under the guise of democracy holders of public office maintain their power by taxing the creators of wealth, the "makers," and giving the spoils to the "takers" – the undeserving masses who do not produce wealth. Buchanan's solution was to use the legal system to protect the owners of capital. MacLean writes:[27]

> For liberty to thrive, Buchanan now argued, the cause must figure out how to put legal—indeed, constitutional—shackles on public officials, shackles so powerful that no matter how concerned they were with their own re-elections, they would no longer have the ability to respond to those who used their numbers to get government to do their bidding.

Buchanan's public choice theory essentially states that a society is not free unless every citizen has the right to veto its decisions.[28] This meant that no one should be taxed against their will by using votes to take money they did not earn to promote the interest of the undeserving taker majority. This taking includes government taxing to support public education, public health and welfare, and environmental protection. The function of the state is to protect and promote the interests of wealth and surplus value creation. Freedom is a word applied to the market superorganism, not to individual humans. Mont Pelerin member Richard Posner writes:[29] "The function of criminal sanction in a capitalist market economy, then, is to prevent individuals from bypassing the efficient market."

• • •

Neoliberals focus with laser-like intensity on promoting the market as a godlike entity to be served all at costs. This explains both the predictability of neoliberal policies and their apparent contradictions. Mirowski outlines the "full spectrum" approach of neoliberalism:[30]

> [O]ne of the reasons that the neoliberals have come to triumph over all their ideological rivals in recent years is that they have managed to venture beyond any simplistic notion of a single "fix" for any given problem, but always strive instead to invent and employ a broad spectrum of different policies, from the most expendable short-term expedients to medium term politics to long-horizon utopian projects, all of which may appear to outsiders as distinct and emanating from different quarters, but in fact turn out inevitably to be nicely integrated so as to produce the eventual capitulation of nature and society to the market.

The neoliberal response to regulation is unrelated to any particular problem the regulation addresses. The response to tobacco regulation, curbing CFCs to protect the ozone layer, or curtailing sulfur emissions is exactly the same. All regulations curbing the market are bad no matter how compelling the need to protect the public good.[31] Regulation itself is the enemy.

The neoliberal response to climate change shows the full spectrum approach. The first stage is *denial,* as in the promotion of climate change skepticism by numerous neoliberal think tanks such as the American Enterprise Institute, the Heartland Institute, and the Cato Institute. The second stage is to *promote a market solution* to the problem, as in carbon trading schemes. The third is to *promote technological solutions* such as geoengineering and nuclear power. Seemingly contradictory policies, as in the Heartland Institute's climate change denialism and its simultaneous promotion of geoengineering as a solution to climate change, make sense when they are seen in the "full spectrum neoliberal Pharmacopoeia."[32] No matter what the particular issue is, the underlying purpose of the NTC approach is to promote the market and protect it from regulation. The market is never wrong and any attempt to regulate it puts the economy on the slippery slope to socialism. Because of the frailty of human nature, markets need to be protected from misguided attempts to regulate it. On the one hand, neoliberalism decries government interference in the market, and on the other hand, it supports government policies, and especially government spending, to actively promote growth and expansion.

Climate change is an existential threat to the human species, but avoiding catastrophic environmental change means actively curtailing many sectors of the economy and aggressively regulating how energy is produced and consumed. The NTC recognizes this threat. Vaclav Klaus, former president of the Czech Republic, made this clear in a talk to the Mont Pelerin Society about climate change:[33]

> ... the current world-wide dispute is not about temperature or CO_2. It is another variant of the old, well known debate: freedom and free markets vs. dirigisme, political control and regulation, or in other words, spontaneous evolution vs. the masterminding of human activity from above. It is again the old Misesian and Hayekian dilemma asking what is and what should be dominant: human action or human design ... In the past, the market was undermined mostly by means of socialist arguments with slogans like: "stop the immiseration of the masses". Now, the attack is led under a more seductive slogan: stop the immiseration (or perhaps destruction) of the Planet. I consider environmentalism and its currently strongest version – climate alarmism – to be, at the beginning of the 21st century, the most effective and, therefore, the most dangerous vehicle for advocating drafting and implementing large scale government intervention and for an unprecedented suppression of human freedom.

Klaus sees any regulation as a threat to the superorganism and thus to human freedom. Either it is allowed to spontaneously unfold through "human action" or it is undermined by "human design." Neoliberal opposition to regulation, from smoking, to ozone depletion, to climate change, is based not on science but on ideology. The market must be allowed to "naturally" evolve without human interference.

• • •

The market-driven assault on the earth's biosphere has produced a growing chorus of "ecomodernists" paradoxically calling for more markets, more economic growth, and more corporate subsidies in the name of environmental protection. Ecomodernism is a phenomenon clearly showing the connection between economic policy, the market superorganism, and neoliberalism. Promoted by the neoliberal Breakthrough Institute (BTI), ecomodernism is a poster child for Mirowski's description of the NTC. Neoliberal environmentalism supports the expansion of the superorganism at the expense of human welfare and environmental integrity. Whatever the environmental problem, the solution is to let modernization through the market have its way. Ecomodernists see the absorption of the nonhuman world by the market economy as a triumph, not a disaster.[34,35,36,37,38] Ecomodernists are explicit about the state's role in promoting the expansion of the markets and protecting it from regulation. The BTI's website statement "What We Believe" includes:

> We believe that technology and modernization are at the foundation of human progress. We believe that human prosperity and an ecologically vibrant planet are not only possible, but also inseparable. We believe the market is a potent force for change, but that long-term government investment is required to accelerate technological progress, economic growth, and environmental quality.[39]

BTI publications usually start out with observations sympathetic about caring for the environment: "Human success has come at the expense of nonhuman life." But then the narrative quickly shifts to obfuscation and denialism: "Although many of humankind's environmental impacts have grown in absolute terms, several have plateaued or have started to decline, and most impacts have declined on a per-capita basis."[40] By the "per-capita" logic, if wildlife populations decline by 50 percent but human populations increase by 60 percent (which has been the case in the last fifty years), then wildlife populations must be recovering. The BTI argument flies in the face of evidence of massive declines in land vertebrate, insect, and ocean fish populations in recent decades.[41]

Consider the Breakthrough approach to the following environmental concerns:

Climate change – the answer to climate change is nuclear energy financed by governments. "In contrast to the tried, tested, and failed model of emissions reduction commitments, policy makers should replace targets and timetables with a pragmatic framework that emphasizes energy innovation, resilience, and human development." "If renewables cannot scale fast enough to address climate change, what can? Just nuclear."[42] Nuclear power advocacy is a good example of the NTC approach – deny climate change exists and at the same time call for massive public funding for private "climate change" projects in the name of environmental protection. In fact, calculations show that massively replacing fossil fuel power plants with nuclear power would have little effect on atmospheric CO_2 levels.[43]

Wildlife poaching – following the neoliberal playbook as outlined by Mirowski, and Oreskes and Conway, first comes denial and obfuscation by questioning the data about wildlife loss: "Elephants live over far too vast an area for a complete, scientifically rigorous census for all of Africa." Secondly, markets are not the problem: "In their rush to blame the plight of elephants on Chinese demand for ivory, Western journalists leave out the other factors that are equally or even more important, but far less dramatic." According to the Breakthrough Institute, elephants are disappearing because of habitat loss due to inefficient agricultural practices that market forces will automatically correct. Thirdly, the problem can be solved by technology. The technological solution is more energy and capital-intensive agriculture that would (somehow) free up land for wild animals. There is no need to set aside preserves because the return of wild nature will happen naturally through modernization.[44]

Likewise, there is no need to regulate bushmeat trade because with modernization everyone will become wealthy, shop in supermarkets, and abandon their reliance on bushmeat. In fact, the bushmeat trade is driven by global market incursion, not local subsistence hunting. The demand for exotic animal meat comes from upscale Chinese citizens, Middle Eastern Sheiks, and wealthy Africans in cities from Kinshasa to Paris and London. The market for timber is devastating primates as logging roads provide access to remote areas.[45] The Breakthrough Institute enthusiastically supports trophy hunting as the market-based solution to preserve charismatic species like lions, elephants, and rhinos. The reality of "lion factories" breeding lions solely to be hunted paints a different picture. More "canned" hunting will not protect wild species.

The ecomodernist solution to everything is to let the market superorganism have its way. It paints a dystopian future with the complete harnessing of the nonhuman world to serve the needs of the global market economy. The wholesale looting of nature is seen as a blessing, not a curse. Breakthrough president Michael Shellenberger writes:[46]

> The apocalyptic vision of ecotheology warns that degrading nonhuman natures will undermine the basis for human civilization, but history has shown the opposite: the degradation of nonhuman environments has made us rich. We have become rather adept at transferring the wealth and diversity of nonhuman environments into human ones. The solution to the unintended consequences of modernity is, and has always been, more modernity – just as the solution to the unintended consequences of our technologies has always been more technology.

Ecomodernism is not modern at all. The Ecomodernist Manifesto repeats all the cosmologies[47] about human nature and human progress that have been around for centuries – agriculture was "invented" by humans to make us more efficient and prosperous. Progress, technology and modernization have always made everyone better off. There is no mention of poverty except the implicit assumption that poverty is simply a lack of modernization. Chris Smaje, in a critique of the Ecomodernist Manifesto writes:[48]

> There is no sense that processes of modernization *cause* any poverty. So there is no mention here of the vast literatures on the changing and varied economic fortunes of the many civilisations that have come and gone, or the changing and varied ideas they've had about themselves. There's nothing on uneven development, historical cores and peripheries, proletarianisation, colonial land appropriation and the implications of all this for social equity. The ecomodernist solution to poverty is simply more modernization.

Ecomodernism employs the full spectrum approach of neoliberalism. First denial and obfuscation, then propose a market solution, then salvation by technology. The core agenda of the NTC and ecomodernism is unwavering support of a "regimented controlled society dedicated to the doctrine of 'spontaneous order'."[49] The only way forward is to submit to the will of the market. Mirowski writes:

> [F]or neoliberals, humans can never be trusted to know whether the biosphere is in crisis or not, because both nature and society are dauntingly complex and evolving; therefore, the neoliberal solution is to enlist the strong state to allow the market to find its own way to the ultimate solution. It can accomplish this only if the invariant character of the market is allowed to manifest itself in all its glorious resilience.[50]

• • •

It is commonly asserted that humans are different than social insects because we have free will and we act intentionally. Human society is not an ant colony but we should have no illusions about how much "freedom to choose" we actually have. The transition to agriculture set into motion forces that led to a higher level of social organization whose focus became the generation of economic surplus. This higher-order organization called forth new modes of production, the reorganization of labor, and policing mechanisms that constrained individual behavior and reinforced surplus maximization. Downward causation in social insect colonies brought forth genetically based mechanisms to protect the ultrasocial order by controlling the actions of individual workers. When human society became ultrasocial, downward causation called forth institutions, belief systems, and political movements that reinforce the goal of surplus production, and that defend those at the top who control the economic process and the distribution of that surplus.

Ultrasocial societies need to protect themselves from the potentially disruptive forces of individual initiative. The greatest internal threat to insect societies is reproduction by workers and this is enforced by a variety of mechanism to detect and eliminate non-queen breeders. The biggest threat to the human superorganism is that individuals have the capacity to realize that the system does not work in their interest and that it is possible to change it. Throughout history policing against this threat has taken two forms, violent suppression and belief systems supporting the subordination of the masses to the "needs" of the ultrasocial system. The power of the elites depends on the success of the superorganism through continued expansion and exploitation.

Contemporary neoliberalism is an example of the parallel evolution of social insect and human societies after agriculture. The ultrasocial superorganism is not passive. To protect itself it employs a variety of genetic (ants and termites) and social (human) mechanisms. An analysis of NTC ideology ties together the major themes of this book, ultrasociality, downward causation, group selection, and belief systems supporting unconstrained economic growth and exploitation. The proponents of neoliberalism explicitly recognized that market capitalism acts as if it is a kind of all-knowing superorganism. Hayek drew heavily on biological theories of group selection in his political philosophy. He saw the conflict between evolved human emotions like altruism and a preference for fairness, and the impersonal rationality of the market. But he sided with the market and called for the suppression of individual human emotions that undermined its internal dynamic. Exposing neoliberal ideology as the philosophy protecting the market superorganism lends support for active governmental policies asserting human agency and control of the ultrasocial system.

The next chapter presents a "minimal bioeconomic program" to begin to assert human control over the market economy superorganism. Most of the proposals presented have been widely discussed and they are politically feasible if we explicitly recognize and directly confront the power of the market superorganism to generate political "antibodies" to protect itself. Even if all these proposals were enacted, we would still be part of a system dependent upon expansion and resource exploitation. But we could begin to move toward an evolutionary path that would be sustainable, egalitarian, and nonexploitative.

Part III
BACK TO THE FUTURE

Human greatness does not lie in wealth or power, but in character and goodness. People are just people, and all people have faults and shortcomings, but all of us are born with a basic goodness.
Anne Frank

A minimal bioeconomic program would curb the major abuses of unchecked global capitalism. Polices include maximum and minimum limits to income and wealth, universal affordable health care and education, and an expansion of protected wild areas. Implementing these policies would not solve the basic contradiction of global capitalism – an inherently expansionary system within a finite planet – but it would buy time to make the transition to a sustainable society less catastrophic.

Our hunter-gatherer past is a guide to an equitable and sustainable future. Current research in behavioral and neuroscience shows that humans are a flexible species with innumerable possible ways of living. Selfishness and exploitation are no more a part of human nature than cooperation and caring about others and the natural world.

There are many plausible future scenarios for the human species, including collapse, a gradual disintegration, an optimist's utopia, a technological/cyborg dystopia, and a golden age of decentralized barbarism. Given the likelihood of drastically higher global temperatures and a return to the climate instability of the Pleistocene, I argue that the most likely long-run future is a return to the hunting and gathering way of life of the Pleistocene.

8 TAMING THE MARKET
A Minimal Bioeconomic Program[1]

> Abolish the rich and you will find no more poor.
> *De Divitiis (On Riches)*, "The Sicilian Britain," fifth century

The domination of neoliberalism on political discourse has stifled discussions of social and environmental policy options and blocked policy responses to the growing fault lines in the global economy. Power is increasingly concentrated in the hands of those who benefit the most from the continued destruction of nature and the exploitation of human labor. Antidemocratic far-right governments are taking power all over the world. But the excesses of the system illuminate the problems we face and clarify what needs to be done. Currently, the progressive left lacks a coherent, compelling program to match the philosophical sophistication and organization of the Neoliberal Thought Collective. The impotency of the Occupy Wall Street movement showed this clearly. Simply documenting the faults of the economic system will lead nowhere unless it is coupled with a coherent understanding of the evolutionary forces that led to its dominance, namely, the drive for surplus accumulation and the ubiquity of belief systems supporting the commodification of people and nature.[2] Recognizing the inherent conflict between the requirements of the higher-level market superorganism (growth and exploitation) and the well-being of individuals at lower levels in the hierarchy can help focus the political debate. Understanding how we got here is a precursor to a clear vision for a new path forward.

Seeing the market as an evolved ultrasocial entity with its own "goals" antithetical to human well-being provides the following insights:

- Today's environmental and social problems began with the widespread adoption of agriculture thousands of years ago when human societies came to resemble social insect colonies. Ultrasocial societies are by nature expansionary and exploitative.
- The latest and most virulent expression of human ultrasociality is the global market economy. Like an autonomous living organism it survives by extracting "nutrients" from its environment. Like any organism it will do what it must to insure the flow of natural resources and human labor necessary for its survival and expansion.
- There exists an inherent conflict between the market superorganism and human well-being. With ultrasociality individuals become expendable in the service of the global market superorganism.

For most of human existence we lived in small groups where decisions about where and when to move, what to eat, and how to distribute resources were based on face-to-face interactions and the good of individual members of the group. With agriculture, control of the social dynamic passed from transparent bottom-up group consensus based on give-and-take among individuals to the top-down invisible control of the ultrasocial superorganism. Invisible control is still control. Recognizing this leads us to challenge the neoliberal discourse about "freedom" ("Who are you to tell people what to do?"). We are being "told" what to do by an evolved entity whose expansionary dynamic is in conflict with individual well-being and our long-run viability as a species.

• • •

How do we begin to tame the excesses of the global market to buy some time to make the transition to a viable evolutionary path? A good beginning is Georgescu-Roegen's Minimal Bioeconomic Program. His suggestions include: Eliminate all instruments of war, fairly distribute the material fruits of the economy to all; reduce the human population to a level that could be fed by organic agriculture; and eliminate fashion and consumerism.[3] These proposals are radical but in Georgescu's view they are only the first step toward a just and ecologically sustainable economy. Georgescu was correct in calling this program "minimal." For example, relying solely on organic agriculture would get us back to where we were around the year 1900, but at that time humans already dominated the biosphere and were rapidly exterminating earth's other higher life forms. The policy suggestions to come are merely the first step in reforming an inherently unsustainable and unstable system. But reform and revolution can be complementary. Enacting the policies outlined shortly can begin to move the human economy toward a fundamentally different system that breaks the imperative of accumulation and expansion.

With earth's population approaching 8 billion, we cannot rapidly return to a hunting and gathering economy, barring a collapse of human civilization. We can, however, work to implement policies that curb the worst excesses of the global market. The following ideas have been around for a long time. There is nothing new here and since so much has been written about each of these policy recommendations, I will not elaborate on them. With these policies we can begin to tame the superorganism and move toward an environmentally and socially sustainable evolutionary path. Then we will be in a better position to manage the inevitable end of the evolutionary dynamic that keeps the system expanding. These policies may seem politically naive but all of them have been extensively analyzed, most have broad public support, and many of them have been successfully implemented in a number of countries. If put into place they would have the potential to change the basic character of market capitalism and pave the way for more radical structural change. Furthermore, they incorporate some of the features of hunter-gatherer societies that worked to promote ecological and social harmony for most of our history as a species. These policies include the following:

Halt the Most Egregious Assaults on the Natural World
Climate Change

The increase in greenhouse gases over the past few decades is one of the most dramatic indicators of the Anthropocene. Over the past 800,000 years atmospheric concentrations of CO_2 varied between 180 ppm and 280 ppm.[4] CO_2 levels during this period are tightly correlated with temperatures and sea levels. Fluctuations of 50 ppm around the average of 230 ppm were enough to push the earth between warm periods comparable to today's warm climate to extremely cold ice age conditions. In May 2020 atmospheric CO_2 levels at Mauna Loa, Hawaii reached 418 ppm, an increase of over 100 ppm since the middle of the twentieth century.[5] The discernible human impact on the atmosphere is recent and sudden. The change in CO_2 is usually stated something like, "CO_2 levels are about 100ppm higher than preindustrial levels." This is true but almost all the increase has come after 1950 or so, within one human lifetime. In spite of all the coverage of climate catastrophes and dire warnings from every major (and minor) climate change organization for decades, no substantial reductions in atmospheric carbon due to climate policies have taken place.

When CO_2 levels in the past were as high as today's, the earth's climate was dramatically different. During the Middle Miocene, some 10–14 million years ago, CO_2 levels were lower than today's (around 350 ppm), but temperatures were 3–6°C warmer and sea levels were 25–40 meters higher.[6] Further back in time, around 56 million years ago, the earth experienced the Paleocene–Eocene Thermal Maximum (PETM) when temperatures rose by 8°C or more. The origins of the PETM carbon influx are hotly debated. Candidates include volcanic activity, a release of methane clathrates, and massive forest fires. The PETM CO_2 event lasted only about 1,000–10,000 years but its effects lasted 200,000 years. The rate of heating was estimated to be 0.025°C per 100 years compared to the projected rate of 2–5°C per 100 years over the next few centuries.[7] If past climate regimes are approximate indicators of what we can expect in the future, large, abrupt, and unpredictable changes will occur for centuries, if not millennia, to come. The scientific consensus is that delaying substantial emission reductions for even a few more years will court disaster.

It is clear that drastic climate change policies are needed. Most importantly, recognize that avoiding catastrophic climate change is a collective problem requiring collective and globally enforceable policy solutions. According to the final COP24 report of December 2018 (blocked from adoption by the United States, Russia, and Saudi Arabia): "Keeping to the preferred target would need rapid, far-reaching and unprecedented changes in all aspects of society." If warming is to be kept to 1.5°C this century, then emissions of carbon dioxide will have to be reduced by 45 percent by 2030,[8] that is, within the next ten years, an impossible goal.

Climate change is an existential threat. It is such a serious threat that policy responses should not be constrained by parochial, short-run cost-benefit calculations. Actions to avoid catastrophe should be based on the best science, not on vague, imprecise, and unreliable estimates about the future economic impacts of climate change measured by the present discounted value of projected GDP growth.[9] The most recent climate change reports[10] are increasingly dire about the consequences of greenhouse gas emissions. Recent climate modeling has improved our understanding of the role of clouds in the earth's hydrological cycle and the results are not encouraging. It appears to be more likely that positive cloud feedback – with warming low-level clouds decreasing and high-level clouds increasing – worst-case scenarios are more likely to occur and more likely to be severe.[11,12] Climate scientists say that to avoid a catastrophic rise in average temperature, the world should begin immediately to cut CO_2 emissions and reduce them to near zero by 2050. We are already locked into significant temperature increases over today's levels but it makes a huge difference whether these increases are in the range of 2°C, or 3–6°C, or even higher. We need aggressive, enforceable worldwide policies to achieve rapid decarbonization.

- Keep coal in the ground. Coal is by far the most abundant fossil fuel and its future use is the key to how much the earth will warm in coming centuries. Estimates of fossil fuel reserves vary widely because of the inherent uncertainty with terms like "recoverable reserves" and "economically recoverable reserves" that can change suddenly with changes in technology and economic conditions. But some idea of the relative abundance of coal can be gleaned by looking at estimates of remaining years before exhaustion published by the Energy Information Administration (EIA). The EIA estimates that *at current rates of use*, coal reserves will last 150 years, natural gas about 48 years, and oil 46 years.[13] World coal production has leveled off but it has not declined. The decline in coal use is confined to North American and Europe. Countries in Asia and Africa are investing heavily in coal because it is cheap and abundant. There is enough accessible coal to heat the earth to unmanageable levels if a substantial portion of it is burned.
- Reduce total energy use. The major focus of climate change policies has been to find "alternatives" to fossil fuel. But solar energy, wind, and hydro power are not alternatives unless they actually replace fossil fuels.[14] Consider conservation to be a major energy source in energy plans. Focus on reducing total energy use, not adding to the supply by substituting one destructive source for another.

The Loss of Nature

Biodiversity loss is more than the loss of individual species or genetic diversity. What's happening now is nothing short of the annihilation of the nonhuman world as we have known it since our genus *Homo* evolved millions of years ago.[15] In just the last few decades the populations of birds, mammals, fish, reptiles, and invertebrates have plummeted by as much as 70 percent. This is much more than a loss of "nature's services." It is a loss of the connections with nature that created our "humanness" over millions of years. E. O. Wilson suggests that the current epoch should be called the Eremocine – the Age of Loneliness.

Most people are well aware of the loss of charismatic megafauna – the decimation of populations of elephants, tigers, lions, giraffes, and the other species we have admired since we were children. These losses may fill us with sorrow, but our inner voice tells us "this is sad but not a catastrophe." Most of us will never see these animals in the wild. They are invisible as far as their impact on our everyday lives. Even more invisible are organisms directly important to our well-being, namely the insects. Insects are not often discussed as indicators of biodiversity loss, but they are perhaps the most striking example of what's happening to the nonhuman world and the potentially devastating consequences. Insects make up about 75 percent of known species. The number of known species of insects is about 1 million, but insect biologists believe that the true number of insect species is about 8 million.[16] Only eighty-four insect species are protected under the Endangered Species Act, partly because of the prohibition of listing any species that might potentially be a pest.

Those of us who are old enough can remember driving in the countryside with our parents and having the car windshield plastered with insects. Today only an occasional bug causes a smear. Entomologists call this "the windshield phenomenon." Recent studies have shown just how severe insect loss has been. US populations of monarch butterflies have fallen by 90% in the last twenty years, an estimated loss of 1 million individuals.[17] A study of macro-moths in Britain found that two-thirds of the 337 species are in decline, with one-fifth of them declining by over 30% in the last thirty-five years.[18] In perhaps the most comprehensive insect population studies to date, researchers found a 75% decline in flying insect biomass in protected areas in Germany over the past twenty-seven years.[19] Looking at midsummer population peaks, the decline was 82%. A study in Puerto Rico found that insect populations have declined by 90–98% between 1976–1977 and 2011–2013. Declines in other lifeforms associated with these insect losses were found in birds, lizards, and frogs. The researchers blame the decline on climate change. Temperatures in the Puerto Rican rainforest studied have risen by 2°C in recent decades.[20]

The usual suspects in the insect decline are land use changes (loss of habitat) and increasing pesticide use. Human land disturbance has complex and cascading effects. For example, land disturbance is favorable to invasive ants. Invasive ants are partly responsible for insect population declines. It is known that with massive ant invasions, like Argentine ants in California, insect populations suffer. Climate change is also taking its toll on insect populations. Insects are *ectotherms*, meaning that regulation of their body temperatures depends on external, not internal, factors. As such they are particularly susceptible to climate change. Declines due to climate change have already been documented and they are predicted to become more severe as global warming intensifies.[21]

The loss of insects has a cascading effect through ecosystems. Jarvis writes:[22]

> People who studied fish found that the fish had fewer mayflies to eat. Ornithologists kept finding birds that rely on insects for food were in trouble: eight in 10 partridges gone from French farmlands; 50 and 80 percent drops, respectively, for nightingales and turtledoves. Half of all farmland birds in Europe disappeared in just three decades.

Biologists have called the current loss of nature "biological annihilation."[23] What accounts for the massive "defaunation" of the earth? Once again, as throughout the last 10,000 years of human history, agriculture is the main culprit. Land grabbing of the earth's remaining wild areas, large-scale dam projects for irrigation, pesticide use, and massive monoculture plantations are all taking their toll. To save what is left of the richness and diversity of the nonhuman world, two broad policies are required. The first is to prevent the worst-case scenarios for future climate change as outlined. The second is to reduce the human presence on the planet.

• *Protect and expand wild areas and keep markets out* – in *Half Earth*, E. O. Wilson calls for committing half of planet earth's surface to nature.[24] He calls this an emergency solution commensurate with the magnitude of the problem we face: the looming decimation of the nonhuman world. Wilson writes: "I am convinced that only by setting aside half the planet in reserve, or more, can we save the living part of the environment and achieve the stabilization required for our own survival."

Stopping the exploitation of half the planet is not as far-fetched as it sounds. Large areas of the planet are relatively intact – the Amazon River Basin, the greater Serengeti ecosystem, the Congo Basin, and the Sudd wetlands of South Sudan. Furthermore, much of the world is already being depopulated as the forces of globalization push people out of rural areas. For much of the planet, keeping markets out and expanding wild nature could actually improve the quality of life for the humans living there. Projects are underway to protect and restore wilderness areas and establish corridors between them. Projects include the Yellowstone to Yukon conservation initiative, the European Green Belt along the former Iron Curtain boundary, and the Buffalo Commons initiative for the American great plains. The beauty of these projects is that, for the most part, they require little investment except for regulations and easements and scientific information gathering and monitoring. Once established, nature takes care of the details. An example of nature's resilience is the cascading effect of the reintroduction of wolves in Yellowstone Park in 1995, seventy years after they had been exterminated. Monbiot writes (*Feral*, p. 84):

> When they arrived, many of the streamsides and riversides were almost bare, closely cropped by the high population of [elk]. But as soon as the wolves arrived, this began to change. It was not just that they sharply reduced the number of deer, but they also altered their prey's behavior. The deer avoided the places—particularly the valleys and gorges—where they could be caught most easily.
>
> In some places, trees on the riverbanks, until then constantly suppressed by browsing, quintupled in height in just six years. The trees shaded and cooled the water and provided cover for fish and other animals, changing the wildlife community which lived there. More seedlings and saplings survived. The bare valleys began reverting to aspen, willow and cottonwood forests.

Numerous other changes occurred including increases in beaver populations, which created habitats for birds, otters, and moose. The presence of wolves reduced coyote populations, causing a rise in the number of small mammals that in turn increased the numbers of owls, foxes, and badgers.

Several "natural" experiments have occurred in the wake of the unintended consequences of human abandonment of large areas. The contaminated land around Chernobyl and Fukushima, Japan is now abundant with wildlife as is the demilitarized no-man's-land between North and South Korea. When human exploitation ends, nature has an amazing ability to heal itself.

- *Reduce the human population to leave room for other species* – the human population reached 7 billion sometime in 2011. It now stands at close to 7 ½ billion. It is growing at an annual rate of 1.1%, adding about 83 million people per year. Median projections show world population reaching 8.6 billion in 2030; 9.8 billion in 2050; and 11.2 billion by 2100. Longer-term projections are highly speculative and show everything from runaway growth to a population crash down to 2.3 billion in 2300.[25]

The most widely accepted view of population growth is the "demographic transition." If incomes continue to rise in most countries and richer people have fewer children, then world population should peak at 11 billion around the year 2100. But some recent statistics suggest that his view could be wrong. In Europe during the past ten years or so fertility rates have been increasing. According to Oxford University demographer Francesco Billari, this increase in highly developed countries cannot be attributed solely to immigration.[26] Fertility rates fell in Africa for a few years, but they have now leveled off at around 4.6 instead of continuing to drop as the demographic transition predicts. Reasons include lower death rates (particularly from HIV), and the lack of family planning programs partly due to pressure from conservative religious groups.

The effect of the sheer number of people on the planet is staggering. But calculating the human impact on the planet should also take into account the impacts of human farm animals. Humans and their domestic animals account for a staggering 96 percent of total terrestrial vertebrate biomass.[27] The biomass of humans and their livestock is more than twenty times larger than the biomass of wild mammals.[28] Global human appropriation of the planet's net primary energy production (HANPP) doubled during the twentieth century.[29]

The effect of human population growth on the natural world is complicated and depends not only on sheer numbers of people but also on energy and material use and technology. But the current human population is staggeringly high and will likely grow exponentially for the foreseeable future. Even a 1 percent annual growth rate means a doubling every seventy-two years. If the human population suddenly declined by half, to 3½ billion people, at the current rate of growth we would be back to the current population level in one human lifetime. Some of the attacks on population planning by progressives are misguided to say the least. Population policies are dismissed out of hand as "imperialism" or even "genocide."[30] As Paul Ehrlich and other advocates of population control have long argued, population, overconsumption, and destructive technologies are all to blame for the destruction of the natural world as we know it.[31] Decreasing the human population should be a coordinated strategy of family planning, female empowerment, and economic equality. Economic and social security can also play an important role in the sustainability of modern societies. Social security programs and old-age pensions played a decisive role in the reduction in population growth in Kerala (India), China, South Korea, and Sri Lanka. When life is perceived to be secure, people do not need large families to ensure that they will be taken care of in old age. However, all the problems we face are exacerbated by a growing population. As Ehrlich puts it:

> Solving the population problem is not going to solve the problems of racism, of sexism, of religious intolerance, of war, of gross economic inequality. But if you don't solve the population problem, you're not going to solve any of those problems. Whatever problem you're interested in, you're not going to solve it unless you also solve the population problem. Whatever your cause, it's a lost cause without population control.[32]

The earth needs fewer people, not more.

Make the Economy Work for Human Beings

The market economy treats human beings as productive inputs whose worth is measured by how much economic surplus they produce.

The commodification of nature and people is in sharp contrast to the human economies that existed for most of human history. Again, we cannot suddenly return to a hunting and gathering way of life, barring a catastrophic collapse of the human population. We can, however, work to incorporate some of the features of traditional societies that worked to promote ecological and social harmony. The key is to institute policies that support economic security and self-actualization, that is, control over one's life and life choices. Achieving this can be done by recognizing that the remarkable material gains our species have made are the result of hundreds of thousands of years of social evolution, not the individual contributions of an elite few. The following are minimal policies for making the economy work for people, not the market superorganism. If we think of the world's economic surplus as a collective good belonging to every human on the planet, not to an elite few, the possibilities are endless.

- *A Guaranteed Basic Income*

Basic income is the payment of identical amounts of money to all citizens. It is not means tested or adjusted for income level. It recognizes that human civilization is the result of social evolution and the contributions of hundreds of millions of unknown individuals over millennia. Solely by being a member of the species *Homo sapiens*, every human being on the planet deserves a slice of the global economic surplus we produce. Standing in the way of a basic income is an evolved ideology and set of institutions justifying the confiscation of the products of human social evolution by a tiny minority of despots and oligarchs. The collective nature of economic production is even more apparent as capital replaces labor in the twenty-first-century economy. The thousands of inventions and innovations behind the robotics and information technology revolution are not the products of single individuals. Furthermore, the research behind the new technological economy has come from public funding, not the private sector. The costs are paid by all and the benefits should be shared by all. A basic income is an old idea. Napoleon Bonaparte believed that "man is entitled by birthright to a share of the earth's produce sufficient to fill the needs of his existence." Thomas Paine wanted a "citizen's dividend" to compensate for the "loss of his or her natural inheritance, by the introduction of the system of landed property." Even Friedrich Hayek favored the idea of a guaranteed income: "I have always said that I am in favor of minimum income for every person in the country."[33]

Basic income is different from a guaranteed minimum income that does not depend on a means test. It should be seen as a basic human entitlement, not a gift from the state, not as a form of "redistribution." Basic income does not take the place of other social support programs like health care, social security, or education. Need for these programs varies greatly depending on age, gender, and inherited characteristics, and support will vary greatly from person to person. Basic income should not be confused with a guaranteed minimum income advocated by some neoliberals to replace all other assistance programs. Conservative motives for supporting a guaranteed income are (1) to reduce the total amount paid by the government for social programs; and (2) a misguided belief in the rationality of individual choices. The deeply flawed argument is that if people can choose whether they want to spend a given amount of money on health care, education, or anything else, they will always make the correct choice and make themselves better off than they would if spending options were restricted.

- *A Maximum Limit to Income and Wealth*

A basic income for all should be complemented by a confiscatory wealth tax and an upper limit on income. Inherited wealth is at the heart of the evolution of inequality and of the conversion of the commons into private property for private gain.[34] There is an inherent tendency of elites to capture larger and larger shares of the economic surplus. Recent comprehensive studies have shown the persistence of hereditary wealth. In 2017 the median pay for S&P 500 CEOs was $12.1 million, an increase of about 10 percent over the previous year. Broadcom CEO Hock Tan topped the list with a total compensation package of $103.2 million.[35] In the 1950s average CEO salary was about twenty times the salary of the average worker. In 2017 the average CEO made 361 times as much money. Furthermore, even failed CEOs are lavishly rewarded by the current system. The average severance package for CEOs forced out of their jobs was $48 million.[36]

Herman Daly has pointed out that a maximum limit on income and wealth was advocated by all prominent early American statesmen (except Alexander Hamilton).[37] Apologists for unlimited private wealth base their defense on the supposed greater contribution the rich make to surplus generation. But what possible economic justification is there for a single person to be paid $100 million a year? The argument for a ceiling on maximum income is essentially the same as the one for a basic income. Society's ability to generate economic surplus is not the result of the action of a handful of individuals at a point in time. It's the result of the collective intelligence and evolutionary heritage of our species.

A minimum and maximum income would apply to all citizens regardless of personal circumstances. The delivery of the following programs would vary according to the needs of specific population subgroups. But with a basic income and a cap on maximum income these programs would not have to be means tested, greatly reducing their administrative costs.

- *Universal Quality Health Care*

We have seen the inefficiency and irrationality of the US health care system. So much has been written about successful and unsuccessful health care systems that there is no need to go into detail here. In terms of the United States it is by now clear what the broad features of a workable system would look like. A focus on preventative care. Letting the government, as a single buyer, negotiate drug prices, giving some flexibility to states, recognizing the very different health care requirements of urban and rural areas, colder and warmer climates, and differing population subgroups. Use and carefully monitor controlled public experiments to determine what works and what does not. The United States also faces several crises related directly to health care but involving a variety of other factors. Getting control of the addiction crisis will require not only treatment programs, but also mental health counseling, more treatment centers, more innovative law enforcement and incarceration procedures for repeat offenders, and more resources to intercept drugs at borders. The obesity epidemic also needs to be directly addressed with specific policies targeted to specific groups. Another crisis is the growing incidence of families needing counseling and intervention. Child neglect and abuse, in particular, have intergenerational consequences and lies behind much of the violence in American society. Addressing these issues will require spending more money, but this should be covered by the savings generated by a rationally planned health care system. Again, the United States spends twice as much per capita on health care as other advanced economies.

- *Old-Age Security*

Social Security provides income for people past working age. The US social security system was instituted in 1935 under President

Franklin Roosevelt. Along with Medicare, Social Security is one of the most efficient government programs with overhead costs amounting to less than 1.5 percent of outlays.[38] Even with an adequate basic income in place, supplemental programs for the elderly would be needed. The needs of the elderly vary considerably from person to person and place to place. Long-term care will be increasingly important as the population ages. Expanded social security programs could include government-sponsored retirement villages in a variety of areas – urban, rural, rewilded areas, and densely populated cities. People should be given choices about where they want to live. Specialized care for specific medical conditions could be provided in some of the retirement communities and not others. As with providing health care, a key is programs that are flexible and carefully monitored and evaluated.

- *Universal Quality Public Education*

    Access to primary and secondary education should be based on need, not income. College education should be free. The reliance on property taxes to fund primary and secondary education should be eliminated. Free public education through college exists in most European countries. In the United States, as with health care, enough government money is currently spent on education to provide universal free education through college and/or post-secondary vocational training. And with basic needs satisfied by a minimum income, the range of choices could be greatly expanded. Some could pursue apprentice training, others any sort of esoteric studies they desire. Educational opportunities should be coordinated with the aforementioned programs, for example, by drawing on the expertise present in retirement communities.

- *Establish a Department of Well-Being and Happiness*

    The field of "happiness studies" is now well established. We have a good idea of what contributes to human well-being.[39] The department would be responsible for implementing innovative new programs to increase well-being. Two possible initiatives are music and exposure to nature. Making music is a universal human characteristic. A Neanderthal flute has been dated at 43,000 years ago. Music is one thing that brings people together. The department could fund concerts, community music centers, and music instruction. Establishing links to retirement communities is an obvious thing to do. Another well-established contributor to well-being is contact with the natural world.

E. O. Wilson suggests that the term biophilia describes "the connections that human beings subconsciously seek with the rest of life." He believes that the deep feelings humans have with the natural world are rooted in our biology.[40] The positive impacts on health of taking a daily walk in the woods are dramatic. Designing public spaces, parks, and buildings with biophilia in mind has already become an important subfield of architecture and community planning.

• • •

Would the aforementioned policies move society toward long-run sustainability? Given the dire straits our species finds itself in, the policies are minimal first steps toward reasserting human agency over the global economy. But if instituted they would lay the groundwork for more radical change. What would the immediate effects of the policies be? First of all, the nonhuman world would be given some breathing space from the current unprecedented assault on nature. Secondly, the current deterioration in the well-being of the mass of the population would be reversed. These policies would help depressed areas. All over the world rural areas are suffering from economic decline, the collapse of public services, and the outmigration of the young and talented. Revitalizing key support systems – health care, education, and long-term care – would allow rural areas to draw people back to the lifestyle amenities the countryside offers. Thirdly, the policies would create the flexibility to meet the challenges of a rapidly devolving, and possibly disintegrating, economy. People would have the security and the resources to try new flexible ways of making a living without the risk of economic disaster if they fail. These proposals are not particularly radical. The world economy will not cease to function if a few people are not allowed to make $100 million a year, or even $10 million a year. If there is a minimum guaranteed income, everyone will not immediately stop working.

In addition to the policies mentioned, two broad objectives should cut across all these recommendations – abolish all aspects of the human caste system and preserve cultural diversity. Both of these have an evolutionary basis. Humans evolved biologically and socially as a sexual species. We also evolved from populations of hominids whose successful adaptation to changing environments depended on having a diverse range of characteristics for natural selection to act on. Although the woman-as-gatherer, man-as-hunter distinction is not as sharp as once believed, women in most tropical and temperate hunter-gatherer societies supplied the bulk of the food through gathering. Women were not dependent on males for food, although division of labor certainly generated differences in the ability to access means of subsistence. The dependence on gathering contributed to the gender autonomy generally present in the group. Decisions were made with inputs from all members of the hunter-gatherer groups. The more information and the more inputs from different perspectives, the better the decision. The low social status of women and their exclusion from decision-making in many countries today is frequently cited as a major contributor to explosive population growth and economic stagnation. The legacy of slavery and colonialism needs to be directly addressed. Distribution of surplus in the human economy is based on centuries-old institutions, laws, and customs restricting the ability of particular classes of people to share the material wealth the system generates. Most cultures today do not have rigid, legally sanctioned caste systems. But the legacy of slavery and the disdain for the those at the bottom of the economic ladder permeate Western societies. "Reparations" in the form of targeted quality education, health care, and access to jobs and income are necessary to address this legacy.

• • •

For most of human existence we had a wide variety of physical types and a wide variety of cultures. The Inuit of arctic northern North America and the Aborigines of the Australian deserts were able to live sustainably for millennia in environments where contemporary industrial-society humans could not survive without a steady subsidy of resources from the outside. The hunting and gathering lifestyles represented a remarkable and varied response to different environmental conditions. For most of the 2 million plus years of human existence a wide range of lifestyles and economic bases could be found in ecosystems, from desert to tundra to rainforest. Vandana Shiva writes:

> Diversity is the characteristic of nature and the basis of ecological stability. Diverse ecosystems give rise to diverse life forms, and to diverse cultures. The co-evolution of cultures, life forms and habitats has conserved the biological diversity on this planet. Cultural diversity and biological diversity go hand in hand.[41]

With a diversity of cultures, there is a better chance for the human species to withstand shocks, climatic, and otherwise. The growing cultural homogenization of the world economy is particularly vulnerable to environmental and social disruption.

This chapter offers broad policies to address the two crises of ultrasociality central to this book – the loss of the natural world, and expropriation of economic surplus by an elite class. The common thread in the previously mentioned environmental and social policies is: Do not let the market determine public policy. The market is not the solution, the market is the problem. Are these suggestions feasible? In terms of public support the answer is a resounding "yes." In response to the question: "Do you think the federal government should guarantee health care for all Americans, or don't you think so?," Americans favor guaranteed health care for all, by a margin of 62–38 percent.[42] About half of all Americans support a universal basic income.[43] Two-thirds of Americans support free college education.[44] A majority supports aggressive climate change mitigation policies. The problem with implementing these proposals is not a lack of public support, it is the control of the political process by an economic elite who oppose any change that constrains their ability to exploit people and nature.

9 EVOLVING A SUSTAINABLE AND EQUITABLE FUTURE
What Can We Learn from Nonmarket Cultures?

Most recommendations for a sustainable and equitable future stop with a progressive political agenda similar to that outlined in the last chapter. But even if all those programs were enacted, our planet and our species would still be in peril. The growth dynamic and the conditions for increasing inequality would still be in place. Prosperity would still be based on extraction and surplus accumulation. Georgescu-Roegen called sustainable development "snake oil," a worthless concoction packaged to pass as a cure-all for society's ills. Perhaps a more charitable view would be a line from the folk song "Arkansas Traveler": "Sorry mister but you can't get there from here." The global economy is so far from being sustainable that it is fruitless to talk about transforming it with piecemeal reforms into something environmentally benign. We can make things better but it is hard to imagine a sustainable human presence on earth without moving to an entirely new system.

What if all the reforms listed in the last chapter were in place? Climate change would be slowed, giving us more time to prepare for a new climate regime. Half the natural world would be protected as bioreserves. This would give nonhuman species and ecosystems the chance to recover much of their lost richness and resilience. Progressive social programs would give everyone more security, freedom, and flexibility to fare better within the market economy. A maximum income and confiscatory inheritance tax would curb the economic power of elites and limit the ability of elites to form. It would curb incentives for the acquisition of wealth and material goods. An expanded health care system, with universal coverage and a focus on preventive medicine, would mean that people would have longer, more active, lives. With more flexibility in life choices in occupations, education, and leisure activities, the skills of older people could be used in creative ways to foster new lifestyle choices and relieve pressure on the working-age population. These reforms would be an improvement over the existing system, but they would not make the necessary break with an economic system based on the imperative of accumulation and exploitation.

The minimal bioeconomic program would have some negative as well as positive effects. Significantly reducing the population might mean the further depopulation of rural areas and might require resettlement (for example, regrouping the elderly) as populations become so small that they are not viable. Japan is currently experiencing such a demographic change and we can learn from their experience. An aging population would also put pressure on the tax base and the ability to generate enough surplus to support people in retirement.

With the minimal bioeconomic program it is likely that a new caring environment with more security and less stress would generate changes in how humans relate to each other and the natural world. The point is not to have a utopian blueprint for the future. If we strive for flexibility and evolvability, positive new directions for human society will present themselves. New technologies like robotics, biotechnology, and information technologies have some potential if they are used to improve the well-being of human beings, not as a source of private monetary gain and control over labor. The traits that made us human as Pleistocene hunter-gatherers would, hopefully, once again become dominant – cooperation with nonkin, a positive material and emotional bond with the natural world, compassion for others, and other attitudes promoting well-being, fairness, and equality. These traits were weakened with the transition to ultrasociality and the subjugation of individuals to the goal of surplus production. But we can use the examples of nonmarket cultures as a guide to how to live sustainably and equitably. We can also use the negative characteristics of societies that emerged after large-scale agricultural to ascertain what went wrong – unsustainable exploitation of nature, social hierarchies and caste systems, and the cancer of hereditary wealth. The past is our guide to making the transition to a better world. The hunter-gatherer way of life presents a direct challenge to the market economy.[1] In the words of Richard Lee:[2]

> It is not necessary to portray the foragers as paragons of virtue to see the radical alterity of their way of life. Neither is it necessary to postulate that contemporary hunters and gatherers are a baseline from which other forms of society have evolved. It is sufficient to say that whatever the pathways by which they reached their present conditions, the existence of mobile, small-scale, relatively non-exploitative and egalitarian societies based on sharing is prima facie evidence that even in the hard bitten age of global capitalism, other ways of being, other ways of living in the world are possible.

• • •

The Cultural Impediments to Radical Change

What can hunter-gatherers tell us about the impediments to radical change? First of all they show us that the theoretical framework of orthodox economics is seriously flawed as a general description of human social organization. Challenges to economic orthodoxy coming from the descriptions of life in hunter-gatherer societies are (1) the economic notion of scarcity is a social construct, not an inherent property of human existence; (2) the separation of work from social life is not a necessary characteristic of economic production; (3) linking individual well-being to individual production is neither a necessary nor desirable characteristic of economic organization; (4) selfishness and acquisitiveness are aspects of human nature, but not necessarily the dominant ones; and (5) inequality based on class and gender is not a necessary characteristic of human society. These insights offer hope that a new and better economy is possible.

- *Scarcity Is a Social Construct*

The notion of scarcity is the foundation for orthodox economics. Economics is defined as the study of the allocation of limited resources to satisfy near-infinite wants. But scarcity is not a necessary characteristic of human existence or a molder of human nature. As Marshall Sahlins stressed, hunter-gatherers may be considered affluent because they achieve a balance between means and ends by having everything

they need and wanting little more. Asked why he did not plant crops a !
Kung man replied: "Why should we plant when there are so many
mongongo nuts in the world?"[3] As a San song goes, "Those who work
for a living, that's their problem!"[4] Hunter-gatherers have few material
possessions but much leisure time and, arguably, a richer social life than
the "affluent" consumers of the modern world. The market economy
generates scarcity by continually and aggressively creating unlimited wants.
Consumers are conditioned to be addicts requiring a continual flow of
consumer goods. They are in a constant state of deprivation because
addiction can never be satiated. In Sahlins's words: "Consumption is a
double tragedy: what begins in inadequacy will end in deprivation."[5] The
worldwide addiction to material wealth is a drain on our psychological
well-being as well as the biological and geophysical foundations of human
existence.

- *Production Is a Social, Not an Individual, Activity*

    Work in hunter-gatherer cultures is social and cooperative, and
limited to satisfying everyday needs. Immediate-return hunter-gatherers,
such as the Hadza and !Kung, spend only three or four hours per day
doing what we would call economic activities.[6] These include hunting a
large number of animal species and gathering a large variety of plant
material. Successfully fulfilling everyday wants depends on detailed
knowledge about the characteristics and life histories of the plant and
animal species upon which they depend for survival, not on capital
equipment. Hunter-gatherers had the original information economy.
The "means of production" was knowledge, and this knowledge was
freely available to all. Economic life was integrated with rituals, socialization, and artistic expression. The idea that earning a living is
drudgery whose only purpose is to make it possible for us to live our
"real" lives is alien to traditional hunter-gatherers.

- *Linking Production and Distribution Is a Social Construct*

    According to economic theory the distribution of economic
output, what each person receives, depends on how much that individual contributes to producing it – his or her marginal product. There is
no social context, just the given configuration of technology and capital
stock. But other cultures show us that there is no necessary connection
between production by individuals and distribution to individuals. In
many cultures there is no connection between who produces and who

receives the economic output. According to Woodburn, some members of the Hadza do virtually no work their entire lives.[7,8] Many Hadza men gamble with spear points, and many are reluctant to hunt for fear of damaging their gambling "chips," yet these men continue to get their full share of the game animals killed. Distribution of meat among the Ju/'hoansi is a serious social event and they go to great lengths to ensure that the distribution is done exactly right. Lee[9] writes: "Distribution is done with great care, according to a set of rules, arranging and rearranging the pieces for up to an hour so that each recipient will get the right proportion. Successful distributions are remembered with pleasure for weeks afterward, while improper meat distributions can be the cause of bitter wrangling among close relatives." By contrast, market economies, by basing distribution on the isolated productivity of each individual, deny the social nature of production and at the same time fragments the social bonds that help hold other societies together.

- *Private Ownership of the Means of Making a Living Is Incompatible with an Equitable Society*

Accounts by early European explorers and anthropologists indicate that a lack of concern with ownership of personal possessions is a common characteristic of hunter-gatherers. Among the Hadza, the lack of private ownership of things also applies to the ownership of resources.[10] Characterizing the relationship of some hunter-gatherers to the land as "ownership" is a case of imposing Western concepts on people who have very different beliefs about the relationships between people and the nonhuman world. David Riches argues that the term "ownership" should be used only in cases where people are observed denying others the right to use particular resources.[11] The mere act of asking permission may be only a social convention expressing friendly intent and may not be an indication of "legal" control over a resource.

Substitution Is Overrated

Economists are fond of extolling the power of the market to overcome scarcity through substitution. As Robert Solow put it:

> [H]istory tells us an important fact, namely, that goods and services can be substituted for one another. If you don't eat one species of fish, you can eat another species of fish. Resources are,

> to use a favorite word of economists, fungible in a certain sense. They can take the place of each other. That is extremely important because it suggests that we do not owe the future any particular thing. There is no specific object that the goal of sustainability, the obligation of sustainability, requires us to leave untouched. (Robert Solow, Sustainability: An economist's perspective)
>
> Money greatly extends the notion of substitutability by creating a common equivalent between any good or service. With global markets, if there is a demand for something anywhere it can quickly be transformed into money. Perishable and ephemeral things become fungible and storable.
>
> Substitution is a fact of life in all human economies, but it takes a much different, and virulent, form in market societies. In economic markets, no matter what the resource, a substitute for it will always appear if the price is right. However, since the ultimate measure of market value is monetary, all things are reduced to a single common denominator, money. Substitution is based on monetary values that may ignore essential characteristics not related to immediate market functions. According to economic criteria, an economy is sustainable, then, if its ability to generate income is maintained, that is, if the monetary value of its means of production is nondecreasing. By this criterion, it is "sustainable," for example, to cut down a rainforest if the net monetary gain from cutting it is invested for future generations. The type of investment does not matter. It could be another automobile factory, or even a financial investment. Everything is convertible to money and capable of being substituted for something else if the relative prices are right.

Immediate-return hunter-gatherers depend only on their bodies and intelligence to produce their daily sustenance. Mobility is paramount and physical capital is necessarily simple. Capital in a hunter-gatherer world is not a physical thing that can be manipulated and controlled, but rather knowledge that is shared and accessible to all.[12] With this knowledge, hunter-gatherers can quickly construct their material culture. Turnbull writes of Pygmies of Central Africa: "The materials for the making of shelter, clothing, and all other necessary items of material culture are all at hand at a moment's notice."[13] Unlike the manufactured capital of industrial society, hunter-gatherer capital stock is knowledge that is freely given and impossible to control for individual advantage. Furthermore, the lack of preoccupation with acquiring material goods gives hunter-gatherers the freedom to enjoy life. Most of the life activities of hunter-gatherers do not occur at a workplace away from friends and family but in talking, resting, sharing, and celebrating; in short, in being human.

- *Equality Does Not Come Automatically Even in Hunter-Gatherer Societies*

Woodburn describes immediate-return hunter-gatherer societies as "aggressively egalitarian."[14] These societies worked because they actively kept power and authority in check. Inequality as an inevitable result of human nature is another side of the cultural myth of the economic man. The logic of economic rationality justifies as "natural" income differences based on class, race, or gender. Usually, this justification is based on appeals to economic efficiency. Since markets are competitive, higher incomes are the result of more productive work. A trade-off between economic growth and equity is a feature of most economic textbooks. If society errs on the side of too much equity (so the story goes) the incentive to work is lost, production falls, and even the temporary beneficiaries of more income equality end up worse off than before.

The hunter-gatherer literature shows that "economic rationality" is embedded in a set of cultural beliefs, not in objective universal laws of human nature. There are many other ways of behaving that do not conform to the laws of market exchange. The myth of rational economic man may be the basic organizing principle of contemporary capitalism, but it is no more legitimate than the myths that drive Hadza, Aborigine, or !Kung society. Because immediate-return hunter-gatherers lived off the direct flows from nature, it was immediately apparent when the flow of nature's services was disturbed. Sustainability meant sustaining the ability of nature to provide the necessities of life. Hunter-gatherers have displayed the ability to substitute certain natural resources for many others, but care was taken to maintain the flow of nature's bounty.

• • •

Cosmologies That Blind Our Vision of a Better Future

The economic dynamic that began with agriculture generated belief systems that support and perpetuate expansion and exploitation. Sahlins's "cosmologies" guide the way we see ourselves and our place in the cosmos.[15] Three important cosmologies clouding our understanding of the ultrasocial economy and the transition to a better future are (1) the belief in the inevitability of progress; (2) the belief that humans hold a special place in universe; and (3) the belief that individual initiative is the prime mover in human affairs.

- ## *The False Allure of Inevitable Progress*

We judge progress in terms of the technological achievements of civilization and the accomplishments of modern science. We conflate individuals and society. "We" put a man on the moon. "We" discovered DNA and the double helix. "We" created the modern age of technological wonders. Yet few individuals have even a rudimentary understanding of any of these achievements. Progress has come to mean technological achievement, not advancements in individual intelligence, knowledge, or well-being. The meaning of "individual well-being" is a matter of debate among social scientists. But the evidence showing that agriculture made the average person worse off for some 10,000 years opens the door to questions relevant for evaluating our present condition and our future prospects. Has civilization and the industrial revolution truly made people better off? Even if the answer is a tentative "yes," are the years since World War II, a period of relative peace and prosperity, typical, or are they an anomaly?

Progress has become a kind of secular religion whose promise always lies in the future.[16] Technology will solve the problems it has created if only we wait a little longer, as in the old Christian hymn "farther along we'll know all about it, farther along we'll understand why." Things may seem bad now, but just wait a bit and everything will work out for the best.

- ## *The False Allure of Human Exceptionalism*

Perhaps the most contentious implication of human ultrasociality is that social evolution is a consequence of the same mechanistic (i.e., not consciously directed) evolutionary forces that govern other species. Human agency may be overrated or even a pure illusion. It is disturbing to consider that complex aspects of human social structure are in many respects the same as those of "mindless" creatures such as ants and termites. But similar outcomes in insect and human societies suggest common drivers of social evolution independent of intentional behavior and planning. Unlike any other kinds of organisms, agricultural ants, termites, and humans have extremely large-scale city-states, a complex division of labor, and sophisticated communication systems to coordinate economic activity. These similar social features lead to similar outcomes – ecosystem domination and the subjugation of individuals for the goal of surplus production. Ultrasociality challenges the notions of human exceptionalism and intentional behavior at the level of society.

Darwin's heretical idea was not evolution itself but rather that humans are subject to the same impersonal evolutionary forces and natural laws that shape the characteristics of other species. Attributing agriculture, civilization, and human domination of the planet to evolutionary processes common to ants and termites, not to the superiority of the human intellect, is an affront to conventional wisdom. The question of the special place for humans in evolutionary history goes back to the debate between Darwin and the theologian William Paley. The hostility to materialism (what exists in nature is the result of impersonal mechanical processes, not divine guidance) was one reason Darwin delayed the publication of *The Origin of Species* for twenty years.[17] The great successes of biology came about by moving from supernatural to scientific explanations. A pioneer in the field of ultrasocial evolution, Donald Campbell, warned against the presumption of human uniqueness: "I also join [Dobrowski] in distrusting that value-salvage route which lies in worshipping man's conscious experience, as by saving mind as separate from body, or making body all mind, for these too commit the ancient sin of man worshipping himself instead of the purposes and forces beyond any individual's transient being."[18] The belief in human uniqueness has led us to denigrate the complexity of the nonhuman world and the intelligence of other species. Carl Safina observes:

> We're obsessed with filling in the blank for a Mad Libs line that goes: "_____ makes us human." Why? Scratch and sniff the "what makes us human" obsession and you get a strong whiff of something that could fit into that blank: our insecurity.[19]

The pervasive belief in human uniqueness makes it difficult to accept that human society has followed the same blind evolutionary path as social insects. But the recognition that we are trapped in a system we stumbled into through no fault of our own opens the door to asserting human agency and taking control of our future.

- *The False Allure of Selfish Individualism as the Driving Force in Human Affairs*

Sahlins used the term "intellectual vertigo" to describe the feeling one gets from realizing that many "new" ideas have pedigrees going back hundreds if not thousands of years. An example is the notion of "rational economic man," the rugged individual of economic theory. In the standard economic model human nature makes us selfish and narrowly rational. The assumption of "self-regarding preferences" is the starting point for the mathematical proof that competitive markets are the most efficient way to allocate society's scarce resources. As Sahlins points, out the idea that self-interest drives all human relationships goes back hundreds of years in Western cosmology. In 1431 Lorenzo Valla wrote:[20]

> And what is the aim of friendship? Has it been sought for and so greatly praised by all ages and nations for any other reasons than the satisfactions arising from the performance of mutual services such as giving and receiving whatever men commonly need? ... As for masters and servants, there is no doubt their only aim is common advantage. What should I say about teachers and students? ... What finally forms the link between parents and children if it is not advantage and pleasure?

The image of the self-sufficient individual without the need of social bonds has a long pedigree and still dominates the field of economics. Within this cosmology, choices by self-interested individuals drive market economies. Causality only moves upward, from the individual to the larger economy. Since the global market economy is driven by individual choice, it must be "good" in the sense that it must be what people want. Despite the encouraging contributions of behavioral economics in overturning the icon of narrowly rational economic man, the focus is still on the individual to the exclusion of institutions and group-level processes. A major theme of this book is that the evolution of human society is not driven by individual choice, but rather the requirements of making a living. The economic system molds attitudes and belief systems. Causality in social evolution is top-down, not bottom-up.

• • •

Evolutionary biology can teach us a lot about the importance of cooperation and synergy. Diversity and competition drove the evolution of complex life. Life first appeared on earth some 3.8 billion years ago in the form of prokaryotes (bacteria and archaea), one-celled organisms without nuclei or mitochondria. It took about 2 billion years for the next step in complexity to occur, the appearance of eukaryotes, cells with well-defined nuclei and mitochondria. Mitochondria allow cells to capture and use large amount of energy. They originated as prokaryotes but eventually formed a symbiotic relationship with other cells to become eukaryotes, a process known as endosymbiosis.[21] Eukaryotes are about 15,000 times the size of prokaryotes.[22] About 1 1/2 billion years later, 540 million years ago, another giant leap in complexity occurred with the proliferation of complex multicelled life in what is known as the Cambrian explosion. One explanation for the proliferation of complex life in the Cambrian is the evolution of eyes.[23] Eyes paved the way for a much more intense competition among organisms and a new arms race between predators and prey.[24,25] Even in the earliest stages of complex life on earth, a key driver was variety. As more diversity appeared, natural selection was provided with more material to work with, which in turn resulted in even more diversity and complexity.

Today the world is moving toward a single, unified economic system. The result is not only an economic homogenization but also a homogenization of values and beliefs. It is hard for us to see the homogenization of the world because at the same time individual countries and regions are becoming more heterogeneous. Our neighborhoods are becoming more diverse ethnically with international literature, food, and music. We hear more languages and we see goods from all over the world. But differences between countries, for the most part, are becoming less pronounced. The world's major cities are becoming more similar. There are certainly positive aspects of this change but there is a real danger in terms of the ability to adjust to change. We are moving toward a single economic system, market capitalism, with its own unique value system. The values of "WEIRD" societies (Western, Educated, Industrial, Rich, and Democratic)[26] are replacing those of all other cultures as more and more of the world's population come under the domination of the market superorganism.

The values embedded in global capitalism are apparently aberrations – outliers compared to those of myriad other human cultures. Henrich et al. examined the characteristics of sixteen societies around the world, including fourteen small-scale societies, and concluded the following:

Here, our review of the comparative database from across the behavioral sciences suggests both that there is substantial variability in experimental results across populations and that WEIRD subjects are particularly unusual compared with the rest of the species – frequent outliers. The domains reviewed include visual perception, fairness, cooperation, spatial reasoning, categorization and inferential induction, moral reasoning, reasoning styles, self-concepts and related motivations, and the heritability of IQ. The findings suggest that members of WEIRD societies, including young children, are among the least representative populations one could find for generalizing about humans.[27]

Large differences among cultures were found in spacial perception, risk aversion, perception of nature, social motivation (fairness), and views of "self" (independent or embedded in society). Members of WEIRD societies were outliers on measures of all these characteristics. It seems as if the "least representative" values are becoming dominant worldwide.[28] It may be that WEIRD people offer a glimpse of what the future world will look like if the "rationalization" of human life continues – a world of a one-dimensional culture with little variety for cultural selection to work with.

What does all this have to do with human social evolution and moving to a sustainable presence on planet earth? Humans evolved from diverse populations of hominids whose successful adaptation to changing environments depended on having a wide range of characteristics for natural selection to act on. Likewise, human social evolution has been a story of migrations, conquests, and mixing of customs and beliefs. Selection among groups and synergy from new traits was the raw material for human cultural evolution.[29] The dangers of genetic bottlenecks are well known. Equally ominous is the cultural bottleneck as the immense variety of human languages, customs, and belief systems fall victim to the homogenized global economy.

• • •

Social and Biological Evolution

Choice is a feature of biological and cultural natural selection. Sexual selection offers significant fitness advantages by creating more variety for natural selection to work with. Since it dominates multicellular organisms, the fitness of offspring produced by two genders must outweigh the costs. Experiments have shown that female choice is an important feature in enhancing fitness and that natural selection is perfectly consistent with individual choice. For example, Patricia Gowanty did several experiments with mice showing that if female mice are allowed to choose their mates, those offspring are more robust and have higher survival rates than the offspring of females who were not allowed to choose with whom they mate.[30] She even found the same result with fruit flies. Choice can bring more information into play for natural selection to work on.

Judging from historical hunting and gathering societies, and some archaeological evidence,[31] a striking characteristic of hunter-gatherer societies is gender equality in decision-making, although women and men had different, but overlapping, spheres of influence. Although the woman-as-gatherer, man-as-hunter distinction is not as clear as once believed, women in many if not most tropical and temperate hunter-gatherer societies supplied the bulk of the calories through gathering. The dependence on gathering contributes to the relatively high status of women present in hunter-gatherer societies. Communal decisions were made with inputs from all members of hunter-gatherer groups. The more information and diverse insights and opinions, the better the decision. The low social status of women in many countries today is frequently cited as a major contributor to explosive population growth and economic stagnation. Gender equality (autonomy and self-actualization) was a universal human characteristic for most of our history as a species. As Leacock argues, the failure to appreciate the radical transformation of society that came with agriculture and the commodification of production has obscured the effects of this transition on the status of women. She writes:[32]

> The transmutation of production for consumption to production of commodities for exchange (usually along with intensive work on land as a commodity for future use) begins to take direct control of their produce out of the hands of the producers and to create new economic ties that undermine the collectivity of the joint households. Women begin to lose control of their production, and the sexual division of labor related to their childbearing ability becomes the basis for their oppression as

private dispensers of services in individual households. The process is by no means simple, automatic, or rapid, and where women retain some economic autonomy as traders they retain as well a relatively high status.

Cultural diversity is critical for future adaptation to a destabilized world. For most of human existence we had a wide variety of physical types and a wide variety of cultures. The Inuit of northern North America and the Aborigines of the Australian deserts were able to live sustainably for millennia in environments where contemporary industrial-society humans could not survive without a steady subsidy of resources from the outside. The hunting and gathering lifestyle represented a remarkable and varied response to different environmental conditions. For most of the 2 million plus years of human existence a wide range of lifestyles and economic bases could be found in ecosystems from desert to tundra to rainforest. Such diversity is critical to the stability of natural systems. With a diversity of lifestyles, there is also a better chance for the human species to withstand shocks, climatic and otherwise.

If individual perceptions and values are becoming more uniform, what about societies as a whole? Countries seem to be converging in terms of language, clothing, music, food, and technologies. These are usually viewed as positive, or at least benign. But what about some of the negative characteristics of market economies identified earlier? For one thing, class differences seem to be widening. The "underclass" described by Nancy Isenberg seems to be spreading to countries like Japan that traditionally have had more equal income distributions.[33] China now has one of the most unequal income distributions in the world, with a Gini coefficient of .61, just behind the income inequality leader Lesotho.[34] Income inequality is rising even in the Scandinavian countries as automation, the rationalization of production, and the growing information economy driving meritocracy based on verbal and analytical skills take hold worldwide. Likewise, stress-related disorders like obesity and drug addiction are increasing worldwide as country after country adopts the US model.

Accounts of hunter-gatherer societies indicate the importance of consensus and collective decision-making as opposed to the individual-choice obsession of market society. These societies have had mechanisms for social choice that allowed them to make the best choices for the long-term good of the group. By contrast, public policy in industrial societies is increasingly based on market approaches or pseudo-market approaches such as cost-benefit analysis. Market outcomes are based on decisions made by individuals isolated from the rest of society. What is good for isolated individuals in an impersonal market may not be the best for society as a whole. In terms of the social or biological value of ecosystems, for example, it makes little sense for society as a whole to discount them as an individual acting alone would, that is, to claim that they are worth less in the future. From society's point of view it makes little sense to assume that the value of breathable air, drinkable water, or a stable climate continually and sharply declines as a society goes further into the future. Market decisions reflect the interests of individual humans, not necessarily the community, and certainly not the well-being of the rest of the natural world. We make very different choices as individuals than we do as members of families, communities, or nations, or even as world citizens.

We have much to learn from indigenous people. The institution of private property is not the only mechanism to promote efficient resource use. In fact, there is evidence that common property regimes may be more effective in managing resources such as fisheries, even in contemporary capitalist economies, than policies based on the sanctity of individual property rights. Acheson and Wilson[35] argue that peasant and tribal societies practice management policies that are more consistent with the biological patterns and inherent unpredictability of fish stocks. Even among academic economists, theories of common property management are beginning to be taken seriously.[36,37]

• • •

Let us return to the question, "What is human nature?" The answer drives policy recommendations and one's view of the feasibility of positive radical change. If one holds a Hobbesian view that people are by nature selfish and greedy – life is a "war of all against all" – one is likely to support a strong central authority and economic policies motivated by self-interest and wealth acquisition. If one takes a more Rousseauian view that if left alone people will live in harmony, one is more likely to favor policies based on sharing, cooperation, and self-actualization. Discussions of Hobbes and Rousseau usually point out that Hobbes' dim view of human nature came from the turbulent and violent period in which he lived. Jean-Jacques Rousseau's view came out of his rejection of mercantile Europe and the relatively tranquil times in which lived. It is taken for granted that worldviews are shaped by the cultures we grow up in. But does it go deeper than that? The evidence is overwhelming that there is a neurological basis for cultural values. The answer to "What is human nature?" depends on the physical environment, neurology, cultural context, and individual and social history.

Human nature is hardwired by genes and culture. The search for universal human characteristics is complicated by the fact that the human brain continues to develop physically long after birth. The physical structure of the brain can vary depending on external (cultural and environmental) influences. For example, there exist structural differences between the brains of musicians and nonmusicians, attributable to long-term skill acquisition and repetitive training.[38] Brain plasticity allows for a remarkable degree of differentiation in terms of the ability of individuals to adapt to different cultures and behavioral patterns.[39] Chapter 3 discussed the presence in the human brain of Von Economo neurons, also called spindle neurons, that apparently evolved to enable people to make rapid decisions in social contexts.[40] This brain development plasticity gives humans the flexibility to conform to a variety of cultural settings. This helps to create an interdependence and conformity that secures and strengthens the group as a self-referential entity. Much has been written about human sociality, and Von Economo neurons are one of the keys. They are the smoking gun proving other-regarding behavior in humans.

Von Economo neurons are also present in Great Apes and other large social mammals but not in the amount present in humans. The neuroscientist John Allman recounts a remarkable case involving the gorilla Michael, a companion of the famous Koko who taught Michael sign language. Michael had a rich social environment with extensive interaction with humans, other gorillas, and lots of environmental stimulation. Michael could communicate through natural gorilla gestures, American sign language, spoken English, and symbols. He could express himself through art, music, and storytelling.[41] When Michael died in 2000 at the age of 27 an autopsy was performed to examine the structure of his brain. Remarkably, his endowment of Von Economo neurons was many times greater than found in any other gorilla studied, in fact it was in the lower range for humans.[42] If such marked physical brain changes and changes in social behavior can occur in a nonhuman primate from a change in its social environment, imagine the profound change in human cognition and human sociality that came with the change from living in small, always familiar groups to populous, complex societies, massive built environments, complicated technologies, and daily interactions with total strangers.

• • •

What other characteristics of human nature evolved in the 3 million years of Hominid evolution? The still dominant view is that the Pleistocene was one of extreme scarcity where only the strongest and most selfish survived. This is the world view of much of evolutionary psychology, selfish gene advocates, and most economists. But as we have seen, Pleistocene humans were generally well-fed, healthy, and egalitarian. Characteristics such as selfish behavior, warfare, and male domination would have been disadvantageous in small groups whose survival depended on the contributions of each member, and on altruism. But underlying this behavior is "evolvability," a set of possible phenotypic expressions of genes whose presence or absence depends on developmental and environmental circumstances. For the current dilemma of human civilization this is good and bad news. It is not human nature to be greedy and destructive, myriad other kinds of behaviors are possible, but our current belief systems and behavioral characteristics may be hardwired to a culture doomed to self-destruct.

We can learn something about evolved human nature by looking at our primate relatives. In a cooperation game with chimpanzees at the Ngamba Island Chimpanzee Sanctuary in Uganda, a feeding platform with two metal rings was placed outside a testing-room cage with a rope threaded through the rings and the two ends of the rope inside the cage. If the chimpanzee(s) pulled on one end of the rope only, the rope passed through the rings and the food was not obtained. Only if two pulled together could the platform be pulled forward and the food obtained. During repeated tests, the chimpanzees were allowed to recruit partners of their own choice and they quickly learned to recruit those who were the best collaborators. Kin selection is not involved since the chimpanzees at the sanctuary are unrelated orphans from the wild. The authors observe: "Therefore, recognizing when collaboration is necessary and determining who is the best collaborative partner are skills shared by both chimpanzees and humans, so such skills may have been present in their common ancestor before humans evolved their own complex forms of collaboration."[43]

Another universal human behavior is altruism, helping others even at the cost of one's own fitness.[44] Economists tend to be skeptical of altruistic behavior because of the "free rider" problem. Self-regarding individuals can out-compete altruists by taking advantage of their generosity. As an answer to this objection, Henrich et al. propose that altruism arose in humans hand in hand with punishment.[45] Altruistic punishment – punishing others for violating social norms even at cost to oneself – is one way humans deal with free riders and make cooperation work. Apparently, punishing those who do not cooperate actually stimulates the same pleasure centers in the brain that are activated by, for example, eating something sweet.[46] Some evidence indicates that punishing behavior is present in chimpanzees. In one experiment semi-wild chimpanzees were fed at a regular time only after all the chimpanzees in the compound came to the feeding station. Latecomers held up the feeding for all the chimps and these stragglers were punished with hitting and biting. Altruism is universal, but it is a social attribute not a strictly individual characteristic. It must be maintained by enforceable social rules.

Another policy-relevant universal attribute is a sense of fairness. Brosnan and de Waal found that brown capuchin monkeys (*Cebus paella*) exhibit a strong aversion to inequity. In one experiment, monkeys rejected rewards for performing a simple task if they witnessed another monkey receiving a more desirable reward for performing the same task. Pairs of monkeys were trained to exchange a small rock with a human in return for receiving a piece of cucumber. When one monkey saw another receiving a more desirable reward (a grape), the monkey would not only refuse to participate in further exchanges, it would frequently refuse to eat the cucumber reward, sometimes even throwing it toward the human experimenter.[47] Brosnan and DeWaal write:

> People judge fairness based both on the distribution of gains and on the possible alternatives to a given outcome. Capuchin monkeys, too, seem to measure reward in relative terms, comparing their own rewards with those available, and their own efforts with those of others.[48]

These characteristics have profound policy implications that go against the dominant economic policy prescription of providing monetary incentives to rational, selfish individuals.

• • •

In the 1980s Margaret Thatcher famously declared that there is no alternative (TINA) to neoliberal, free market capitalism. In fact there are many examples of societies that thrived with radically different economic systems. Some of these societies changed course almost overnight from teetering on the brink of collapse to being sustainable. These societies do not offer precise blueprints but they do show that radical change is possible and that there are myriad ways to organize a human economy. The description of these noncapitalist economic systems is not meant to advocate any of them but rather to illustrate the myriad possibilities for future cultural evolution and adaptations to the inevitable disruptions to come. Who knows what the future will bring in terms of new forms of human societies? But the more cultural material social evolution has to work with, the more likely some of these new forms will be successful.

Can a Traditional Society Remake Itself? The Case of Tikopia[49,50,51]

The Pacific islands are a kind of natural laboratory to examine the relationship between human cultures and their biophysical base. By about 3,500 years ago the Lapita culture, probably originating in Southeast Asia, had begun to spread throughout the South Pacific, colonizing a variety of island ecosystems of different sizes, soils, vegetation, and degrees of isolation from other islands. Some cultures, such as Easter Island and Mangareva, failed to achieve a sustainable pattern of habitation and disintegrated due to environmental degradation from deforestation and soil erosion that led to the depletion of food resources.[52] A society that escaped the overshoot-and-collapse fate of many other cultures is the island culture of Tikopia. Archaeological data indicate that Tikopia was headed down the same path as Easter Island – with massive deforestation, soil erosion, and a rapidly expanding population – but somehow managed to reverse course and achieve a stable existence. Tikopia is a case study of a successful transition from unsustainability to sustainability.

Tikopia is a small island (5 kilometers^2) located in the Solomon Islands. The island is fertile and surrounded by a rich and diverse coral reef. About 3,000 years ago the Lapita people settled the island and began transforming it through forest clearing for slash and burn agriculture. Many species of native birds were hunted to extinction, and it appeared that the island was headed down the familiar overshoot-and-collapse path. The earliest occupation of Tikopia is called the Kiki phase. It persisted for about 800 years and was characterized by a horticultural base of yams, taro or breadfruit, pigs and dogs, marine resources, and two species of rat. During this period there was a steady decline in protein intake due to the overexploitation of wild game.[53] The next cultural phase, the Sinapupu, was characterized by the disappearance of turtles and other native food sources, widespread forest clearance, and soil erosion. There was a decline in the numbers of wild birds, fish, and shellfish. Domestic animals were substituted for wild sources as indicated by a dramatic increase in pig bones. During the Tuakamali Phase beginning around 1200 CE, landscape alteration increased and the island's coasts were significantly expanded by infilling. Erosion continued as a result of deforestation and other unsustainable agricultural practices.[54]

Sometime around 1700 CE archaeological evidence shows that the Tikopia culture changed dramatically. Pigs and dogs were eliminated from the island, slash and burn agriculture was replaced with a "complex system of fruit and nut trees forming an upper canopy, with aroids, yams, and other shade tolerant crops under these." Species of fish that were once a significant portion of the diet were no longer eaten and the ethnographic record shows that they became forbidden. The people of Tikopia adopted a variety of customs to impose zero population growth. The history of Tikopia's transition to sustainability shows two key changes that led to sustainable habitation – a stable population and sustainable agriculture. Achieving both these conditions involved complex interactions between individual incentives, sanctioned cultural behavior, and a reliance on environmental resilience. Population and agriculture were the focal points for the dramatic change in the relationship between Tikopia's cultural and environmental systems.

The transition to sustainability was no accident. It was the result of a culture taking control of, and changing the course of, its evolutionary destiny. The anthropologist Raymond Firth visited the islands in the 1930s and found that the residents were keenly aware of the relationship between the island's resources – its ability to produce food – and the size of the population. When referring to the population of the island, Tikopians used the expression *fakatau kit e kai*, which means "measured according to the food."[55] Firth documented four direct checks on population: contraception, infanticide, celibacy of males in large families, and as a last resort expelling large numbers of the island's population. These behavioral patterns were reinforced by the moral code of Tikopia reflected in the *Fono of Rarokoka*, a ceremonial proclamation delivered annually by the chief or one of his assistants. The resort to infanticide and expulsion may seem cruel by modern standards, but these harsh measures helped to insure the stability of Tikopia for millennia. In the twentieth century, Christian missionaries succeeded in abolishing the old customs on population control and a direct result was an increase in Tikopia's population increased from 1,278 in 1929 to 1,753 by 1952, when two cyclones destroyed half of Tikopia's crops. The cyclone and the large population led to widespread famine, with disaster being averted only by just-in-time food aid from the British Solomon Islands' colonial government.[56] After the famine, Tikopia's chiefs limited the population to 1,115 by resettling the excess population on other islands. Agricultural sustainability was achieved by micromanaging each crop and the integration of the entire agricultural system. Jared Diamond[57] writes:

> Virtually the whole island is micromanaged for continuous and sustainable food production, instead of the slash-and-burn agriculture prevalent on many other Pacific islands. Almost every plant species on Tikopia is used by people in one way or another: even grass is used as a mulch in gardens, and wild trees are used as a food source in times of famines.

As a response to the periodic famines, edible wild trees from the remaining original rainforest, not normally eaten in good times, are left alone as insurance during times of severe need. Like the system of population control, agricultural practices are regulated by institutions designed to insure sustainable production and consumption. The annual proclamation of *fono* also contains specific references to harvesting coconuts and taro. Without domestic animals, maintaining a reliable source of protein is essential. This protein comes from marine fish and shellfish whose sustainable harvest is insured by *tapus* on harvesting administered by the chiefs. A complicated system of rules regulates the entire agricultural system of Tikopia. These *tapus* are associated not only with resource conservation, but also integrated with kinship restrictions, mourning, and other traditional customs. According to Firth, observing *tapus* is considered to be the duty of all Tikopians. Customs are followed not so much due to coercion but because of cultural solidarity and obligations agreed to by all Tikopians.[58]

Many past societies followed the pattern of overshoot because they became locked into unsustainable practices and they could not overcome the inertia of sunk costs.[59] Tikopia was able to overcome this inertia through a combination of good fortune and foresight. The first Tikopians landed on a geologically young and fertile island with a productive reef, a saltwater bay that could be transformed into a freshwater lagoon, and areas with slopes too steep to cultivate that preserved some of the original forest. Tikopia also had a small population of around 1,000 inhabitants. This was apparently a small enough group so that factions and rival clans did not develop (unlike Easter Island). Judging from Firth's accounts the political structure was democratic with the chiefs' power arising from consensus rather than coercion. This probably made it possible to take drastic steps when necessary, such as the extermination of all the pigs on the island. The island was close enough to other islands for trade to take place (again, unlike Easter Island), so that new kinds of sustainable tree crops could be introduced as the adverse effects of slash and burn agriculture became apparent. Finally, the horticultural system was flexible enough so that the transition to sustainable agriculture could be accomplished without a major change in the economic life of the island.

Does a Fragile Environment Promote Sustainability? The Case of Ladakh[60,61]

The kingdom of Ladakh is located high in the Himalayas, within Indian-controlled Kashmir, with valleys that begin 3,000 meters above sea level and mountains that rise to 6,000 meters. It is a culture in a fragile environment that was sustainably inhabited for thousands of years. The traditional culture of the people of Ladakh evolved to carefully interact with the fragile mountain environment. They wasted nothing, recycled everything, and kept within the ability of the ecosystem to dilute the pollution they generated. Their Buddhist religion encouraged practices that kept the population from growing – polyandry was practiced and many women were nuns and many men celibate priests. The result was a stable population of around 100,000 in an area of 115,000 square kilometers.

The growing season is short, and water and soils must be carefully managed. The suitability of land for farming varies considerably and land is measured not in hectares but in the time needed for plowing it (one day, two days, etc.).[62] The growing season lasts only four months a year, rainfall is near zero, and the land is poor in nutrients. Nevertheless, traditional Ladakh was self-sufficient in all but a few agricultural products and domestic goods. Sustainability was accomplished through carefully coordinated micromanagement of land and water. Water management is an example of how Ladakhi culture, ecological knowledge, and cooperation were integrated at the village level. Traditionally the only source of water was glacial summer melt from the Himalayas. Channels several kilometers long carried water from the high mountains to the villages. A complex system of small channels was used to provide water to individual farmers based on an equally complex distribution system. Who gets how much water and when they get it was determined by custom, environmental conditions, and negotiations at the village level and higher.

Some agricultural land was individually owned and some was owned by monasteries. Land was never divided but passed to the eldest son or eldest daughter. Plots were small, only one or two hectares, yet they produced high yields due to the intense and careful management of each plot. Barley was the staple crop but wheat, peas, vegetables, and mustard were also grown. Each extended family took care of its members from products of the land – food, shelter, and clothing – either directly or through small-scale exchange. Ladakhis traded with the outside world only for exotic items like tea, salt, stones for making jewelry, and metals needed to make tools and utensils.

Nick Wilson describes the efficiency of the Ladakhi agricultural system:

> Nothing is wasted, animal dung becomes fuel, human dung goes to the fields (the traditional Ladakhi toilet is an efficient composting design), even old gonchas, the all purpose wool cloak, may be used to patch irrigation channels. The scattered and meagre wild plants, too, are used for fuel, fibre and labour. A village's animals are taken to high pastures (phu) during summer, by everyone on a rotational basis. Nearer the snow there is more water and hence fodder, and dung is collected and butter and hard cheese made for the winter ahead.[63]

Traditional Ladakh was sustainable because it had to be. Any mistake in such a harsh environment had immediate and obvious negative consequences. To survive the harsh climate the social system also had to be stable and harmonious. Commentators marvel at the sense of harmony and holism and the vision of interconnectedness of nature and people. To a remarkable degree, social relations are based on sharing and a sense of community. Extended families are the core of Ladakh society, but there also exists larger formal groupings of ten families (called chutso) and village counsels made up of representatives from each chutso.

As Helena Norberg-Hodge so eloquently documents, traditional, peaceful and harmonious Ladakh exists no more. Roads have been built to remote villages; trade, commerce, and Western media have come to Ladakh with predictable consequences for traditional society. She has spent decades observing Ladakh, and writes:

> During the early years of my stay in Ladakh, I visited a particularly beautiful Village. Out of curiosity I asked a young man to show me the poorest house in his village. He thought for a moment and then he said, "We don't have any poor houses here." Eight years later I visited the same village again, and I heard the same man saying to a tourist, "Oh, please help us Ladakhis, we are so poor." Within eight years his perception of his own culture had changed dramatically. From thinking that there was no poverty, he now saw everyone as poor. How could the Ladakhis' self-esteem, which had seemed so unassailable, crumble in a few short years following the advent of Western influence?[64]

Trade and the possibilities for substituting import goods for traditional ones have undermined Ladakhi society as well as its traditional agricultural system.

Can a Hierarchical State Society Be Egalitarian? The Case of the Incas[65]

The case of Tikopia is instructive but may be of limited relevance since it was a small-scale island society with a simple economy. The land area of Tikopia was about 5 square kilometers and its pre-contact population was only about 1,000 people. Ladakh was also relatively small and isolated from the outside. By contrast, the Inca Empire stretched for 4,000 kilometers and included present-day Peru and parts of Ecuador, Bolivia, Columbia, Chile, and Argentina. It originated in the highlands of Peru in the 1400s and ended with the

Spanish conquest in 1572. Its population is estimated to have been around 10 million people.

During its more than 100-year-long reign, the Incas established one of the most interesting complex economies ever described. It was a dual economy with subsistence agriculture and other essential activities directed by peasant households and local administrators, and another surplus-generating economy organized and administered by the Inca State. The Inca Empire stretched the length of South America from the equatorial north to the cold south, and each climatic zone had considerable vertical variation because of the Andes. Peasant cultivators had claims to productive resources including land of different environmental zones, labor, and the management of agricultural and other biodiversity.[66] The food consumption needs of the people were met by their own autonomous cultivation of a great variety of local crops. Agriculture was also the base for the state-run redistributive economy. Surplus agricultural production was confined to a few crops such as maize and potatoes that could be easily stored and transported. The state also provided other necessities of life including clothing, textiles, and cloth. The surplus produced by peasant labor was carefully and meticulously collected and stored and it was redistributed to all in equal allotments, not based on need.

John Murra has called the Inca agricultural system "ecological complementarity." Villages were integrated across elevations – up and down the steep mountain topography. Farmers might walk a day or two to work a field in a distinct district that produced fruit or crops not possible to grow in the main village. This not only assured a variety of food, it also had the desirable social consequence of promoting cooperation and reciprocity among localities. Michael Moseley writes:

> The model of vertical complementarity posits that mountain communities maintained satellite colonies of villagers in far-flung ecological zones in order to secure distant commodities. Occupied on a seasonal or year-round basis, colonists work their community's economic satellites to grow low-altitude produce or to obtain resources such as salt or seaweed. Products from distant enclaves are returned to the home settlement for redistribution in the community. Villagers reciprocate by looking after the colonists' fields, herds, and kindred, and expatriates retain full rights and privileges in their highland

homeland. Indeed, unwavering commitments to reciprocity bind economic satellites to their home community by insuring just recompense for those who work distant holdings.[67]

The most remarkable feature of the Inca economy was the lack of money, markets, or a merchant class. McEvan writes:

> With only a few exceptions found in coastal polities incorporated into the empire, there was no trading class in Inca society, and the development of individual wealth acquired through commerce was not possible ... A few products deemed essential by the Incas could not be produced locally and had to be imported. In these cases several strategies were employed, such as establishing colonies in specific production zones for particular commodities and permitting long-distance trade. The production, distribution, and use of commodities were centrally controlled by the Inca government. Each citizen of the empire was issued the necessities of life out of the state storehouses, including food, tools, raw materials, and clothing, and needed to purchase nothing. With no shops or markets, there was not need for a standard currency of money, and there was nowhere to spend money or purchase or trade for necessities.[68]

The Incas engaged in local exchange in small fairs through barter of products they produced and unneeded items they received from the government. No money was used. According to Rowe:[69] "As the government levied no property taxes, only labor, a thrifty and industrious family could accumulate considerable movable property and diversify it through trade." Commerce was a government monopoly and was practiced only with outsiders, not among themselves. The tax system was based on labor, not money, so the "tax" went directly to producing specific goods. Currency speculation was impossible. In return, everyone was provided with the necessities of life. Perhaps because the tax was in the form of labor to produce specific goods, local administrators knew what was a tolerable level of work. The duration of onerous work, like mining, was limited to one month a year.

The Inca had a class system with hereditary rulers. The Emperor class was relatively small, consisting of the Emperor, his immediate family, and consorts. There was an administrative class made up mostly of Incas, although administrators were also selected from local populations. The number of actual Incas was quite small, maybe as few as 15,000, to administer 10 million people. Almost all the population were "commoners." Although Inca society did have an upper class, it successfully dealt with problems of distribution of surplus and the pernicious effects of money. Inca leaders recognized it was in their self-interest to take care of the population.

• • •

Humans are in the grip of a highly successful result of natural selection – ultrasociality – a form of social organization likely to doom our current way of life if we do not devise effective ways to control its negative consequences. The affluence some of us enjoy – longer lifespans, access to education and technology – is a very recent phenomenon and it is far from certain that it can continue. The next decades are likely to see an increase in human pressure on the earth's biophysical systems, and an increase in the glaring inequalities characterizing our species during the last 10,000 years. Our current predicaments are not gene-based. They have risen out of the material base of human economies and the associated cultural adaptations and supporting institutions.

Ecomodernists see the Anthropocene as the age of human control of the planet but this is an illusion. "We" are not in control. It may appear that individuals are "choosing" to transform nature and society, but the market superorganism is making the key decisions about resource use and surplus distribution. We have little choice within that narrow framework. If there is hope for the future, it should begin with facing daunting challenges squarely. Whether dealing with climate change, the ravaging of biodiversity, or pervasive grinding poverty and inequality, we must first determine the root cause of the problems in historical and evolutionary contexts. Then, regardless of current political feasibility, determine what needs to be done to begin the transition to a system not driven by the imperative of accumulation and the logic of market allocation. We need a "decoupling," the separation of economic activity from environmental destruction, but the ecomodernists have it backward. More technology and more modernization will not save us. What does the future hold? Can we rejoin nature, regain our humanity, and decouple from the global market and modernity?

10 RECLAIMING HUMAN NATURE
The Future Will Be Better (Eventually)

At this point most commentaries about the human prospect, even the gloomiest ones, wax poetically about the resilience of the human species and tell us that our compassion, intelligence, and our technology will get us through dark times. Viewing our current predicament in the context of past civilizations tells a different story. The general historical pattern is expansion, a period of stability, then a slow deterioration or rapid decline. But in the past if one society collapsed, others still flourished elsewhere. Today's crises are different because they are worldwide. We face an unprecedented global deterioration in the earth's life support systems. The negative effects of climate change and the absorption of nature by the market economy are accelerating and the social order is rapidly destabilizing. Other existential threats to the environment include ocean acidification,[1] soil degradation,[2] deforestation,[3] air pollution, and plastic pollution. Social and political instability is increasing, driven by environmental disruption accelerating inequality, and carefully orchestrated misinformation campaigns. The Covid-19 pandemic shows the fragility of the global economy and the social limits to rational collective responses to crises.

Two extreme possibilities loom. The first is sudden collapse or gradual disintegration from the synergistic effects of environmental disruption, pollution, energy shocks, financial instability, income inequality, and the associated social upheavals. A second prospect, perhaps more ominous, is that the system will continue with business-as-usual growth and extraction, and human society will evolve into some form of totalitarian technological dystopia. Wild nature will disappear and human domination of the biosphere will keep growing, powered by ever more elaborate technologies and new sources of energy like methane clathrates. Humans will be bioengineered to fit the needs of the brave new world of the cyborg superorganism. Omnipresent surveillance and control will ensure obedience. Between these extremes lies a range of possibilities, some plausible and some not.

The quick answer to the question "What are our prospects?" is who knows? No species has been in the position of today's *Homo sapiens*. We have a good understanding of our origins, a good idea of where we are headed, and a good idea of what needs to be done to avoid calamity. As the social insects show us, other species have established complex technologies, language, and economic systems that enabled them to dominate the planet. But unlike humans, these species do not have the *potential* to redirect their own evolution. We can reflect on what our future might look like based on past history and speculations about what might develop. Here are some plausible scenarios.

Sudden Collapse

A strong case can be made for a sudden catastrophic collapse of human society and a massive die-off of *Homo sapiens*.[4] A BBC report on civilization collapse states:[5]

> Societies of the past and present are just complex systems composed of people and technology. The theory of "normal accidents" suggests that complex technological systems regularly give way to failure. So collapse may be a normal phenomenon for civilisations, regardless of their size and complexity. We may be more technologically advanced now. But this gives little ground to believe that we are immune to the threats that undid our ancestors. Our newfound technological abilities even bring new, unprecedented challenges to the mix. And while our scale may now be global, collapse appears to happen to both sprawling empires and fledgling kingdoms alike. There is no reason to believe that greater size is armour against societal dissolution. Our tightly-coupled, globalized system is, if anything, more likely to make crisis spread.

Predictions of collapse are based on a few broad themes: (1) resource exhaustion, particularly fossil fuel depletion; (2) nuclear war and the resulting environmental and social chaos; (3) financial collapse and the resulting global economic and social disintegration; (4) a global pandemic even more virulent than the Covid-19 outbreak; and (5) the annihilation of the nonhuman biosphere. The last and greatest threat comes from climate change and the resulting social instability, and the collapse of industrial agriculture. Climate change is so certain to cause major disruptions that it is treated in more detail in a separate section. Although the proximate causes differ considerably, Joseph Tainter is correct when he identifies the ultimate cause of past collapses as the increasing costs of complexity. The complexity and specialization that come with ultrasociality bring advantages at first, but increasing fragility makes the system more vulnerable to environmental degradation, resource constraints, and the destabilizing effects of inequality, administrative complexity, and invasion.

- *Resource exhaustion* has a long pedigree among potential causes of collapse. Its advocates are sometimes referred to as Neo-Malthusians – referring to the simple Malthusian idea that population growth will eventually outstrip the ability of a society to feed itself. Contemporary versions begin with the idea that the ability of a society to continue to grow will be comprised by inevitably increased scarcities in natural resources, particularly energy. The most sophisticated argument was made by Nicholas Georgescu-Roegen in *The Entropy Law and the Economic Process.*[6] He takes the Second Law of Thermodynamics, the entropy law, as his starting point. Entropy is a measure of the disorder of a closed thermodynamic system. Over time, disorder increases, it never decreases. Energy, and according to Georgescu-Roegen, materials, are continually transformed from usable to unusable forms. Humans, like all other living things, survive by taking low entropy resources from the environment and discharging them as high entropy waste. With agriculture and later the industrial revolution, the human economy changed from living off the *flows* of low entropy solar energy from nature to living off *stocks* of solar energy stored as fossil fuels. The "mineralogical bonanza" is finite and sooner or later technological advances will be unable to compensate for the inexorable unfolding of the entropy law. An example of a practical application of the entropy law to economics is Charles Hall's concept of the energy return on energy invested (EROEI) – a measure of the amount of direct and indirect energy it takes to get an equivalent unit of energy.[7] Hall estimates that, for petroleum, the EROEI has fallen from about 100:1 at the turn of the twentieth century to about 10:1 for new wells today. The arguments for resource exhaustion and the empirical evidence for the exhaustion of particular resources are compelling. But it must be said that the ability of the global economy superorganism to find and extract the energy and resources it needs to survive and grow has been consistently underestimated. The limits or tipping points to economic growth seem more likely to come first from the pollution side than from the extraction side.

- *Nuclear war* as a prelude to collapse is not as widely discussed as it was during the Cold War but it is still a clear and present danger. A major nuclear exchange between two countries or even a rogue nuclear terrorist attack could have catastrophic consequences, including deaths and destruction from radiation fallout and possibly a decades-long nuclear winter. There could be hundreds of millions of immediate casualties and the secondary effects of famine and social collapse would threaten civilization as we know it. Even a limited nuclear exchange would substantially increase the probability of future exchanges and pave the way for a major nuclear war. The increasing political instability in some of the most stable countries in the world – including the United States, the United Kingdom, and Europe – is a cause for concern, as the chance of unstable leaders blundering into a nuclear war increases. In March 2020 researchers reported the results of a scenario in which India and Pakistan engaged in a limited nuclear exchange:[8]

> Tens of millions of people die in the blasts. That horrifying scene is just the beginning. Smoke from the incinerated cities rises high into the atmosphere, wrapping the planet in a blanket of soot that blocks the sun's rays. The planet plunges into a deep chill. For years, crops wither from California to China. Famine sets in around the globe.

In the coming years it is likely that more countries will have nuclear weapons, and probably with increasingly unstable leaders. New generations of ever more deadly cyber weapons are raising the stakes even higher.

- *Financial collapse* is a favorite candidate for doomsday theorists, especially after the near catastrophe in 2008. Historical examples of economic collapse triggered by financial crises include the Dutch

Tulip bubble of 1637, the South Sea bubble of 1720, Weimar Germany's hyperinflation in the 1930s, and the Wall Street collapse of 1929. Financial crises seem to be more frequent in recent decades and include the US savings and loan crisis of 1989–1991, the Asian financial meltdown of 1997–1998, and the 2008 global market crash. Financial crashes in the past have led to substantial declines in economic activity and real hardship for millions in the countries involved. But is it possible that a financial collapse could lead to worldwide collapse of civilization? So far one would have to say that the ultrasocial economy has been successful in adapting and adjusting to financial crises. Even though great hardships have fallen on individuals, particularly those at the bottom, the system itself has always survived. Attempts to constrain the excesses of the financial sector have always called forth new ways for finance to thwart regulation and find new ways to extract surplus value from the economy. Is the financial situation different today? Much has been written about the "financialization" of capitalism. The financial sector of the US economy increased from about 3% of GDP in 1960 to about 8% in 2018. Trading in equity markets grew from 24% of US GDP in 1985 to 34% in 1995, to 163% in 2015.[9] The current crisis in financialization is only the latest incarnation of a fundamental problem with the surplus generating economy, the ability of elites to extract existing surplus from the system rather than produce new surplus. This can take the form of currency manipulation, confiscation of common property, or orchestrating favorable tax breaks and governmental protection from competition. The temptation to engage in nonproductive rent extraction grows as opportunities for productive investment decrease. The financialization of everything is part of the Hayekian dream of applying the logic of the market to all aspects of life.[10]

- *Global pandemics* have been a favorite topic of science fiction movies and books for decades. The interconnectedness of the world's population and the vulnerability to the spread of new diseases have been apparent since outbreaks of AIDS, SARS, MERS, and Ebola. Still, nothing seems to have prepared the world for the social panic and economic devastation of the Covid-19 virus. It has exposed not only the fragility of the world's health systems but also the vulnerability of supply chains, financial markets, and the difficulty of coordinating very different economies and political systems to achieve a common goal. The virus also showed the importance of foresight and a coordinated swift response. Countries that acted quickly to contain the disease – Iceland, New Zealand, South Korea, and Vietnam for example – were spared the worst effects. Other countries that were slow to react – Brazil, Russia, and the United States – suffered needless deaths and longer disruptions.

If nothing else, the Covid-19 outbreak showed the vulnerability of complex systems to ecological shocks and the reality that humans are biological species, not purely economic agents. The shutdown of the world's economies also exposed the conflict between the human economy and the environment – pollution levels were down, wildlife reappeared in newly empty cities, and CO_2 emissions fell substantially. The outbreak also showed the ability of right-wing leaders to convince their followers to ignore science and reason in the quest to protect the market at all costs.

- *The Annihilation of the Nonhuman World* – will the annihilation of nonhuman nature cause civilization to collapse? So far, the collapse of fish, vertebrate, bird, and amphibian populations has not affected economic growth. Replacing the "free gifts of nature" by market activities may actually have a positive effect on the economy. Take the case of bees in the apple-growing region of Maoxian County, China. By the 1990s, bee populations had crashed due to pesticide use and forest clearance. Pollination had to be done by humans using cigarette filters and feathers. It seemed to be a clear example of inefficiency and the economic folly of destroying nature's services. But it turned out that replacing the unpaid services of bees with paid human labor actually helped the local economy. The area's apple growers actually preferred humans to bees because they could work in rainy and windy conditions and they eliminated the need for male pollinator trees, thereby increasing the number of apple-producing trees.[11] There is an irreconcilable conflict between the market economy and the nonhuman biosphere. Whether this conflict will lead to economic collapse is an open question.

A Business-as-Usual Ultrasocial Dystopia

What if society does not collapse and the ultrasocial system continues to evolve in the direction it is headed? One likely future would be a science fiction dystopia of barricaded enclaves of technological elites, surrounded by the vast majority of semi-literate starving masses. The human domination of the planet will continue to increase and what is left of wild nature will disappear altogether. Democracy will disappear. Inequality will increase to the point where the bulk of the world's population lives at a subsistence level. New technologies for surveillance and control will protect the elite and keep the population under control. The elite will employ genetic engineering to "improve" themselves so as to better fit into the brave new world of high-technology abundance for the few. In spite of dire warnings from prominent scientists, Stephen Hawking for example, the mantra in the scientific community seems to be "Remake humans for a smart society."[12] If there is a mismatch between the characteristics of humans and the needs of the superorganism, it is humans who must be changed. They must be made to adapt to, and love, their servitude. As Aldous Huxley observed in the foreword to *Brave New World*:[13]

> There is, of course, no reason why the new totalitarianisms should resemble the old. Government by clubs and firing squads, by artificial famine, mass imprisonment and mass deportation, is not merely inhumane (nobody cares much about that nowadays), is demonstrably inefficient and in an age of advanced technology, inefficiency is a sin against the Holy Ghost. A really efficient totalitarian state would be one in which the all-powerful executive of political bosses and their army of managers control a population of slaves who do not have to be coerced, because they love their servitude.

Another dystopian possibility is that robots will become sentient and, with their superior intelligence, decide that humans are a threat to their existence and decide to exterminate us. A disturbing insight from group selection is that "sentience" is not a necessary condition for the natural selection of "intelligence." Beehives and ant colonies act as if they are intelligent, yet they are not sentient. To take this idea further, if natural selection can work on nongenetic entities then the locus of evolution need not be a living organism. As long as the entity being selected can reproduce and be differentially selected, it can evolve through natural selection. Robots could rise to dominance through the same mechanical forces of natural selection that produced ultrasociality.

Figure 10.1 Ultrasocial totalitarianism

A New Optimist Paradise

Another possibility for future human society is that the "new optimists" are right and the future of the human species will be brighter and brighter. This is the neoliberal vision of a market- and technology-driven utopia. In spite of the seemingly endless parade of calamities we read about every day – the converging catastrophes of climate disruption, biodiversity loss, and economic catastrophe – a chorus of prominent commentators seem immune to the news. *New York Times* columnist Nicholas Kristof writes: "2018 was the best year in the history of humanity," a sentiment shared by Matt Ridley (*The Rational Optimist*), Stephen Pinker (*Enlightenment Now*), Johan Norberg (*Progress: Ten Reasons to Look Forward to the Future*), and Michael Shermer (*The Moral Arc*).[14] This optimism is based on evidence for an increased material standard of living for a higher percentage of the world's population, driven mostly by the economic growth of China and India in recent decades, and a quaint faith in progress tinged with an Enlightenment disdain for "primitive" cultures.

It is true that the material standard of living for much of the world's population has increased in recent decades. The percentage of the world's population living in abject poverty (living on less than $1.90 a day according to the World Bank) has fallen below 10 percent; the child mortality rate is about one-sixth of what it was in 1950; and the percentage of people with access to electricity and clean drinking water has increased dramatically. The average human lifespan in 1950 was about forty-eight years, today it's over seventy-two years. Per capita incomes are rising in most countries. Oliver Burkeman, in a critique of the new optimists, acknowledges that the world's poorest have become better off in recent decades[15] but asks "What's wrong with this rosy picture?" Is it true that today's pessimism about the future (65 percent of Brits and 81 percent of the French think the world is becoming worse off), is merely an evolutionary adaptation, a survival-enhancing cautiousness, that is maladaptive in the modern world?

There are many reasons to be skeptical of the claims of the new optimists. First of all, humans have been around for hundreds of thousands of years with myriad types of economies and social systems, so is it prudent to assume that the existing system and the improvements in the human condition during the last 100 years or so will continue indefinitely? Secondly, the new optimists make almost no mention of the environmental calamities caused by the improvements in material living standards. Third, the complexity and interconnectedness of the modern world means have laid the foundations for hard-to-anticipate disruptions that could lead to global collapse. Finally, the dramatic increase in well-being indicators since 1950 is the direct result of the explosion in economic output. Total gross world product was about $US 1.1 trillion in 1900, about $4 trillion in 1950, and a staggering $77 trillion in 2014. Fossil fuel consumption was 6,000 terawatt-hours in 1900; 20,000 terawatts in 1950; and 131,000 terawatts in 2018. It seems unlikely that these levels of economic output and energy use can continue indefinitely as the new optimists would have us believe.

Lurking behind the new optimists' arguments is the neoliberal faith in markets and a visceral hostility to anything that threatens the existing economic order. If the human condition is better than ever, and improving every day, it is folly to make changes in the system that brought us to this point. And the system that brought us to the Golden Age of happiness is free market capitalism. Ridley writes: "The evidence is overwhelming that markets do not just make people richer, they make people nicer too, less likely to fight and more likely to help each other."[16] Ridley is a climate change skeptic, best known as the chairman of the Northern Rock bank when it collapsed, and had to be bailed out by British taxpayers in 2007. Steven Pinker is an ardent enthusiast for global market capitalism, arguing that it is a direct product of the Enlightenment and has produced the advances in living standards we have enjoyed over the past few centuries. Shermer's defense of capitalism, and his dismissal of its critics, echoes Hayek's belief that we must cast aside our "primitive instinct" for equality:

> Why do people distrust free markets? Part of the answer can be found in our history. Because we lived for so long in small groups of a couple of dozen to a couple of hundred people in hunter-gatherer communities in which everyone was either genetically related or knew one another intimately, most resources were shared, wealth accumulation was almost unheard of, and excessive greed and avarice was punished. Thus, we naturally respond to a free market system in which conspicuous wealth is paraded as a sign of success with envy and anger. Call it evolutionary egalitarianism.[17]

The new optimists minimize the negative trends toward increasing inequality and environmental catastrophe either by saying "things aren't so bad" or "we can easily deal with these problems." The underlying message is that free markets brought us a Golden Age and we should be thankful and leave things alone. The response to their critics is to accuse them of being "irrational," and lacking faith in science and reason.

Disintegration of the State and a New Golden Age of Barbarism

Judging from past collapses, even a gradual or partial collapse of the world order could ultimately be very good for the average person. Economic growth and its ravenous effects would stop. The human population would be significantly reduced. The iron grip of the elite on the bulk of the world's population would be relaxed. According to James Scott, after past collapses the return to barbarism was a positive change. He makes a strong case that the average person was better off after past state societies collapsed, and that the period from the first appearance of states until their complete hegemony some 5,000 years later was a "golden age of barbarians."[18] Barbarians had the autonomy to pursue limited agriculture, foraging, and hunting, and they had the opportunity to take some of the spoils of the state through raiding and pillaging.

But past collapses did not have to deal with the massive climate changes that future generations will have to deal with. The term "barbarians" implies that there will also be non-barbarians, perhaps remnants of the old order living in isolated, gated communities protected from those living outside the compounds of the privileged. It is likely that this would be a temporary situation given the fragility of isolated high-tech communities dealing with extreme climate change, energy shortages, and the need for more defense and more elaborate technologies just to maintain the status quo.

• • •

The Inevitability of Destabilizing Climate Change

Climate change, with all its related destabilizing effects, presents the clearest threat to the continuation of civilization as we know it. We have likely passed the point of no return in terms of avoiding catastrophic effects. Current research indicates that the effects of global warming will be worse than previously thought. For example, warming in the Arctic and Antarctic is being felt much earlier than predicted because warmer ocean currents are melting sea ice from below.[19] Sea levels are now expected to rise between 6 and 16 feet by the end of this century.[20] In the long run the melting of Antarctica could raise sea levels by 50 feet or more. Since most of the world's population lives in coastal areas this will cause massive population movements, inevitably leading to violent conflicts. In addition to the loss of habitable land area, sea level rise and the intensification of extreme weather events will have numerous secondary effects such as the contamination of drinking water and the salinization of vast areas of farmland.

Climate change is all the more worrying given its role in the collapse of so many earlier societies – the Mayan, Harrapan, Angkor Watt, and the Akkadian Empire to name a few. These collapses were due to regional changes in climate. The climate changes predicted in the coming decades will also differ greatly by region. It could be argued that regions less affected will have the resources to help the others get through the crisis, especially in dealing with food shortages. But the predicted effects are so severe and so widespread that it will be difficult to simultaneously deal with food shortages, water shortages, massive migration, and loss of infrastructure on a planetary scale.

A troubling fact about today's climate change challenge is that it will come much faster and will be more pronounced than previous climate changes. A 50 ppm change around the Pleistocene CO_2 average of 240 ppm was enough to drive the earth in and out of ice ages. The atmospheric CO_2 increase that will occur from 1950 to the year 2100 will be in the range of 200–400 ppm – from 5 to 10 times greater. And CO_2 levels will continue to increase after that unless drastic measures are taken very soon. It is hard to imagine how human civilization as we know it can survive such a drastic and rapid change.

In spite of international efforts to curb greenhouse gases, CO_2 emissions have grown at an annual rate of 3 percent per year since 2000, compared to 1.1 percent per year in the decade of the 1990s.[21] In view of the magnitude of emission increases, the amount of fossil fuel still remaining to be burned, and the inertia of the world's economic and political systems, the chances of limiting the CO_2 level to one consistent with the Holocene's stable climate regime are slim. Emissions scenarios by the Intergovernmental Panel on Climate Change (IPCC) include a worst-case, carbon-intensive scenario projecting a level of 1,370 ppm by 2100.[22] By some estimates CO_2 levels could reach 2,000 ppm within a few centuries if the readily available coal, petroleum, and natural gas are burned.[23] Climatologist James Kasting believes that the most likely scenario is that atmospheric CO_2 will peak at about 1,200 ppm sometime in the next century.[24] A climate-carbon model developed by Bala et al. has the business-as-usual CO_2 peak occurring around the year 2300 at 1,400 ppm.[25] Obviously, if CO_2 levels reach these extremes, abrupt and catastrophic climate events are inevitable. The scientific consensus is that delaying substantial emission reductions for even a few more years will court disaster.

Will technology save us? Carbon capture is the favored technological fix but it is in its infancy. Given the urgency of the climate change problem, it seems unlikely that this technology can make a real difference anytime soon. Even if large-scale CO_2 capture becomes feasible, two problems exist. First, even with the tremendous increase in knowledge and modeling about climate change, major uncertainties remain.

We are still finding major previously unknown effects of climate change, for example, the recent conclusion that the oceans have absorbed as much as 60 percent more CO_2 than previously thought. It seems highly unlikely that we can precisely target the exact amount of CO_2 removal needed to keep the earth at a given temperature. Secondly, the regional impacts of temperature increases will differ greatly, and this has serious geopolitical consequences. Some parts of the world – Russia, Canada, and the Nordic countries for example – may benefit substantially from temperature increases. Even if the technology is feasible, will these nations agree to atmospheric CO_2 reductions? Renewable energy is not a solution to the climate crisis unless it reduces the absolute, not the relative, amount of fossil fuel use. Increasing renewable energy merely adds to the total amount of energy available for more economic growth, more population growth, and more land appropriation by humans. Adding solar and wind technologies to the supply of energy may lower the price of fossil fuels and result in a greater use of them.

Will "peak carbon" save us? Fossil fuels are a finite resource and eventually the energy cost of extracting specific forms of energy will increase until it equals the value of the energy obtained from it.[26] Solid analyses have shown declines in the EROEI for a variety of fossil fuels. Nevertheless, peak energy researchers have consistently under-estimated the ability of the market superorganism to find and develop new energy sources – hydraulic fracturing is the latest case in point. Who would have believed, at the height of the energy crisis in the 1970s, that US oil production would be at record levels in 2018? In November 2018 the United States exported more oil and fuel than it imported for the first time since World War II. New energy technologies are on the horizon. Will harnessing methane clathrates create a new abundant and evermore dangerous source of energy? In any case, it is clear that drastic policies are needed. Keep fossil fuels in the ground.[27] Consider conservation to be a primary source in energy plans. Focus on reducing total energy use, not adding to the supply by substituting one destructive energy source for another. As Paul Ehrlich put it: "Giving humans cheap energy is like giving a child a loaded gun." Most importantly, recognize that avoiding catastrophic climate change is a collective problem requiring collective and globally enforceable policy solutions. According to the final COP24 report of December 2018 (blocked from adoption by the United States, Russia, and Saudi Arabia): "Keeping to the preferred target would need rapid, far-reaching and unprecedented changes in all aspects of society." If warming is to be kept to 1.5°C this century, then emissions of carbon dioxide will have to be reduced by 45 percent by 2030,[28] that is, within the next ten years, an impossible goal.

Climate change projections are increasingly alarming as they become more accurate, for example, by refining the effects of sunlight reflected by clouds as the earth warms, and modifying projections using past warming events to calibrate the interactions between CO_2, temperature, sea level rise, and feedback effects. The IPCC's (2014) noneffective climate policies, continued high emissions projection for 2100, is a warming of 4°C (RCP8.5).[29] The IPCC optimistic scenarios (RCP2.6, RCP4.5) assume not yet feasible geoengineering schemes to remove atmospheric CO_2. The current lack of effective policies to deal with climate change, even in the face of dire warnings, suggests that high emissions projections represent the most plausible climate change scenarios.[30] Brown and Caldeira[31] suggest that there is a 93 percent chance that temperature increases will exceed 4°C by the end of this century. A report by the World Bank warns:

> Without further commitments and action to reduce greenhouse gas emissions, the world is likely to warm by more than 3°C above the preindustrial climate. Even with the current mitigation commitments and pledges fully implemented, there is roughly a 20 percent likelihood of exceeding 4°C by 2100. If they are not met, a warming of 4°C could occur as early as the 2060s. Such a warming level and associated sea-level rise of 0.5 to 1 meter, or more, by 2100 would not be the end point: a further warming to levels over 6°C, with several meters of sea-level rise, would likely occur over the following centuries.[32]

The alteration of the earth's atmosphere by human activity is a very recent and rapid phenomenon. Most of the human-caused increase in atmospheric CO_2 has occurred since 1950. Seventy-five percent of fossil fuel burning and anthropogenic CO_2 in the atmosphere has occurred since 1970. Most of the 1°C increase in the earth's average temperature since preindustrial times has occurred since 1980. The effects of anthropogenic CO_2 emissions are just beginning to be felt. The inaction of governments, even in the face of increasingly dire warnings, indicates that business-as-usual climate change projections constitute the most credible climate change scenario. It seems unlikely that the policies required to keep warming at manageable levels will be implemented. Annual emissions have increased substantially since the Kyoto Protocol twenty years ago. No major industrial country is on track to meet the commitments of the Paris agreement.[33]

• • •

After the Mega-Greenhouse: Our Hunter-Gatherer Future[34]

The very long-term consequences of climate change have received relatively little attention.[35,36,37] Most projections of global warming focus on either the year 2100 or the effects of a doubling of CO_2 (from the preindustrial level of 275 ppm to 550 ppm). The lack of attention to the very long run is a serious shortcoming, since integrated carbon-climate models project that if CO_2 from current in situ fossil fuel resources continues to be released into the atmosphere, the peak concentration of atmospheric CO_2 could exceed 1,400 ppm by the year 2300, and the average global temperature could warm by 8°C or more.[38,39] CO_2 remains in the atmosphere centuries or even millennia after its release. Archer suggests that 300 years is a good average lifetime number for CO_2 and that 17–33% of the CO_2 will remain in the atmosphere 1,000 years after it is emitted.[40] Montenegro et al.[41] suggest that released carbon may stay in the atmosphere an average of 1,800 years or longer. According to Archer and Brovkin: "Ultimate recovery takes place on time scales of hundreds of thousands of years."[42] A CO_2 level of 1,400 ppm would increase the risk of a rise in temperature as high as 20°C, which will certainly have catastrophic consequences for all life on earth. It is sobering to consider that current levels of CO_2 are higher than at any time in the last 15 million years.[43]

The determining variable for the earth's temperature is the amount of CO_2 in the atmosphere, not emission rates or changes in emission rates. Future increases in total atmospheric CO_2 depend on the total amount of fossil fuel carbon burned. Around 4,000 gigatons (10^9 tons) of carbon is stored in the earth's active environment, in soils, forests, the surface ocean, and the atmosphere. The amount of carbon currently stored in fossil fuels (5,400 gigatons) is almost eight times the amount currently in the atmosphere (700 gigatons).[44,45] This fossil fuel carbon – mostly stored in coal – is so vast that if it continues to be released, currently feasible mitigation options such as moderately reducing CO_2 emission rates, limited sequestration, and reforestation will have a negligible effect on the ultimate atmospheric concentration of CO_2.[46,47] Even if climate change mitigation policies reduce CO_2 emission rates, atmospheric CO_2 concentrations will continue to rise until emissions fall to the natural removal rate. The effects of fossil fuel burning are irreversible on a time scale relevant to humans.

Agriculture will likely be impossible in the post-Holocene climate. Climate change will affect agriculture in a number of ways including sea level rise, higher average temperatures, heat wave extremes, changes in rainfall patterns, and the loss of biological diversity. Lesser understood changes include the effects on agricultural pests, soil composition, and CO_2 levels. Two major concerns are (1) increasing unpredictability of the weather; and (2) differing regional impacts on food production. A 2008 study found that southern Africa could lose 30 percent of its maize crop by 2030 due to the negative effects of climate change. Losses of maize and rice crops in South Asia could also be significant.[48]

Climate stability was the major reason why agriculture was possible in the Holocene. With the future climate instability already locked into the system by recent human activity, we will most likely return to the climate volatility of the Pleistocene. Future volatility will not, of course, follow exactly the same pattern, but the instability of the Pleistocene is a rough guess as to what might occur. Agriculture was impossible in the past under abrupt and unpredictable climate conditions and is likely to be impossible when a similar pattern returns. Increased climate volatility could occur quite soon. According to Batissti:[49]

> By 2050, under a typical middle-of-the-road emissions scenario, you're looking at a doubling of the volatility for grains in the mid-latitudes. In places like China, the U.S., Europe, Ukraine— the breadbasket countries of the world—the volatility from year-to-year just from natural climate variability at a higher temperature is going to be much higher. The impact on crops is going to be greater and greater.

Moving crops north to avoid warmer temperature is not generally feasible because of poor quality soils in places like northern Canada and Russia. Also, temperature fluctuations will be greater toward the poles. Growing intensively managed crops on the massive scale required to support billions more people will be prohibitively expensive in terms of the energy required alone.

The ability of agriculture to adapt to climate change will depend on the rapidity of changes as well as their severity. The effects of temperature increases on the oceans will be a major stress factor on agricultural output. According to Hansen et al., during the last intergla- cial, about 140,000 years ago, the earth was about 1°C warmer than today and sea levels were 6–9 meters higher with evidence of extreme storms.[50] Their modeling implies that a 2°C warming would cause an eventual shutdown of the North Atlantic current, an ice melt in the North Atlantic and Southern oceans causing increased temperature gradients and more severe storms, and sea level rise of several meters within a very short time span of 50–150 years. Fischer et al. write:[51]

> A global warming average of 1–2°C with strong polar amplifi- cation has, in the past, been accompanied by significant shifts in climate zones and the spatial distribution of land and ocean ecosystems. Sustained warming at this level has also led to substantial reductions of the Greenland and Antarctic ice sheets, with sea-level increases of at least several meters on millennial timescales. Comparison of paleo observations with climate model results suggest that, due to the lack of certain feedback processes, model-based climate projections may underestimate long-term warming in response to future radia- tive forcing by as much as a factor of two, and thus may also underestimate centennial-to millennial-scale sea-level rise.

According to low, medium, and high emission scenarios, depending on the total amount of carbon released by human activity, Greenland will be ice free by about 2,500, 4,000, or 6,000 years from now, causing a 4 meter rise in sea levels. In the high emission scenario, the melting of Antarctic ice sheets will result in a 45 meter sea level rise within 10,000 years.[52]

The ocean conveyor belt, or thermohaline circulation, moves a massive amount of water around the planet and plays a major role in regulating the earth's temperature. Its movement is driven by the sinking of the current near Iceland due to evaporation and increasing salinity. Wallace Broecker has called the ocean conveyor belt "the Achilles' heel of the climate system." Broecker estimates that were it not for the belt's current course, average winter temperatures in Europe would drop by

20 degrees or more. According to him, "There is surely a possibility that the ongoing buildup of greenhouse gases might trigger yet another of these ocean re-organizations, and thereby the associated atmospheric changes. Were this to happen a century from now, at a time when we struggle to produce enough food to nourish the projected population of 12 billion to 18 billion, the consequences could be devastating."[53]

Another threat to agriculture partially due to climate change, the loss of pollinators, is already underway.[54] Recent studies have shown just how severe insect loss has been. US populations of monarch butterflies have fallen by 90% in the last twenty years, an estimated loss of almost 1 million individuals.[55] In perhaps the most comprehensive insect population studies to date, researchers found a 75% decline in flying insect biomass in protected areas in Germany over the past twenty-seven years.[56] A study in Puerto Rico found that insect populations have declined by 90–98% between 1976–1977 and 2011–2013. Declines associated with these insect losses were found in birds, lizards, and frogs. The researchers blame the decline on climate change. Temperatures in the Puerto Rican rainforest studied have risen by 2°C in recent decades.[57]

Increasing temperatures will have a devastating effect on agricultural productivity, especially given the sensitivity of grains to temperature extremes. It is estimated that 60% of the calories consumed by humans come from just three grains: corn, rice, and wheat. Modeling by Battisti and Naylor[58] indicates a greater than 90% probability that future average growing season temperatures will exceed the most extreme seasonal temperatures recorded between 1900 and 2006 for most of the tropics and subtropics. During the record heat in Europe in summer 2003, maize production fell by 30% in France and 36% in Italy. A 2008 study found that southern Africa could lose 30% of its maize crop by 2030 due to the negative effects of climate change. Losses of maize and rice crops in South Asia could also be significant.[59]

It is difficult to establish a direct cause-and-effect relationship between climate change and social conflict, but the correlations are suggestive.[60] The wars in Darfur and Syria and the massive migrations out of North Africa have been linked to droughts. The climatologist Michael Mann observed: "The Syrian uprising was driven by another drought that was the worst drought on record – the paleo record suggests the worst in 900 years. Drought is a big one, it's behind a lot of the conflict we see."[61] As climate change accelerates, migrations will be driven not only by drought, sea level rise, and the uninhabitability of much of South Asia and the Middle East because of extreme temperatures. Peter Clark et al. write:[62] "Given that deglacial warming led to a profound transformation of Earth and ecological systems, the projected warming of 2.0–7.5°C above the already warm Holocene conditions (at much faster rates than experienced during deglaciation) will also reshape the geography and ecology of the world." Mass migration and the resulting conflicts over water and food will most likely destabilize future societies. Our ability to adapt our global industrial agriculture system through technological advances and energy intensification will be severely compromised. Agriculture will once again be impossible.

• • •

Hunter-Gatherers in the Twenty-Second Century

For most of the history of our species, humans survived, and even thrived, in an unstable climate, with an economy based on face-to-face cooperation, simple and flexible technologies, and an intimate knowledge of every aspect of the food sources they depended on. A return to the climate instability of the Pleistocene will force us to return to the way of life that made us human.

Collapse is not a necessary prerequisite to a hunter-gatherer future for our species. We may be able to avoid collapse and have some sort of semi-orderly contraction of the human population and our impact on the biosphere. But with the environmental stress on agriculture from future climate change and the inevitable decline in food production, the number of humans on the planet will plummet. The dominant culture of exploitation and materialism will give way to an immense variety of cultures adapted to local ecosystems. It may take only decades or stretch out over centuries. As human populations shrink, and grain agriculture becomes impossible, state societies as we know them will disappear. One can envision a relatively slow decline in food production as climate change becomes more and more pronounced, and a decline in population and economic output. The decrease in economic surplus will increasingly constrain the ability of states to maintain their monopoly on violence and their ability to control the population. It may be unlikely, but if the effects of climate change are gradual enough, a soft landing to a nonagricultural economy may be possible. When we revert to hunting and gathering at some point in the future, policies we implement today can make the transition easier and improve the survival prospects for our descendants.

We do not have to "save the planet." It will be fine without us after we're gone. When human exploitation ends, the natural world will regain its lost richness. In the twenty-second century and beyond the natural world will most likely be able to support populations of human hunter-gatherers. Rapid evolution will occur in "new" territories sparsely occupied by humans. The recovery of plants and animals will depend on the severity of climate change impacts on the biological world, for example, the amount of inhabitable land after sea level rise and increases in lethal regional temperatures. Given nature's resilience when human pressure is removed, there is reason to be optimistic about the recovery of the nonhuman world. There will be some wildlife slaughter in the period of the contraction – there is a massive number of guns on the planet – but the limiting factor will be ammunition, which will run out quickly. Most of it will be used on other humans if history is any guide.

Without the fossil fuel bonanza of the twentieth century, and given future climate instability, water shortages, and degraded soils, large-scale grain agriculture will be impossible. Our industrial agricultural system is already beginning to fail because of climate change. The major crops we depend on are already showing signs of stress due to climate change. About half the world's population depends on rice as a major source of calories.[63] Rice production will be affected by sea level rise and an increase in average temperature. Higher temperatures result in increased sterility of rice plants and a larger net energy loss at night because plants are more active then at higher temperatures. Kucharik and Serbin[64] estimated that each additional $1°C$ increase in summer temperature would cause a decline in the output of corn and soybeans by 13% and 16%, respectively. Wheat is also being adversely affected by climate change. A simulation model by Asseng, Foster, and Turner[65] using Australian data, found that variations in average growing season temperatures of $2°C$ can cause reductions in grain production of 50%.

Suppose there is a precipitous decline in the human population and our species is once again characterized by isolated bands of hunter-gatherers. Would agriculture eventually return? Probably not. (1) temperatures would be too instable to support major grain crops; (2) currently grown varieties of rice, wheat, and corn could not survive without human help; and (3) human hunter-gatherers in the Pleistocene did not "choose" agriculture and would be unlikely to do so in the future.[66]

• • •

Even if we take the view that civilization as we know it will disappear in the coming centuries, we can still enhance the chances of our long-run survival. Furthermore, we can do this by implementing policies we should be doing anyway. We should do what we can to keep climate change as manageable as possible. It makes a big difference whether the earth heats by 3 °C or 6°C. We should preserve as much of the nonhuman biosphere as possible by halting the current biological annihilation. We should expand and protect large-scale bio-preserves and keep markets out of them. If we return to hunting and gathering, our chances of survival as a species are hampered by the homogenization of human culture. Species are more likely to adapt to drastic environmental changes if they are genetically diverse, and if they have a variety of possibilities to adjust to new situations. Humans have adapted to a variety of environments by evolved myriad cultural institutions compatible with specific local conditions. Nonmarket cultures still exist and we should do everything we can to preserve their integrity. The more cultural variety there is after civilization's demise, the more likely some cultures will survive.

In terms of policy responses, one thing is clear. Standard economic analysis is of no use in policy valuations of the very long-term effects of climate change. Its valuation perspective is that of a self-regarding individual making decisions in the immediate present. Any positive discount rate, no matter how small, will reduce the long-term benefits of climate change mitigation (avoided costs) to near zero.[67] Furthermore, standard theory and policy recommendations are based on surveys of human "preferences," almost invariably on the preferences of Western people living in market economics. Henrich, Heine, and Norenzayan[68] documented the biases of preference surveys and concluded that people in WEIRD societies (Western, educated, industrial, rich, and democratic) hold world views that are outliers in terms of most human cultures. Economics, or indeed science, cannot be used to answer questions of ethics and value judgments. As Peter Clark et al. put it: "An evaluation of climate change risks that only considers the next 85 years [to 2100] of climate change impacts fails to provide essential information to stakeholders, the public and the political leaders who will ultimately be tasked with making decisions about policies on behalf of all, with impacts that will last for millennia."[69]

Rewilding – protecting and restoring large wild areas – will leave more possibilities for humans and the nonhuman world. Whenever the conversation turns to keeping nature wild some people immediately go on the attack with "What about people? You care about nature more than humans!" But rewilding is not about keeping out humans, it's about keeping out markets and the industrial economy. The inherent conflict is between nature and economic exploitation, not between nature and people. Reconnecting with the natural world makes us more human, not less.

Climate change has been a major diver in the biological and social evolution of the human species. For some 97 percent of our existence we lived as hunter-gatherers in the Pleistocene, a geological epoch characterized by extreme climate swings from ice ages to warm periods. Agriculture, perhaps the major social evolutionary transition in our history, was made possible by the unusually warm and stable climate of the Holocene. That climate stability is already being under-mined by the fossil fuel CO_2 injected into the atmosphere by the indus-trial economy. The climate system will be overwhelmed if we continue to burn fossil fuels for just a few more decades. Without climate stability and the cheap, abundant energy of the twentieth century, it is unlikely that agriculture will continue to be possible in the twenty-first century, and beyond. Civilization will either collapse or gradually disappear over the coming centuries.

The fact that civilization is likely to end does not mean that we should give up on climate change mitigation, radically changing the world's industrial agriculture system, social justice, or the rest of a progressive political agenda. Our prospects for survival will dramatic-ally improve if we hold temperature increases to $3\,^\circ C$ rather than 6–$8\,^\circ C$, and if we institute social and environmental policies to reduce the worst impacts of climate change. In the long run, the vision of returning to a hunting and gathering way of life is wildly optimistic compared to the technological dystopias envisioned by science fiction writers and social philosophers. Every characteristic that defines us as a species – compas-sion for unrelated others, intelligence, foresight, and curiosity – evolved in the Pleistocene. We became human as hunters and gatherers and we can regain our humanity as we decouple from the ultrasocial economy.

NOTES

1 The Ultrasocial Origin of Our Existential Crisis

1 Gowdy and Krall, Agriculture and the evolution of ultrasociality.
2 Richerson, Boyd, and R. Bettinger, Was agriculture impossible during the Pleistocene?
3 Biraben, The rising numbers of humankind.
4 Bocquet-Appel, When the world's population took off.
5 Larsen, The agricultural revolution as environmental catastrophe.
6 Gowdy and Krall, Agriculture and the evolution of human ultrasociality.
7 Crespi, Insectan apes.
8 Schultz, In search of ant ancestors.
9 Fittkau and Klinge, On biomass and tropic structure.
10 E. O. Wilson, One giant leap.
11 E. O. Wilson, *The Social Conquest of Earth*, p. 117.
12 Hölldobler and E. O. Wilson, *The Leafcutter Ants*, p. 7.
13 Diamond, *Collapse*.
14 Ponting, *A New Green History*.
15 Scheidel, *The Great Leveler*.
16 Tainter, *The Collapse of Complex Societies*.
17 Bar-On, Phillips, and Milo, The biomass distribution on earth.
18 Smil, *Harvesting the Biosphere*.
19 Jones, Human influence comes of age.
20 Steffen, Cruzen, and McNeill, The Anthropocene.
21 Bar-On, Phillips, and Milo, The biomass distribution on earth.
22 Barnosky, Hadley, Bascompte, et al. Approaching a state shift in earth's biosphere.
23 Anderson and McShea, Individual *versus* social complexity.
24 Burkhardt, Individual flexibility and tempo in the ant.
25 Crespi and Yanega, The definition of eusociality.
26 Mattison, Smith, Shenk, and Cochrane, The evolution of inequality.
27 Scheidel, *The Great Leveler*.
28 Oxfam, 2016, *An Economy for the 1%*. www.oxfam.org/en/pressroom/pressre leases/2016-01-18/62-people-own-same-half-world-reveals-oxfam-davos-report

29 Jablonka and Lamb, *Evolution in Four Dimensions.*
30 Pigliucci and Müller, *Evolution: The Extended Synthesis.*
31 Hayek, *The Road to Serfdom.*
32 Mirowski, *Never Let a Serious Crisis Go to Waste.*
33 Funtowicz and Ravetz, Science for the post-normal age.

2 The Evolution of Ultrasociality in Humans and Social Insects

1 Margulis, *Symbiotic Planet.*
2 Maynard Smith and Szathmáry, *The Major Transitions in Evolution.*
3 D. S. Wilson, Multilevel selection and major transitions.
4 D. S. Wilson and E. O. Wilson. Rethinking the theoretical foundations of sociobiology.
5 Keller, *Levels of Selection in Evolution,* p. 60.
6 Martínez and Moya, Natural selection and multi-level causation.
7 Campbell, Legal and primary-group social controls.
8 Campbell, The two distinct routes.
9 Richerson and Boyd, The evolution of human ultra-sociality.
10 Turchin, The puzzle of human ultrasociality.
11 E. O. Wilson, *The Social Conquest of Earth.*
12 Campbell, Legal and primary-group social controls, p. 160.
13 Frith and Frith, The social brain.
14 Wexler, *Brain and Culture.*
15 Quoted in Nowak and Highfield, *Super Cooperators,* p.158.
16 Hölldobler and E. O. Wilson, *The Superorganism.*
17 Aanen and Boomsma, Social-insect fungus farming.
18 Mueller and Gerardo, Fungus-farming insects.
19 Aanen and Boomsma, Social insect fungus farming, p. R1014.
20 Engel, Gramaldi, and Krishna, Termites.
21 Engel, Gramaldi, and Krishna, Termites, p. 8.
22 Sanderson, Biomass of termites.
23 Zimmerman, Greenberg, Wandi, and Crutzen, Termites.
24 Hölldobler and Wilson, *The Leafcutter Ants,* pp. 11–12.
25 Wong, Tiny termites dig a world of their own.
26 Roberts, Todd, Aanen, et al., Oligocene termite nests.
27 Barden and Grimaldi, Adaptive radiation.
28 Barden and Grimaldi, Adaptive radiation, p. 1.
29 Barden and Grimaldi, Adaptive radiation, p. 519.
30 Benckiser, Ants and sustainable agriculture.
31 Hölldobler and E. O. Wilson, The Leafcutter Ants.
32 Schultz and Brady, Major transitions in ant agriculture.
33 Martin, The biochemical basis.
34 Benckiser, Ants and sustainable agriculture.
35 Mueller, Kardish, Ishak, et al., Phylogenetic patterns.
36 Quoted in Boyd & Ruth, Leafcutter ants' success. www.sciencedaily.com/releases/2018/05/180509104921.htm
37 Flannery, The superior civilization, *The Superorganism.*
38 Maynard Smith and Szathmáry, *The Major Transitions in Evolution.*
39 Dawkins, *The Selfish Gene.*
40 See the discussion in Jablonka and Lamb, *Evolution in Four Dimensions,* and Pigliucci and Müller, *Evolution: The Extended Synthesis.*

41 See the discussion in E. O. Wilson, *The Social Conquest of Earth*.
42 Quoted in D. S. Wilson, Truth and reconciliation for group selection.
43 Wynne-Edwards, *Animal Dispersion*.
44 Hamilton, The genetical evolution of social behavior.
45 Trivers, The evolution of reciprocal altruism.
46 Ruse, *Sociobiology: Sense or Nonsense*.
47 E. O. Wilson, *Sociobiology*.
48 E. O. Wilson, *The Meaning of Human Existence*, p. 69.
49 See the important and controversial *Nature* paper by Nowak, Tarnita, and Wilson, The evolution of ultrasociality.
50 E. O. Wilson, *The Meaning of Human Existence*, pp. 70–71.
51 See Wilson and Wilson, Rethinking the theoretical foundations of sociobiology.
52 van den Bergh and Gowdy, A group selection perspective.
53 Wade, Group selection among laboratory populations.
54 Muir, Group selection for adaptation.
55 Goodnight, Heritability at the ecosystem level.
56 Goodnight and Stevens, Experimental studies of group selection.
57 Grinsted, Agnarsson, and Bilde, Subsocial behaviour.
58 Jablonka and Lamb, *Evolution in Four Dimensions*.
59 Mariette and Buchanan, Prenatal acoustic communication.
60 Jablonka, interview with D. S. Wilson in *This View of Life*.
61 Yan, Bonasio, Simola, et al., Eusocial insects as emerging models.
62 Yan, Simola, Bonasio, et al., DNA methylation in social insects.
63 Jablonka and Lamb, *Evolution in Four Dimensions*, p. 158.
64 Hodgson, *From Pleasure Machine to Moral Communities*.
65 Yan, Simola, Bonasio, et al., DNA methylation in social insects.
66 Gowdy, Darwinian economics.
67 Richerson and Boyd, *Not by Genes Alone*.
68 Hodgson and Knudsen, *Darwin's Conjecture*.
69 Hodgson, *Economics and Evolution*.
70 De Waal, *Primates and Philosophers*.
71 Safina, *Beyond Words*.
72 Jablonka and Lamb, *Evolution in Four Dimensions*, p. 189.
73 E. O. Wilson, *The Social Conquest of Earth*, p. 10.
74 D. S. Wilson and Sober, Reviving the superorganism.
75 Dawkins, The descent of Edward Wilson.
76 Pinker, The false allure of group selection.
77 Richerson and Boyd, *Not by Genes Alone*.
78 D. S. Wilson, Human groups as units of selection.
79 Sober and D. S. Wilson, *Unto Others*.
80 Spencer, War and early state formation.
81 Choi and Bowles, The coevolution of parochial altruism and war.
82 Turchin, *War and Peace and War*.
83 Campbell, Legal and primary-group social controls, p. 161.
84 Okasha, *Evolution and the Levels of Selection*, p. 178.
85 D. S. Wilson, Truth and reconciliation, section XIX.
86 Okasha, *Evolution and the Levels of Selection*, p. 112.
87 E. O. Wilson, *The Social Conquest of Earth*, p. 146.
88 Shik, Hou, Kay, Kaspari, and Gillooly, Towards a general life-history model.
89 E. O. Wilson and Hölldobler, Eusociality: origin and consequences, p. 13368.
90 Beshers and Fewell, Models of division of labor in social insects.

91 Hölldobler and Wilson, *The Superorganism*, pp. 47–48.
92 Thorne, Evolution of eusociality in termites, p. 27.
93 Wagner and Altenberg, Complex adaptations and the evolution of evolvability.
94 Michod and Nedelcu, On the reorganization of fitness, p.64.
95 Mueller, Gerardo, Six, and Schultz, The evolution of agriculture in insects, p. 564.
96 Anderson and McShea, Individual *versus* social complexity.
97 Diamond, The worst mistake.
98 Lambert, Health versus fitness.
99 Larsen, The agricultural revolution as environmental catastrophe.
100 Ryan and Jethá, *Sex at Dawn*.
101 Kahn, The tyranny of small decisions.

3 Our Hunter-Gatherer Heritage and the Evolution of Human Nature

1 Hublin, Ben-Ncer, Bailey, et al. New fossils from Jebel Irhoud, Morocco.
2 Stringer and Galway-Witham, On the origin of our species.
3 Sahlins, *The Original Affluent Society*, p.4.
4 Braidwood, *The Near East and the Foundations for Civilization*, p. 157.
5 Lee and I. Devore, *Man the Hunter*.
6 Lee, *Forward* to *Limited Wants, Unlimited Means*.
7 Sahlins, *Stone Age Economics*.
8 Sahlins, The original affluent society.
9 Bird-David, Beyond the original affluent society.
10 Lee, foreword to *Limited Wants, Unlimited Means*.
11 Wallace, *The Malay Archipelago*, Chapter XL, p. 460.
12 See the discussions by J. Solway and R. Lee, Foragers, genuine or spurious: Situating the Kalahari San in history.
13 Lee, Art, science, or politics?
14 Alvard, Evolutionary ecology and resource conservation.
15 Keely, *War before Civilization*.
16 Krech, *The Ecological Indian*.
17 Pinker, *The Better Angels of Our Nature*.
18 Boehm, Egalitarian behavior.
19 Boehm, Impact of the human egalitarian syndrome.
20 Pennisi, Our egalitarian Eden.
21 Culotta, Latest skirmish over ancestral violence.
22 Fry and Söderberg, Lethal aggression.
23 Ryan and Jethá, *Sex at Dawn*.
24 Larsen, The agricultural revolution as environmental catastrophe.
25 See the discussion of this in Ryan and Jethá, *Sex at Dawn*.
26 Kelly, *The Foraging Spectrum*.
27 www.ted.com/talks/steven_pinker_on_the_myth_of_violence
28 Panter-Brick, Laydon and Rowley-Conway, Lines of inquiry, p. 2.
29 Woodburn, Egalitarian societies, p.88.
30 E. O. Wilson, *The Social Conquest of Earth*.
31 Weiner, Xu, Goldberg, Liu, and Bar-Josef, Evidence for the use of fire.
32 Henrich, Boyd, Bowles, Camerer, Fehr, and Gintis, *Foundations of Human Sociality*.
33 Trivers, *Social Evolution*.
34 D. S. Wilson, *Does Altruism Exist?*

35 Nowak and Highfield, *Supercooperators*, p. 168.
36 Harari, *Sapiens*, p. 21.
37 Hoffman et al., U-Th dating of carbonate crusts.
38 Larbey, Mentzer, Ligouis, and Wurz, Cooked starchy food in hearths.
39 Joordens, d'Errico, Wesselingh, et al., *Homo erectus* at Trinil on Java.
40 Bar-Yosef and Belfer-Cohen, From Africa to Eurasia.
41 Pappu, Gunnell, Akhilesh, et al., Early Pleistocene presence of Acheulean hominins.
42 Scott and Gibert, The oldest hand-axes in Europe.
43 Joorderns et al., Postcranial evidence *Homo erectus* at Trinil.
44 www.newscientist.com/article/mg16522280.300-gimme-shelter.html, http:news.bbc .co.uk/1/hi/sci/tech/733747.stm
45 Lordkipanidze et al., Postcranial evidence from early *Homo* erectus at Trinil.
46 Ackerman, Mackay, and Arnold, The hybrid origins of modern humans.
47 Zimmer, In Neanderthal DNA.
48 Posth, Wissing, Kitagawa, et al., Deeply divergent archaic mitochondrial genome.
49 Nielsen, Akey, Jakobsson, et al., Tracing the peopling of the world.
50 Harman, New DNA analysis shows ancient humans interbred with Denisovans.
51 Slon, Mafessoni, Vernot, et al., The genome of the offspring of a Neanéerthal mother.
52 Hershkovitz, Weber, Quam, et al., The earliest modern humans.
53 Stringer and Galway-Witham, On the origin of our species.
54 Berger, Hawks, de Ruiter, et al., *Homo nadeli*, a new species of the genus *Homo*.
55 Wolpoff, Hawks, and Caspari, Multiregional, not multiple origins, p. 129.
56 Richerson, Boyd, and Bettinger, Was agriculture impossible during the Pleistocene.
57 Cepelewicz, Interspecies hybrids play a vital role in evolution.
58 Pennisi, Hybrids spawned Lake Victoria's rich fish diversity.
59 Margulis, *Origin of Eukaryotic Cells*.
60 Sutcliffe, When Neanderthals replaced us.
61 www.abroadintheyard.com/20-physical-traits-inherited-from-neanderthal
62 White, Asfaw, DeGusta, et al., Pleistocene *Homo sapiens* from Middle Awash, Ethiopia.
63 Desmond Clark, Beyene, Wolde, et al., Stratigraphic, chronological and behavioral contexts.
64 Stringer, Out of Ethiopia.
65 Balzeau, Grimaud-Hervé, Détroit, et al., First description of the Cro-Magnon endocast.
66 Rightmire, The human cranium from Bodo, Ethiopia.
67 Wexler, *Brain and Culture*, p. 3.
68 Sherwood, Subiaul, and Zadiszki, A natural history of the human mind.
69 Allman, Watson, Tetreault, and Hakeem, Intuition and autism, p. 379.
70 www.reddit.com/r/collapse/comments/6zpj5y/a_depressed_man_with_a_smiling_ face_jorgen
71 Martin, 40,000 of extinctions on the planet of doom.
72 Grayson and Meltzer, A requiem for North American overkill.
73 A metanalysis of references to Pleistocene extinctions found a striking difference between archaeologists and ecologists. The majority of archaeologists believed that climate change, not human "overkill," was primarily responsible for megafauna demise. Ecologists, on the other hand, were much more likely to accept Paul Martin's hypothetical scenario. Nagaoka, Rick, and Wolverton, The overkill model and its impact.
74 Monbiot, *Feral*.

75 Price, Louys, Faith, Lorenzen, and Westaway, Big data little help in megafauna mysteries.
76 See the discussion in Smil (2013, pp. 78–88).
77 Cooper, Turney, Hughen, McDonald, and Bradshaw, Abrupt warming events.
78 Slezak, Megafauna extinction.
79 Cooper et al., Abrupt warming events, p. 605.
80 MacDonald, Beilman, Kuzmin, et al., Pattern of extinction of the woolly mammoth in Beringia.
81 Lyons, Amatangelo, Behrensmeyer, Bercovici, et al., Holocene shifts.
82 Aggregated pairs occur because of the advantages of interspecies cooperation (zebras and wildebeests or leaf-cutter ants and their fungi, for example) or shared habitat preferences. Two-agent cooperation is the most evolutionarily stable state compared to multi-agent cooperation.
83 Dietl, Different worlds.
84 Lyons et al., Holocene shifts, p. 80.
85 Camposa, Willerslev, Sher, et al., Ancient DNA analyses exclude humans.
86 Hill Jr., Hill, and Widga, Later Quaternary *Bison* diminution, p. 1752.
87 Hansford, Wright, Rasoamiaramanana, et al., Early Holocene human presence in Madagascar.
88 Lawler, Scarred bird bones reveal early settlement on Madagascar.
89 www.zmescience.com/ecology/animals-ecology/elephant-bird-extinction-042332
90 Mooney, Harrison, Bartlein, et al., Late Quaternary fire regimes of Australasia, p. 28.
91 Berndt and Berndt, *The World of the First Australians*, p. 108.
92 Frith and Frith, The social brain.
93 Boehm, Impact of the human egalitarian syndrome.
94 Pennisi, Our egalitarian Eden.
95 Woodburn, Egalitarian Societies, p. 438.
96 Leacock, Women's status in egalitarian society.
97 Leacock, Women's status in egalitarian society, p. 143.
98 Hawkes, O'Connell, and Blurton Jones, Hazda meat sharing, p. 130.
99 Boehm, Egalitarian behavior.
100 Woodburn, Egalitarian societies.
101 Dyble, Salali, Chaudhary, et al., Sex equality can explain, p. 796.
102 Mittnik, Massey, Knipperet, et al., Kinship-based social inequality.
103 Gibbons, Bronze age inequality and family life.
104 Borgerhoff Mulder, Bowles, Hertz, et al., Intergenerational wealth transmission.
105 Carneiro, The chiefdom: Precursor of the state.
106 Lee, Primitive communism and the origin of social inequality, p. 239.
107 Spikins, Needham, Tilley, and Hitchens, Calculated or caring?
108 Trinkaus and Sébastien, External auditory exostoses and hearing loss in the Shanidar 1 Neanderthal.
109 Quoted in *Science Daily*, www.sciencedaily.com/releases/2018/03/180313130443.htm
110 Gracia et al., Craniosynostosis in the Middle Pleistocene human cranium.
111 Bonmatí, Gómez-Olivencia, Arsuaga, et al., Middle Pleistocene lower back and pelvis.
112 Walker, Zimmerman, and Leakey, A possible case of hypervitaminosis A in Homo erectus.
113 Flannery, *The Future Eaters*.
114 Gamble, *Time Walkers*.
115 Lee, foreword to *Limited Wants, Unlimited Means*, p. x.

4 The Agricultural Transition and How It Changed Our Species

1 Price and Bar-Yosef, The origins of agriculture, p. S168.
2 McCorriston and Hole, The ecology of seasonal stress and the origins of agriculture.
3 Cohen, *The Food Crisis in Prehistory*.
4 Zvelebil and Rowley-Conway, Foragers and farmers in Atlantic Europe.
5 Flannery, Archaeological systems theory and early Mesoamerica.
6 Binford, Post Pleistocene adaptations.
7 Cohen, *The Food Crisis in Prehistory*.
8 Price and Bar-Yosef, The origins of agriculture.
9 McCorriston and Hole, The ecology of seasonal stress, p. 49.
10 Diamond, The worst mistake.
11 Larsen, The agricultural revolution as environmental catastrophe.
12 Bowles, Cultivation of cereals by the first farmers.
13 Rindos, *The Origins of Agriculture*.
14 Richerson, Boyd, and Bettinger, Was agriculture impossible during the Pleistocene.
15 Interestingly, a takeoff in fungus-growing ant agriculture may have been triggered by a dramatic shift in climate, a global cooling event that began 35 million years ago. See Handwerk, How ants became the world's best fungus farmers.
16 Branstetter, Ješovnik, Sosa-Calvo, et al., Dry habitats were crucibles of domestication.
17 Arctic Impact Climate Assessment (AICA) 2004, *Impacts of a Warming Arctic*.
18 Bowles and Choi, *Holocene Revolution*. See supporting online material, p. 4.
19 Beerling, New estimates of carbon transfer to terrestrial ecosystems.
20 Bettinger, Richerson, and Boyd, Constraints on the development of agriculture, p. 628.
21 Feynman and Ruzmaikin, Climate stability and the origin of agriculture.
22 Gowdy and Krall, The economic origins of ultrasociality.
23 Bar-Yosef, The Natufian culture in the Levant.
24 McCorriston and Hole, Barley.
25 McCorriston and Hole, Wheat.
26 Kuijt and Finlayson, Evidence for food storage and predomestication granaries.
27 Bar-Yosef, The Natufian culture in the Levant, pp. 164–165.
28 Bar-Yosef, The Natufian culture in the Levant, p. 167.
29 Flannery, Archaeological systems theory.
30 McCorriston and Hole, Wheat.
31 Rindos, *The Origins of Agriculture*.
32 Smith, Diet and attrition in the Natufians.
33 McCorriston and Hole, The ecology of seasonal stress.
34 Belfer-Cohen and Bar-Yosef, Early sedentism in the Near East.
35 Munro, Small game, the Younger Dryas, and the transition to agriculture.
36 McCorriston and Hole, The ecology of seasonal stress, p. 51.
37 Makarewicz, The Younger Dryas and hunter-gatherer transitions to food production, p. 217.
38 Holbrook, Clark, Jeanson, Bertram, Kukuk, and Fewell, Emergence and consequences of division of labor in associations of normally solitary sweat bees, p. 301.
39 Carneiro, A theory of the origin of the state.
40 Turchin, *War and Peace and War*.
41 Turchin, The puzzle of human ultrasociality.
42 Cox, Crop domestication and the first plant breeders.
43 Larsen, The agricultural revolution as environmental catastrophe, p. 12.

44 Cohen and Crane-Kramer, *Ancient Health*.
45 Lambert, Health versus fitness.
46 The Upper Pleistocene number is based on the Kaplan et al. (2000) estimate for contemporary hunter-gatherers. Life expectancy estimates are notoriously difficult to compare because of differences in infant mortality, the effects of wars and epidemics, and so on.
47 Gurven and Kaplan, Longevity among hunter-gatherers, p. 322.
48 Balzeau, Grimaud-Hervé, Détroit, et al., First description of the Cro-Magnon 1 endocast.
49 Beals, Smith, Dodd, et al., Brain size, cranial morphology, climate, and time machines.
50 Liu, Tang, Ge et al., Increasing breadth of the frontal lobe.
51 Ruff, Trinkaus, and Holliday, Body mass and encephalization in Pleistocene Homo.
52 Hawks, Selection for smaller brains in Holocene human evolution.
53 Henneberg, Decrease of human skull size in the Holocene.
54 Henneberg and Steyn, Trends in cranial capacity and cranial index.
55 Henneberg, Decrease of human skull size, p. 395.
56 Liu et al., Increasing breadth of the frontal lobe.
57 Hawks, Selection for smaller brains in Holocene human evolution.
58 Riveros, Seid, and Wcislo, Evolution of brain size in class-based societies of fungus-growing ants (*Attini*).
59 The brain of leaf-cutter ants is remarkably large, accounting for 15% of their body mass compared to 2% for humans (Seid, Castillo, and Wcislo).
60 Darwin noted that "the brain of the ant is one of the most marvelous atoms of matter in the world, perhaps more marvelous than the brain of man" (quoted in William Wcislo, Big brains, little bodies).
61 Holbrook, Barton and Fewell, Division of labor increases with colony size.
62 Smith, *Wealth of Nations*, p. 62.
63 Moffett, *Adventures among the Ants*, p. 70.
64 Anderson and McShea, Individual *versus* social complexity, p. 211.
65 Crespi and Yanega, The definition of eusociality.
66 Anderson and McShea, Individual *versus* social complexity.
67 Burkhardt, Individual flexibility and tempo in the ant.
68 A. Smith, *Wealth of Nations*, p. 735
69 Marx, *The Origin of Family*.
70 Dunbar, Coevolution of neocortical size, p. 681.
71 Quoted in Dunbar, p. 687.
72 Prentiss, Foor, Cross, and Harris, The cultural evolution of material wealth based inequality.
73 Pringle, The ancient roots of the 1%.
74 Ariely, *Predictably Irrational*.
75 Edwards and Pratt, Rationality in collective decision-making by ant colonies.
76 Edwards and Pratt, Rationality in collective decision-making by ant colonies.
77 Mueller, Rehner, and Schultz, The evolution of agriculture in ants.
78 Geary and Bailey, Hominid brain evolution.
79 "A hunter gatherer who did not correctly conceive a solution to providing food or shelter probably died, along with his/her progeny, whereas a modern Wall Street executive that made a similar conceptual mistake would receive a substantial bonus and be a more attractive mate." Crabtree, Our fragile intellect.
80 McAuliffe, If modern humans are so smart, why are our brains shrinking?
81 Geary and Bailey, Hominid brain evolution.

82 Mithen, Did farming arise from a misapplication of social intelligence?
83 Barrett, Henzi, and Rendall, Social brains, simple minds.
84 Mithen, Did farming arise from a misapplication of social intelligence?, p. 705.
85 Frith and Frith, The social brain.
86 Brian Wexler, *Brain and Culture*.
87 Crabtree, Our fragile intellect, part II.
88 McDaniel, Big-brained people are smarter, p. 337.
89 Rushton and Ankney, Whole brain size and general mental ability: A review.
90 van Valen, Brain size and intelligence in man.
91 Rushton and Ankney, Whole brain size.
92 Reardon, Seidlitz, Vandekar, et al., Normative brain size variation.
93 Van Essen, Scaling of human brain size.
94 Crabtree, Our fragile intellect, part I, p. 1.
95 Zeder, Emshwiller, Smith, and Bradley, Documenting domestication.
96 Scott, *Against the Grain*, p. 81.
97 Brace and Ryan, Sexual dimorphism and human tooth size differences.
98 Wilson, *The Social Conquest of Earth*.
99 Sanderson, Jaiteh, Levy, et al., The human footprint and the last of the wild.
100 Smil, *Harvesting the Biosphere*.
101 Wilson, *The Social Conquest of Earth*, pp. 116–117.
102 Korb, Termites.
103 King, Warren, and Bradford, Social insects dominate.
104 Folgarait, Ant biodiversity and its relationship to ecosystem functioning.
105 Diamond, *Collapse*.
106 Weiss and Bradley, What drives societal collapse?
107 Weiss, Courty, Wetterstrom, et al., The genesis and collapse of third millennium North Mesopotamian civilization.
108 Rosen and Rivera-Collazo, Climate change, adaptive cycles, and the persistence of foraging.
109 Weiss and Bradley, What drives societal collapse?
110 Quoted in Ponting, *New Green History*, p. 119.
111 Aanen and Boomsma, Social-insect fungus farming, p. 1014–1016.
112 Benckiser, Ants and sustainable agriculture.
113 Boehm, Impact of the human egalitarian syndrome.
114 D. S. Wilson, Ostrom, and Cox, Generalizing the core design principles.
115 Anderson and McShea, Individual *versus* social complexity, p. 219.
116 D. S. Wilson, Ostrom, and Cox, Generalizing the core design principles.
117 Of course, "good" and "bad" are human value judgments that cannot be applied to ant societies.

5 The Rise of State Societies

1 Collyer, The real roots of early city states.
2 Scott, *Against the Grain*.
3 Wright, *A Short History of Progress*, pp. 50–51.
4 Benckiser, Ants and sustainable agriculture.
5 Arranz-Otaegui, Carretero, Ramsey, Fuller, and Richer, Archaeobotanical evidence reveals the origins of bread.
6 Scott, *Against the Grain*, p. 46.

7 Zeder, The origins of agriculture in the Middle East.
8 Scott, *Against the Grain*, p. 57.
9 Ponting, *A New Green History*, p. 56.
10 Ponting, *A New Green History*, p. 57.
11 Scott, *Against the Grain*, pp. 120–121.
12 Nissen, *The Early History of the Ancient Near East*.
13 Scott, *Against the Grain*, p. 121.
14 Ponting, *A New Green History*, pp. 59–60.
15 Matthew and Boyd, Punishment sustains large-scale cooperation.
16 Turchin, *War and Peace and War*.
17 Ponting, *A New Green History*, p. 65.
18 Larsen, The agricultural revolution as environmental catastrophe.
19 Ponting, *A New Green History*, pp. 58–59.
20 Scott, *Against the Grain*, p. 12.
21 Scott, *Against the Grain*, p. 122.
22 Diamond, *Collapse*.
23 Weiss and Bradley, What drives societal collapse?, pp. 609–610.
24 Weiss, Courty, Wetterstrom, et al., The genesis and collapse of third millennium North Mesopotamian civilization.
25 Rosen and Rivera-Collazo, Climate change, adaptive cycles, and the persistence of foraging.
26 Tainter, *The Collapse of Complex Societies*, p. 61.
27 Scheidel, *The Great Leveler*, chapter 2.
28 Schiedel, *The Great Leveler*, p. 64.
29 Tainter, *The Collapse of Complex Societies*.
30 Thompson, Complexity.
31 Weiss et al., The genesis and collapse of third millennium North Mesopotamian civilization.
32 Weiss, *Megadrought and Collapse*.
33 Ponting, *A New Green History*, p. 70.
34 Ponting, *A New Green History*, p. 71.
35 Hoggarth, Breitenbach, Culleton, et al., The political collapse of Chichén Itzá.
36 Tainter, *The Collapse of Complex Societies*.
37 Thompson, Complexity, p. 615.
38 Boserup, *The Conditions of Agricultural Growth*.
39 Scott, *Against the Grain*, p. 156.
40 Finley, Was Greek civilization based on slave labor?, p. 164.
41 Beckwith, *Empires of the Silk Road*, p. 76.
42 Ponting, *A New Green History*, p. 89.
43 Ponting, *A New Green History*, p. 87.
44 Quoted in Scott, *Against the Grain*, p. 139.
45 Scott, *Against the Grain*, p. 144–146.
46 Algaze, Initial social complexity, 220–222.
47 Quoted in Scott, *Against the Grain*, p. v.
48 Isenberg, *White Trash*, pp. 21–22.
49 Isenberg, *White Trash*, p. 27.
50 Polanyi, *The Great Transformation*, p. 37.
51 Biraben, The rising numbers of humankind.
52 Steffen, Cruzen, and McNeill, The Anthropocene, p. 848.

53 Landes, *The Unbound Prometheus*, p. 97.
54 Georgescu-Roegen, *The Entropy Law and the Economic Process*.
55 Hall and Klitgaard, *Energy and the Wealth of Nations*.
56 Hou, Kaspari, Zanden, and Gillooly, Energetic basis of colonial living.
57 Shik, Hou, Kay, Kaspari, and Gillooly, Towards a general life-history model.
58 Bruce and Burd, Allometric scaling.
59 Chaisson, Energy rate density.
60 Hall and Klitgaard, *Energy and the Wealth of Nations*.
61 Piketty, *Capital in the Twenty First Century*.
62 Steffen, Cruzen, and McNeill, The Anthropocene.
63 Lawton, Road kill.
64 Diamond, *Collapse*.
65 United Nations 2013, Population projections.

6 The Modern State/Market Superorganism

1 Polanyi, *The Great Transformation*, p. 73.
2 Scheidel, *The Great Leveler*.
3 Michaels, *Political Parties*.
4 Piketty, *Capital in the Twenty-First Century*.
5 Gordon, Control without hierarchy, p. 143.
6 Mazzucato, *The Entrepreneurial State*.
7 Mazzucato, *The Value of Everything*.
8 Mazzucato, www.youtube.com/watch?v=p4DhbjZ74IQ.
9 Wikipedia "Tesla," https://en.wikipedia.org/wiki/Tesla.
10 www.commonwealthfund.org/publications/fund-reports/2017/jul/mirror-mirror-2017-international-comparison-reflects-flaws-and
11 Vallas, Kleinman, and Biscotti, Political structures.
12 Brill, Bitter pill.
13 Rosenthal, *An American Sickness*.
14 Rosenthal, Who's profiting from your outrageous medical bills?
15 https://nces.ed.gov/programs/coe/indicator_cmd.asp
16 https://en.wikipedia.org/wiki/Education_in_the_United_States
17 Porter, Education gap between rich and poor is growing wider.
18 Brill, *Tailspin*, p. 22.
19 www.npr.org/2016/04/18/474256366/why-americas-schools-have-a-money-problem
20 https://worldpopulationreview.com/state-rankings/per-pupil-spending-by-state
21 Mirowski, *Never Let a Serious Crisis Go to Waste*, p. 83.
22 MacLean, *Democracy in Chains*.
23 Ratnieks and Wenseleers, Policing insect societies.
24 Sketch from *Karl Marx Capital in Lithographs* by Hugo Gellert, 1934.
25 Scheidel, *The Great Leveler*.
26 Brill, *Tailspin*.
27 Hickel, Global inequality.
28 Gregory Clark, G. *The Son Also Rises*.
29 Oreskes and Conway, *Merchants of Doubt*.
30 Gilens and Page, Testing theories of American politics, p. 575.

7 Neoliberalism: The Ideology of the Superorganism

1 Campbell, Downward causation.
2 R. W. Sperry, A modified concept of consciousness.
3 Campbell, Downward causation, p. 180.
4 Mirowski, *Never Let a Serious Crisis Go to Waste.*
5 Mirowski and Plehwe, *The Road from Mont Pelerin.*
6 Hayek, *The Road to Serfdom*, pp. 204–205.
7 Hayek, *The Road to Serfdom*, pp. 204–205.
8 Rand, *The Virtue of Selfishness.*
9 Rand, *Atlas Shrugged.*
10 D'Souza, *The Virtue of Prosperity.*
11 http://thinkprogress.org/politics/2011/08/09/291865/bruning-raccoon-welfare
12 http://www.businessinsurance.com/article/20140501/NEWS08/140509985
13 Mirowski, *Never Let a Serious Crisis Go to Waste*, p. 61.
14 Oreskes and Conway, *Merchants of Doubt.*
15 Mirowski, Is this water or is it the Neoliberal Thought Collective?
16 Horowitz, Hayek, the family and social individualism.
17 Angner, The history of Hayek's theory of cultural evolution.
18 Hayek, *Studies in Philosophy*, p. 67.
19 Hayek, *Studies in Philosophy*, p. 70.
20 Hayek, *Law, Legislation and Liberty*, p. 155.
21 D. S. Wilson, The road to ideology: How Friedrich Hayek became a monster.
22 D. S. Wilson, Love Hayek, love Darwin.
23 Peck, *Constructions of Neoliberal Reason*, p. 3; quoted in Mirowski, *Never Let a Serious Crisis Go to Waste*, p. 54.
24 Bromley, Environmental regulations, p. 677.
25 MacLean, *Democracy in Chains*, p. xxvii.
26 Buchanan, *The Limits of Liberty.*
27 MacLean, *Democracy in Chains*, p. xxvii.
28 Monbiot, A despot in disguise.
29 Quoted in B. Harcourt, *The Illusion of Free Markets.*
30 Miowski, *Never Let a Serious Crisis Go to Waste*, p. 336.
31 Oreskes and Conway, *Merchants of Doubt.*
32 Mirowski, *Never Let a Serious Crisis Go to Waste*, p. 336.
33 Klaus, Current global warming alarmism.
34 Baskin, Paradigm dressed as epoch.
35 Crist, The reaches of freedom.
36 Hamilton, The Theodicy of the "Good Anthropocene."
37 Smaje, Dark thoughts on ecomodernism.
38 Sullivan, Banking nature.
39 http://thebreakthrough.org/about/mission
40 Blomqvist, Nordhaus, and Shellenberger, *Nature Unbound.*
41 World Wide Fund, *Living Planet Report 2014.*
42 http://thebreakthrough.org/index.php/issues/energy/renewables-and-nuclear-at-a-glance
43 Gilland, Nitrogen, phosphorous, carbon and population.
44 http://thebreakthrough.org/index.php/programs/conservation-and-development/stop-blaming-china-for-the-epidemic-of-elephant-killings
45 Stanford, *Planet without Apes.*
46 http://thebreakthrough.org/index.php/journal/past-issues/issue-2/evolve

47 Gowdy, Dollimore, Wilson, and Witt, Economic cosmology and the evolutionary challenge.
48 Smaje, Dark thoughts on ecomodernism.
49 Mirowski, *Never Let a Serious Crisis Go to Waste*.
50 Mirowski, *Never Let a Serious Crisis Go to Waste*, p. 336.

8 Taming the Market: A Minimal Bioeconomic Program

1 From Georgescu-Roegen, Energy and economic myths.
2 A major obstacle to confronting the totally of the market is the denial of its existence by many progressives. David Graeber of Occupy Wallstreet fame writes: "The very notion that we exist in a totalizing system is itself the core ideological idea that we need to overcome." Quoted in Mirowski, *Never Let a Serious Crisis Go to Waste*, p. 370. See Mirowski's discussion of the left's acceptance of the myth of the "timelessness" of the capitalist system in *Never Let a Serious Crisis Go to Waste*, p. 17.
3 Georgescu-Roegen, Energy and economic myths.
4 Lüthi, Le Floch, Bereiter, et al., High resolution carbon dioxide concentration record.
5 The Mauna Loa data are available at ftp://aftp.cmdl.noaa.gov/products/trends/co2/co2_mm_mlo.txt.
6 Tripati, Roberts, and Eagle, Coupling of CO_2 and ice sheet stability.
7 Kump, The last great global warming.
8 www.bbc.com/news/science-environment-46496967
9 Gowdy, Valuing nature for climate change policy.
10 Intergovernmental Panel on Climate Change, Fifth Assessment report.
11 Williams, Hewitt, and Bodas-Salcedo, Use of short-range forecasts.
12 Palmer, Short-term tests validate long-term estimates of climate change.
13 British Petroleum, World reserves of fossil fuels.
14 Gowdy and Juliá, Global warming economics in the long run.
15 Gowdy, The value of biodiversity.
16 Entomological Society of America, ESA position statement on endangered insect species.
17 Jarvis, The insect apocalypse is here.
18 Conrad, Warren, Fox, Parsons, and Woiwod, Rapid decline of common widespread British moths.
19 Hallmann et al., More than 75% decline.
20 Lister and and Garcia, Climate-driven declines in arthropod abundance.
21 Maes, Titeux, Hortal, et al., Predicted insect diversity declines under climate change.
22 Jarvis, The insect apocalypse is here.
23 Ceballos, Ehrlich and Dirzo, Biological annihilation.
24 E. O. Wilson, *Half Earth*, p. 3.
25 Projections of population growth. Wikipedia. https://en.wikipedia.org/wiki/Projections_of_population_growth; United Nations. World population prospects. https://esa.un.org/unpd/wpp/Publications
26 Knight, Can we be sure the world's population will stop rising?
27 Human biomass also depends critically on human diet and especially obesity. Walpole et al. write: "If all countries had the BMI distribution of the USA, the increase in human biomass of 58 million tonnes would be equivalent in mass to an extra 935 million people of average body mass, and have energy requirements equivalent to that of 473 million adults."
28 Bar-On, Phillips, and Milo, The biomass distribution on Earth.

29 Krausmann, Erb, Gingrich, et al., Global human appropriation of net primary production.
30 Much of the contraception-as-imperialism literature comes from the Catholic church (www.cultureoflife.org/2005/08/17/population-imperialism), but it also comes from the "progressive" left, for example "After studying the evidence, it's clear that there is a conscious scheme to control the human population through both cultural and biological means, which allows the elite to sustain or elevate their power and wealth." (www.rooshv.com/the-end-goal-of-western-progressivism-is-depopulation)
31 Ehrlich and Ehrlich, The Population Explosion.
32 www.azquotes.com/quote/1079647
33 Quotes are from Wikipedia. Guaranteed minimum income. https://en.wikipedia.org/wiki/Guaranteed_minimum_income
34 Borgerhoff Mulder et al., Intergenerational wealth transmission.
35 www.cnbc.com/2018/05/09/how-much-the-5-highest-paid-ceos-earn.html
36 www.forbes.com/sites/dianahembree/2018/05/22/ceo-pay-skyrockets-to-361-times-that-of-the-average-worker/#11ebffa7776d
37 Daly, Steady State Economics, p. 54.
38 Brill, Tailspin, p. 289.
39 Layard, Happiness: Lessons from a New Science.
40 E. O. Wilson, Biophilia.
41 Shiva, Monocultures of the Mind, p. 65.
42 https://talkingpointsmemo.com/dc/poll-americans-overwhelmingly-favor-universal-health-care-until-taxes-are-mentioned
43 www.cnbc.com/2018/02/26/roughly-half-of-americans-now-support-universal-basic-income.html
44 www.nbcnews.com/feature/college-game-plan/two-thirds-americans-support-free-college-tuition-n620856

9 Evolving a Sustainable and Equitable Future: What Can We Learn from Nonmarket Cultures?

1 Gowdy, Hunter-gatherers and the mythology of the market.
2 Lee, Non-capitalist work, p. 9.
3 Lee, What hunters do for a living, p. 33.
4 Lee, The Dobe Ju/'hoansi.
5 Sahlins, Original affluent society, p. 4.
6 Barnard and Woodburn, Property, power and ideology in hunter-gatherer societies.
7 Woodburn, Egalitarian societies.
8 Testart, The significance of food storage among hunter-gatherer.
9 Lee, The Dobe Ju/'hoansi, p. 50.
10 Woodburn, An introduction to Hadza ecology.
11 Riches, Hunter-gatherer structural transformations.
12 See the discussion in Veblen, Professor Clark's economics.
13 Turnbull, The Mbuti Pygmies, p.19.
14 Woodburn, Egalitarian societies.
15 Sahlins, The sadness of sweetness.
16 Gowdy, Progress and environmental sustainability.
17 Gould, Darwin and Paley meet the invisible hand.
18 Campbell, Downward causation.
19 Safina, Beyond Words, p. 281.
20 Quoted in Marshall Sahlins, The sadness of sweetness, p. 399.

21 Margulis, *Origin of Eukaryotic Cells.*
22 All eukaryotes descended from a single common ancestor. According to some biologists, the appearance of eukaryotes, and thus all complex life on earth, was a single fluke event that occurred just once in 2 billion years. Others think that life could have originated many times.
23 Contrary to the claims of creationists, the evolution of eyes is well-understood and certainly does not contradict Darwinian natural selection. Calculations show that complex eyes could have evolved from light-sensitive cells in a relatively short period of time. New Scientist, *How Evolution Explains Everything,* pp. 98–101.
24 New Scientist, *How Evolution Explains Everything about Life.*
25 Schwab, *Evolution's Witness.*
26 Henrich, Heine, and Norenzayan, The weirdest people in the world?
27 Henrich, Heine, and Norenzayan, The weirdest people in the world, p. 61.
28 A cautionary warning to Henrich et al. is given by Richard Shweder, who makes the point that reported cultural differences reflect different cultural-specific responses to different experimental designs, not differences in "human nature." Shweder, Donald Campbell's doubt.
29 Corning, *Synergistic Selection.*
30 Gowanty, Free female mate choice.
31 Dyble, Salali, Chaudhary, et al., Sex equality can explain.
32 Leacock, Women's status, p. 161.
33 www.japantimes.co.jp/news/2018/07/13/business/poverty-japan-underclass-struggles-achieve-upward-mobility/#.XBPPxmhKg2w
34 www.forbes.com/sites/sarahsu/2016/11/18/high-income-inequality-still-festering-in-china/#3258c9121e50
35 Acheson and Wilson, Order out of chaos.
36 Berkes, *Common Property Resources.*
37 Hanna, Folke, and Maler, *Rights to Nature.*
38 Gaser and Schlaug, Brain structures differ between musicians and non-musicians.
39 Wexler, *Brain and Culture.*
40 Balter, Brain evolution studies go micro.
41 The Gorilla Foundation, Learning from Michael. www.koko.org/index.php?q=learning-michael
42 Allman et al., The von Economo neurons, p. 62. www.koko.org/index.php?q=learning-michael.
43 Melis, Hare, and Tomasello, Chimpanzees recruit the best collaborators, p. 1297.
44 D. S. Wilson, *Does Altruism Exist?*
45 Henrich et al., Costly punishment across human societies.
46 Vogel, The evolution of the golden rule.
47 Brosnan and de Wall, Monkeys reject unequal pay.
48 Brosnan and de Waal, Monekys reject unequal pay, p. 299.
49 Gowdy, Darwinian selection and cultural incentives.
50 Gowdy and Erickson, Resource use, institutions and sustainability.
51 McDaniel and Gowdy, *Paradise for Sale.*
52 Bahn and Flenley, *Easter Island, Earth Island.*
53 Kirch and Yen, *Tikopia.*
54 Kirch and Yen, *Tikpia,* p. 332.
55 Firth, *We, the Tikopia.*
56 Diamond, *Collapse,* p. 291.
57 Diamond, *Collapse,* p. 288.
58 Firth, *Primitive Polynesian Economy,* pp. 230–236.

59 Janssen, Kohler, and Scheffer, Sunk-cost effects and vulnerability to collapse.
60 Norberg-Hodge, *Ancient Futures*.
61 McDaniel and Gowdy, *Paradise for Sale*, pp. 90–94.
62 Norberg-Hodge, *Ancient Futures*, p. 13.
63 Wilson, Cold, high and dry.
64 https://ratical.org/many_worlds/ladakh.html
65 Information about the Incas is taken from the following sources. Original Spanish accounts are listed in Rowe, *Inca Culture*; Murra, *The Economic Organization of the Inca State*; Zimmerer, Agricultural biodiversity and peasant rights.
66 Zimmerer, Agricultural biodiversity and peasant rights.
67 Moseley, *The Incas and Their Ancestors*, p. 45.
68 McEwan, *The Incas: New Perspectives*.
69 Rowe, *Inca Culture*, p. 270.

10 Reclaiming Human Nature: The Future Will Be Better (Eventually)

1 www.nationalgeographic.com/environment/oceans/critical-issues-ocean-acidification
2 Baveye, Baveye, and Gowdy, Soil "ecosystem" services and natural capital.
3 https://helpsavenature.com/deforestation-statistics
4 Morgan, World on fire.
5 BBC, Are we on the road to civilization collapse?
6 Georgescu-Roegen, *The Entropy Law*.
7 Hall, Balogh, and Murphy, What is the minimum EROI that a sustainable society must have?
8 Witze, How a small nuclear war would transform the planet.
9 https://data.worldbank.org/indicator/CM.MKT.TRAD.GD.ZS?view=chart
10 Storm, Financialization and economic development.
11 Gowdy, Krall, and Chan, The parable of the bees.
12 "Where to from here? Remaking humans for smart society," *Nature*.
13 Huxley, *Brave New World*.
14 See the discussion of these authors in Oliver Burkeman, Is the world really better than ever? *The Guardian*, July 28, 2017.
15 Burkeman, Is the world really better than ever?
16 Ridley, www.rationaloptimist.com/blog/free-markets-and-free-trade.
17 Shermer, https://michaelshermer.com/2008/01/why-people-dont-trust-free-markets.
18 Scott, *Against the Grain*.
19 DeConto and Pollard, Antarctic model raises prospect of unstoppable ice collapse.
20 https://climatenexus.org/climate-issues/science/antarctic-warming
21 Raupach et al., Global and regional drivers of accelerated CO_2 emissions.
22 Kintisch, IPCC tunes up for its next report.
23 Kump, Reducing uncertainty about carbon dioxide as a climate driver.
24 Kasting, The carbon cycle, climate, and the long-term effects of fossil fuel burning.
25 Bala et al., Multicentury changes in global climate and carbon cycle.
26 Hall et al., Hydrocarbons and the evolution of human culture.
27 Gowdy and Juliá, Global warming economics in the long run.
28 www.bbc.com/news/science-environment-46496967
29 IPCC, *Climate Change 2014: Synthesis Report*. The RCP8.5 scenario has been dismissed as a "worst case scenario," but it is also the most likely case since it assumes no meaningful policy action in the next few decades.

30 Gabbatiss, Worst-case global warming predictions are the most accurate, say climate experts.
31 Brown and Caldeira, Greater future global warming.
32 World Bank, Turn down the heat, p. xiii.
33 Wallace-Wells, *The Uninhabitable Earth*.
34 Gowdy, Our hunter-gatherer future.
35 Bala et al., Multicentury changes in global climate and carbon cycle.
36 Gowdy and Juliá, Global warming economics.
37 Kasting, The carbon cycle.
38 Bala et al., Multicentury changes in global climate and carbon cycle.
39 Kasting, The carbon cycle.
40 Archer, Fate of fossil fuel CO_2 in geologic time.
41 Montenegro et al., Long term fate of anthropogenic carbon.
42 Archer and Brovkin, The millennial atmospheric lifetime of anthropogenic CO_2, p. 283.
43 World Bank, Turn down the heat, p. xiv.
44 Archer and Brovkin, The millennial atmospheric lifetime of anthropogenic CO_2.
45 Kasting, The carbon cycle.
46 Caldeira and Kasting, Insensitivity of global warming potentials.
47 Matthews and Caldeira, Stabilizing climate requires near-zero emissions.
48 Lobell et al., Prioritizing climate change adaptation needs for food security in 2030.
49 Quoted in Wallace-Wells, *The Uninhabitable Earth*.
50 Hansen et al., Ice melt, sea level rise and superstorms.
51 Fischer, Meissner, and Zhou, Paleoclimate constraints, p. 474.
52 Peter Clark et al., Consequences of twenty-first-century policy, p. 364.
53 Smith, Wallace, and Broecker, who helped popularize term "global warming," dies at 87.
54 United Nations, Fourth National Climate Assessment.
55 Jarvis, The insect apocalypse is here.
56 Hallmann et al., More than 75 percent decline over 27 years in total flying insect biomass in protected areas.
57 Lister and Garcia, Climate-driven declines in arthropod abundance.
58 Battisti and Naylor, Historical warnings of future food insecurity.
59 Lobell et al., Prioritizing climate change adaptation needs.
60 Burke, Hsiang, and Miguel, Climate and conflict.
61 Quoted in Wallace-Wells, 2017.
62 Peter Clark et al., Consequences of twenty-first-century policy for multi-millennial climate and sea-level change, p. 363.
63 Nguyen, Global climate changes and rice food security.
64 Kucharik and Serbin, Impacts of recent climate change on Wisconsin corn and soybean yield trends.
65 Asseng, Foster, and Turner, The impact of temperature variability of wheat yields.
66 Gowdy and Kralll, Agriculture and the evolution of human ultrasociality.
67 The so-called social discount rate is not "social." It is still based on the perspective of an individual at a point in time.
68 Henrich, Heine, and Norenzayan, The weirdest people in the world?
69 Peter Clark et al., Consequences of twenty-first-century policy for multi-millennial climate and sea-level change.

REFERENCES

Aanen, D. & Boomsma, J. (2006). Social-insect fungus farming. *Current Biology*, 16(24), 1014–1016.

Acheson, J. & Wilson, J. (1996). Order out of chaos. *American Anthropologist*, 98, 579–594.

Ackerman, R., Mackay, A., & Arnold, M. (2016). The hybrid origins of modern humans. *Evolutionary Biology*, 43, 1–11.

Algaze, G. (2001). Initial social complexity in Southwestern Asia: The Mesopotamian advantage. *Current Anthropology*, 42, 199–233.

Allman, J., Tetreault, N., Hakeem, A., et al. (2011). The von Economo neurons in the frontoinsular and anterior cingulate cortex. *Annals of the New York Academy of Sciences*, 1225.

Allman, J., Watson, K., Tetreault, N., & Hakeem, A. (2005). Intuition and autism: A possible role for Von Economo neurons. *Trends in Cognitive Science*, 9, 367–373.

Alvard, M. (1998). Evolutionary ecology and resource conservation. *Evolutionary Anthropology*, 62–74.

Anderson, C. & McShea, D. (2001). Individual versus social complexity, with particular reference to ant colonies. *Biological Reviews*, 76, 211–237.

Angner, E. (2002). The history of Hayek's theory of cultural evolution. *Studies in the History and Philosophy of Biological and Biomedical Sciences*, 33, 695–718.

Archer, D. (2005). Fate of fossil fuel CO_2 in geologic time. *Journal of Geophysical Research*, 110, C09S05, https://doi.org/10.1029/2004JC002625.

Archer, D. & Brovkin, V. (2008). The millennial atmospheric lifetime of anthropogenic CO_2. *Climatic Change*, 90, 283–297.

Arctic Impact Climate Assessment (AICA) (2004). *Impacts of a Warming Arctic*. Cambridge: Cambridge University Press.

Ariely, D. (2008). *Predictably Irrational*. New York: HarperCollins.

Arranz-Otaegui, A., Gonzalez Carretero, L., Ramsey, M. Fuller, D., & Richter, T. (2018). Archaeobotanical evidence reveals the origins of bread 14,400 years ago in northeastern Jordan. *Proceedings of the National Academy of Science*, 115, 7925–7930.

Asseng, S., Foster, I., & Turner, N. (2011). The impact of temperature variability of wheat yields. *OPEN DATA*. https://doi.org/10.1111/j.1365-2486.2010.02262.x

Bahn, P. & Flenley. J. (1992). *Easter Island, Earth Island*. London: Thames and Hudson.

Bala, G., Caldeira, K., Mirin, A., et al. (2005). Multicentury changes in global climate and carbon: Results from a coupled climate and carbon model. *Journal of Climate*, 18, 4531–4544.

Balter, M. (2007). Brain evolution studies go micro. *Science*, 315, 1208–1212.

Balzeau, A., Grimaud-Hervé, D., Détroit, F., Holloway, R. L., Combès, B., & Prima, S. (2013). First description of the Cro-Magnon 1 endocast and study of brain variation and evolution in anatomically modern Homo sapiens. *Bulletins et Mémoires de la Société d'Anthropologie de Paris*, 25, 1–18.

Bar-On, Y., Phillips, R., & Milo, R. (2018). The biomass distribution on earth. *Proceedings of the National Academy of Science*, https://doi.org/cp29.

Bar-Yosef, O. (1998). The Natufian culture in the Levant, threshold to the origins of agriculture. *Evolutionary Anthropologist*, 6, 59–177.

Bar-Yosef, O. & Belfer-Cohen, A. (2001). From Africa to Eurasia—early dispersals. *Quaternary International*, 75, 19–28.

Barden, P. & Grimaldi, D. (2016). Adaptive radiation in socially advanced stem-group ants from the Cretaceous. *Current Biology*, 26, 1–7.

Barnard, A. & J. Woodburn. (1988). Property, power and ideology in hunter-gatherer societies: An introduction. In T. Ingold, D. Riches, and J. Woodburn, eds. *Hunters and Gatherers*, vol. 2. Oxford: Berg.

Barnosky, A., Hadley, E., Bascompte, J., et al. (2012). Approaching a state shift in earth's biosphere. *Nature*, 486, 52–58.

Barrett, L., Henzi, P., & Rendall, D. (2007). Social brains, simple minds: Does social complexity really require cognitive complexity? *Philosophical Transactions of the Royal Society of London B: Biological Sciences*, 362 (1480), 561–575.

Baskin, J. (2015). Paradigm dressed as epoch: The ideology of the Anthropocene. *Environmental Values*, 24, 9–29.

Battisti, D. & Naylor, R. (2009). Historical warnings of future food insecurity with unprecedented seasonal heat. *Science*, 323, 240–244.

Baveye, P., Baveye, J., & Gowdy, J. (2016). Soil "ecosystem" services and natural capital: Critical appraisal of research on uncertain ground. *Frontiers in Environmental Science*, 4, article 41. https://doi.org/10.3389/fenvs.2016.00041.

BBC. (2019). Are we on the road to civilization collapse? www.bbc.com/future/ story/20190218-are-we-on-the-road-to-civilisation-collapse

Beals, K., Smith, C. Dodd, S., et al. (1984). Brain size, cranial morphology, climate, and time machines. *Current Anthropology*, 25, 301–330.

Beckwith, C. (2009). *Empires of the Silk Road: A History of Central Eurasia from the Bronze Age to the Present*. Princeton, NJ: Princeton University Press.

Beerling, D. J. (1999). New estimates of carbon transfer to terrestrial ecosystems between the last glacial maximum and the Holocene. *Terra Nova*, 11, 162–167.

Belfer-Cohen, A. & Bar-Yosef, O. (2000). Early sedentism in the Near East – A bumpy ride to village life. In I. Kuijt, ed. *Life in Neolithic Farming Communities: Social Organization, Identity, and Differentiation*. Dordrecht: Kluwer Academic/Plenum, pp. 19–37.

Benckiser, G. (2010). Ants and sustainable agriculture. *Agronomy and Sustainable Development*, 30, 191–199.

Berger, L. et al. (2015). *Homo nadeli*, a new species of the genus *Homo* from the *Dinaledi* chamber, South Africa. *eLife*. www.ncbi.nlm.nih.gov/pmc/articles/ PMC4559886

Berkes, F. (1989). *Common Property Resources: Ecology and Community Based Sustainable Development*. London: Bellhaven.

Berndt R. & Berndt, C. (1988). *The World of the First Australians*. Canberra: Aboriginal Studies Press.

Beshers, S. & Fewell, J. (2001). Models of division of labor in social insects. *Annual Review of Entomology*, 46, 413–440.

Bettinger, R., Richerson, P., & Boyd, R. (2009). Constraints on the development of agriculture. *Current Anthropology*, 50, 627–631.

Binford, L. (1968). Post-Pleistocene adaptations. In L. Binford and S. Binford, eds. *New Perspectives in Archaeology*. Piscataway, NJ: Aldine, pp. 313–341.

Biraben, J.-N. (2003). The rising numbers of humankind. *Population & Societies*, 394, 1–4.

Bird-David, N. (1992). Beyond "the original affluent society": A culturalist reformulation with CA comment. *Current Anthropology*, 33, 25–47.

Blomqvist, L., Nordhaus, T., & Shellenberger, M. *Nature Unbound: Decoupling for Conservation*. http://thebreakthrough.org/images/pdfs/NatureUnbound.pdf

Bocquet-Appel, J.-P. (2011). When the world's population took off: The springboard of the Neolithic demographic transition. *Science*, 333, 560–561.

Boehm, C. (1993). Egalitarian behavior and reverse dominance hierarchy. *Current Anthropology*, 34, 227–254.

Boehm, C. (1997). Impact of the human egalitarian syndrome on Darwinian selection mechanisms. *American Naturalist*, 150, 100–121.

Bonmatí, A. Gómez-Olivencia, A., Arsuaga, J-L, et al. (2010). Middle Pleistocene lower back and pelvis from an aged human individual from the Sima de Los

Huesos site, Spain. *Proceedings of the National Academy of Sciences*, 107, 18386–18391.

Boomsma, J., Fjerdingstad, E. & Frydenberg, J. (1999). Multiple paternity, relatedness and genetic diversity in Acromyrmex leaf-cutter ants. *Proceedings of the Royal Society B*, 266, 249–254.

Borgerhoff Mulder, M., Bowles, S., Hertz, T., et al. (2009). Intergenerational wealth transmission and the dynamics of inequality in small-scale societies. *Science*, 326, 682–688.

Boserup, E. (1965). *The Conditions of Agricultural Growth: The Economics of Agrarian Change under Population Pressure*. Chicago: Aldine.

Bowles, S. (2011). Cultivation of cereals by the first farmers was not more productive than foraging. *Proceedings of the National Academy of Science*, 108(12), 4760–4765.

Bowles, S. & Choi, J.-K. (2012). *Holocene Revolution: The Co-evolution of Agricultural Technology and Private Property Institutions*. Santa Fe, NM: Santa Fe Institute.

Boyd, J. & Ruth, D. (2018). Leafcutter ants' success due to more than crop selection. *Science Daily*. www.sciencedaily.com/releases/2018/05/180509104921.htm

Brace, L. & Ryan, A. (1980). Sexual dimorphism and human tooth size differences. *Journal of Human Evolution*, 9, 417–435.

Braidwood, R. (1957). *The Near East and the Foundations for Civilization*. Eugene: Oregon State System of Higher Education.

Branstetter, M., Ješovnik, A., Sosa-Calvo, J., et al. (2017). Dry habitats were crucibles of domestication in the evolution of agriculture in ants. *Proceedings of the Royal Society B*, 284: 20170095. http://dx.doi.org/10.1098/rspb.2017.0095

Brill, S. (2013). Bitter pill. *Time Magazine*. February 20.

Brill, S. (2018). *Tailspin: The People and Forces behind America's Fifty-Year Fall–and Those Fighting to Reverse It*. New York: Alfred Knopf.

British Petroleum. (2018). World reserves of fossil fuels. https://knoema.com/infographics/smsfgud/bp-world-reserves-of-fossil-fuels

Bromley, D. (2007). Environmental regulations and the problem of sustainability: Moving beyond "market failure". *Ecological Economics*, 63, 676–683.

Brosnan, S. & de Wall, F. (2003). Monkeys reject unequal pay. *Nature*, 425, 297–299.

Brown, P. & K. Caldeira. (2017). Greater future global warming inferred from Earth's recent energy budget. *Nature*, 552, 45–50.

Bruce, A. & Burd, M. (2012). Allometric scaling of foraging rate with trial dimensions in leaf-cutting ants. *Proceedings of the Royal Society of London B*, 279, 2442–2447.

Burke, M., Hsiang, S. & Miguel, E. (2015). Climate and conflict. *Annual Review of Economics*, 7, 577–617.

Buchanan, J. (1975). *The Limits of Liberty*. Chicago: University of Chicago Press.

Burkeman, O. (2017). Is the world really better than ever? *The Guardian*, July 28.

Burkhardt, J. F. (1998). Individual flexibility and tempo in the ant, Pheidole dentata, the influence of group size. *Journal of Insect Behavior*, 11, 493–505.

Caldeira, K. & Kasting, J. (1993). Insensitivity of global warming potentials to carbon dioxide emissions scenarios. *Nature*, 366, 251–253.

Campbell, D. (1974). Downward causation in hierarchically organized biological systems. In F. Ayala and T. Dobzhansky, eds. *Studies in the Philosophy of Biology: Reduction and Related Problems*. London: Macmillan.

Campbell, D. (1982). Legal and primary-group social controls. In M. Gruter and P. Bohannan, eds. *Law, Biology and Culture: The Evolution of Law*. Berkeley, CA: Bepress, pp. 59–171.

Campbell, D. (1983). The two distinct routes beyond kin selection to ultrasociality: Implications for the humanities and social sciences. In D. L. Bridgeman, ed. *The Nature of Prosocial Development: Theories and Strategies*. Academic Press, pp. 11–41.

Camposa, P. et al. (2010). Ancient DNA analyses exclude humans as the driving force behind the Pleistocene musk ox (Ovibos moschatus) population dynamics. *Proceedings of the National Academy of Sciences*, 107, 5675–5680.

Carneiro, R. L. (1970). A theory of the origin of the state. *Science*, 169, 733–738.

Ceballos, G., Ehrlich, P., & Dirzo, R. (2017). Biological annihilation via the ongoing sixth mass extinction signaled by vertebrate population losses and declines. *Proceedings of the National Academy of Sciences*, 114, E6089–E6096.

Cepelewicz, J. (2017). Interspecies hybrids play a vital role in evolution. *Quanta Magazine*, August 24. www.quantamagazine.org/interspecies-hybrids-play-a-vital-role-in-evolution-20170824

Chaisson, E. (2011). Energy rate density as a complexity metric and evolutionary driver. Wiley online library. 27 January. https://doi.org/10.1002/cplx.20323

Choi, J.-K. & Bowles, S. (2007). The coevolution of parochial altruism and war. *Science*, 318, 636–640.

Clark, G. (2014). *The Son Also Rises*. Princeton, NJ: Princeton University Press.

Clark, D., Beyene, G., Wolde, G., et al. (2003). Stratigraphic, chronological and behavioral contexts of Pleistocene Homo sapiens from Middle Awash, Ethiopia. *Nature*, 423, 747–752.

Clark, P., Shakun, J., Marcott, S., et al. (2016) Consequences of twenty-first century policy for multi-millennial climate and sea-level change. *Nature Climate Change*, 6, 360–369.

Cohen, M. (1977). *The Food Crisis in Prehistory: Overpopulation and the Origins of Agriculture*. New Haven, CT: Yale University Press.

Cohen, M. & Crane-Kramer, G. (2007). *Ancient Health: Skeletal Indicators of Agricultural and Economic Intensification*. Gainsville: University Press of Florida.

Collyer, B. (2017). The real roots of early city states may rip up the textbooks. Review of *against the Grain*. *New Scientist*. www.newscientist.com/article/mg23631462-700-the-real-roots-of-early-city-states-may-rip-up-the-textbooks

Conrad, K., Warren, M., Fox, R., et al. (2006). Rapid decline of common widespread British moths provide evidence of an insect biodiversity crisis. *Biological Conservation*, 132, 279–291.

Cooper, A., Turney, C., Hughen, K., Brook, B., McDonald, G., & Bradshaw, C. (2015). Abrupt warming events drove late Pleistocene Holarctic megafaunal turnover. *Science*, 349. 602–606.

Corning. P. (2017). *Synergistic Selection*. Singapore: World Scientific Publishers.

Cox, S. (2009). Crop domestication and the first plant breeders. In S. Ceccarelli, E. P. Guimaraes, & E. Weltizien, eds. *Plant Breeding and Farmer Participation*. Food and Agricultural Organization of the United Nations (FAO), pp. 171–193.

Crabtree, G. (2013a). Our fragile intellect. Part I. *Trends in Genetics*, 29, 1–3.

Crabtree, G. (2013b). Our fragile intellect. Part II. *Trends in Genetics*, 29, 3–5.

Crespi, B. (2014). The insectan apes. *Human Nature*, 25, 6–27.

Crespi, B. & Yanega, D. (1995). The definition of eusociality. *Behavioral Ecology and Sociobiology*, 6, 109–115.

Crist, E. (2015). The reaches of freedom: A response to *An Ecomodern Manifesto*. *Environmental Humanities*, 7, 245–254.

Culotta, E. (2013). Latest skirmish over ancestral violence strikes blow for peace. *Science*, 341, 224.

Daly, H. (1977). *Steady State Economics*. San Francisco: W.H. Freeman.

Dawkins, R. (1976). *The Selfish Gene*. London: Oxford University Press.

Dawkins, R. (2012). The descent of Edward Wilson. *Prospect*. May 24.

DeConto, D. & Pollard, R. (2016). Antarctic model raises prospect of unstoppable ice collapse. Nature https://climatenexus.org/climate-issues/science/antarctic-warming

De Waal, F. (2006). *Primates and Philosophers*. Princeton, NJ: Princeton University Press.

Diamond, J. (1987). The worst mistake in the history of the human race. *Discover Magazine* May 2, 1987, pp. 64–66. http://discovermagazine.com/1987/may/02-the-worst-mistake-in-the-history-of-the-human-race

Diamond, J. (2005). *Collapse: How Societies Choose to Fail or Succeed*. New York: Viking Press.

Dietl, G. (2016). Different worlds. *Nature*, 529, 29–30.

D'Souza, D. (2001). *The Virtue of Prosperity*. New York: Simon & Schuster.

Dunbar, R. (1993). Coevolution of neocortical size, group size and language in humans. *Behavioral and Brain Sciences*, 16(6), 681–735.

Dyble, M., Salali, G., Chaudhary, N., et al. (2015). Sex equality can explain the unique social structure of hunter-gatherer bands. *Science*, 348, 796–798.

Edwards, S. & Pratt, S. (2009). Rationality in collective decision-making by ant colonies. *Proceedings of the Royal Society B*, 276, 3655–3661.

Ehrlich, P. & Ehrlich, A. (1990). *The Population Explosion*. New York: Simon & Schuster.

Engel, M., Gramaldi, D. & Krishna, K. (2009). Termites (Isoptera): Their Phylogeny, classification, and Rise to Ecological Dominance. *American Museum Novitates*, 3650, 1–27.

Entomological Society of America. (2017). ESA position statement on endangered insect species: Protecting endangered insects is the nation's best interest. www .entsoc.org/sites/default/files/files/Science-Policy/ESA-PolicyStatement-Endangered-Species.pdf

Feynman, J. & Ruzmaikin, A. (2018). Climate stability and the origin of agriculture. ONLINE FIRST. https://doi.org/10.5772/intechopen.83344

Finley, M. (1959). Was Greek civilization based on slave labor? *Historia: Zeitschrift fur alte Geschichte*, 8, 145–164.

Firth, R. (1936). *We, the Tikopia*. London: Allen and Unwin.

Firth, R. (1939). *Primitive Polynesian Economy*. London: Routledge.

Fischer, H., Meissner, K., Mix, A., et al. (2018). Paleoclimate constraints on the impact of 2°C anthropogenic warming and beyond. *Nature Geoscience*, 11, 474–485.

Fittkau, E. & Klinge, H. (1973). On biomass and tropic structure of the central Amazonian rain forest ecosystem. *Biotropica*, 5: 2–14.

Flannery, K. (1968). Archaeological systems theory and early Mesoamerica. In B. Meggers, ed. *Anthropological Archaeology in the Americas*. Anthropological Society of Washington, pp. 67–87.

Flannery, T. (1994). *The Future Eaters*. New York: George Braziller.

Flannery, T. (2009). The superior civilization. Review of *The superorganism: The Beauty, Elegance, and Strangeness of Insect Societies*, by B. Hölldobler and E. O. Wilson. *New York Review of Books*, February 26.

Folgarait, P. (1998). Ant biodiversity and its relationship to ecosystem functioning: A review. *Biodiversity and Conservation*, 7, 1221–1244.

Frith, U. & Frith, C. (2010). The social brain: Allowing humans to boldly go where no other species has been. *Philosophical Transactions of the Royal Society of London B*, 365, 165–176.

Fry, D. & Söderberg, P. (2013). Lethal aggression in mobile forager bands and implications for the origins of war. *Science*, 341, 270–273.

Funtowicz, S. & Ravetz, J. (1993). Science for the post-normal age. *Futures*, 31 (7), 735–755.

Gabbatiss, J. (2017). Worst-case global warming predictions are the most accurate, say climate experts. *The Independent*, December 6. www .independent.co.uk/environment/global-warming-temperature-rise-climate-change-end-century-science-a8095591.html

Gamble, C. (1993). *Time Walkers: The Prehistory of Global Colonization.* Cambridge, MA: Harvard University Press.

Gaser, C. & Schlaug, G. (2003). Brain structures differ between musicians and non-musicians. *The Journal of Neuroscience*, 23, 9240–9245.

Geary, D. & Bailey, D. (2009). Hominid brain evolution: Testing climatic, ecological, and social competition models. *Human Nature*, 20, 265–279.

Georgescu-Roegen, N. (1971). *The Entropy Law and the Economic Process.* Cambridge, MA: Harvard University Press.

Georgescu-Roegen, N. (1972). Energy and economic myths. In N. Georgescu-Roegen, ed. *Energy and Economic Myths*. San Francisco: Pergamon Press.

Georgescu-Roegen, N. (1972). The institutional aspects of peasant communities. In N. Georgescu-Roegen, ed. *Energy and Economic Myths*. San Francisco: Pergamon Press.

Gibbons, A. (2019). Bronze age inequality and family life revealed in powerful study. *Science*, 366, 168.

Gilens, M. & Page, B. (2014). Testing theories of American politics: Elites, interest groups, and average citizens. *Perspectives on Politics*, 12, 564–581.

Gilland, B. (2015). Nitrogen, phosphorous, carbon and population. *Science Progress*, 98, 379–390.

Goodnight, C. (2000). Heritability at the ecosystem level. *Proceedings of the National Academy of Science*, 97, 9365–9366.

Goodnight, C. & Stevens, L. (1997). Experimental studies of group selection: What do they tell us about group selection in nature? *The American Naturalist*, 150 (Suppl.), S59–S79.

Gordon, D. (2007). Control without hierarchy. *Nature*, 446, 143.

Gould, S. J. (1990). Darwin and Paley meet the invisible hand. *Natural History*, 99, 8–13.

Gowanty, P. (2000). Free female mate choice in house mice affects reproductive success and offspring viability and performance. *Animal Behavior*, 359, 71–78.

Gowdy, J. (1994). Progress and environmental sustainability. *Environmental Ethics*, 16, 41–55.

Gowdy, J. (1997). The value of biodiversity: Markets, society, and ecosystems. *Land Economics*, 73, 25–41.

Gowdy, J. (ed.) (1998). *Limited Wants, Unlimited Means: A Reader on Hunter-Gatherer Economics and the Environment.* Washington, DC: Island Press.

Gowdy, J. (1999). Hunter-gatherers and the mythology of the market. In R. Lee and R. Devore, eds. *Cambridge Encyclopedia of Hunters and Gatherers.* Cambridge: Cambridge University Press, pp. 391–398.

Gowdy, J. (2006). Darwinian selection and cultural incentives for resource use: Tikopia as a case study of sustainability. *International Journal of Global Environmental Issues*, 6, 348–361.

Gowdy, J. (2013). Darwinian economics. *BioScience*, 63, 824–827.

Gowdy, J. (2013). Valuing nature for climate change policy: From discounting the future to truly social deliberation. In R. Fouquet, ed. *Handbook on Energy and Climate*. Cheltenham: Edward Elgar, pp. 547–560.

Gowdy, J. (2020). Our hunter-gatherer future: Climate change, agriculture and uncivilization. *Futures*, 115, 1–9. https://doi.org/10.1016/j.futures.2019 .102488

Gowdy, J. & Erickson, J. (2000). Resource use, institutions and sustainability: A tale of two Pacific Island cultures. *Land Economics*, 76, 345–354

Gowdy, J. & Juliá, R. (2010). Global warming economics in the long run. *Land Economics*, 86(1), 117–130.

Gowdy, J. & Krall, L. (2013). The ultrasocial origins of the Anthropocene. *Ecological Economics*, 95, 137–147.

Gowdy, J. & Krall, L. (2014). Agriculture and the evolution of human ultrasociality. *Journal of Bioeconomics*, 16(2), 179–202.

Gowdy, J. & Krall, L. (2016). The economic origins of ultrasociality. *Behavioral and Brain Sciences*, 39, 1–60.

Gowdy, J., Krall, L. & Chan, Y. (2013). The parable of the bees: Beyond proximate causes in ecosystem service valuation. *Environmental Ethics*, 35(1), 41–55.

Gowdy, J., Dollimore, D., Wilson, D. S., & Witt, U. (2013). Economic cosmology and the evolutionary challenge. *Journal of Economic Behavior and Organization*, 90S, S11–S20.

Gracia, A., Arsuaga, J. L., and Martinez, I. (2009). Craniosynostosis in the Middle Pleistocene human Cranium 14 from the Sima de los Huesos, Atapuerca, Spain. *Proceedings of the National Academy of Sciences*, 106, 6573–6578.

Grayson, D. & Meltzer, D. (2003). A requiem for North American overkill. *Journal of Archaeological Science*, 30, 585–593.

Grinsted, L., Agnarsson, I., & Bilde, T. (2012). Subsocial behaviour and brood adoption in mixed-species colonies of two theridiid spiders. *Naturwissenschaften*, 99, 1021–1030.

Gurven, M. & Kaplan, H. (2007). Longevity among hunter-gatherers: A cross-cultural examination. *Population and Development Review*, 33(2), 321–365.

Hall, C. & Klitgaard, K. (2011). *Energy and the Wealth of Nations: Understanding the Biophysical Economy*. Berlin: Springer Science and Business Media.

Hall, C., Balogh, S. & Murphy, D. (2009). What is the minimum EROI that a sustainable society must have? *Energies*, 2, 25–47.

Hall, C., Tharakan, P., Hallock, J., et al. (2003). Hydrocarbons and the evolution of human culture. *Nature*, 426, 318–322.

Hallmann, C., Sorg, M., Jongejans, E., et al. (2017). More than 75 percent decline over 27 years in total flying insect biomass in protected areas.

PLOS One. https://doi.org/10.1371/journal.pone.0185809

Hamilton, C. (2015). The theodicy of the "Good Anthropocene." *Environmental Humanities*, 7, 233–238.

Hamilton, W. (1964). The genetical evolution of social behavior, I and II. *Journal of Theoretical Biology*, 7, 1–52.

Handwerk, B. (2017). How ants became the world's best fungus farmers. *Smithsonian Magazine.* www.smithsonianmag.com/science-nature/how-ants-became-worlds-best-fungus-farmers-180962871

Hanna, S., Folke, C., & Maler, K-G. (1996). *Rights to Nature.* Washington, DC: Island Press.

Hansen, J., Sato, M., Hearty, P., et al. (2016). Ice melt, sea level rise and superstorms: Evidence from paleoclimate data, climate modeling, and modern observations that 2°C global warming could be dangerous. *Atmospheric Chemistry and Physics*, 15, 20059–20179.

Hansford, J., Wright, P., Rasoamiaramanana, A., et al. (2018). Early Holocene human presence in Madagascar evidenced by exploitation of avian megafauna. *Science Advances.* www.advances.sciencemag.org/content/4/9/eaat6925

Harari, Y. (2014). *Sapiens: A Brief History of Mankind.* New York: HarperCollins.

Harcourt, B. (2011). *The Illusion of Free Markets.* Cambridge: Cambridge University Press.

Harman, K. (2012). New DNA analysis Shows ancient humans interbred with Denisovans. *Scientific American August* 30, www.yahoo.com/news/dna-analysis-shows-ancient-humans-interbred-denisovans-230000855.html.

Harner, M. (1977). The enigma of Aztec sacrifice. *Natural History*, 86(4), 46–51.

Hawkes, K., O'Connell, J., & Blurton Jones, N. (2001). Hazda meat sharing. *Evolution and Human Behavior*, 22, 113–142.

Hawks, J. (2011). Selection for smaller brains in Holocene human evolution. *John Hawks weblog*, August 22. http://johnhawks.net/research/hawks-2011-brain-size-selection-holocene

Hayek, F. (1944). *The Road to Serfdom.* Chicago: University of Chicago Press.

Hayek, F. (1967). *Studies in Philosophy, Politics and Economics.* Chicago: University of Chicago Press.

Hayek, F. (1979). *Law, Legislation and Liberty.* London: Routledge & Kegan Paul.

Henneberg, M. (1988). Decrease of human skull size in the Holocene. *Human Biology*, 60, 395–405.

Henneberg, M. & Steyn, M. (1993). Trends in cranial capacity. *Biology*, 5, 473–479.

Henrich, J., Heine, S., & Norenzayan, A. (2010). The weirdest people in the world? *Behavioral and Brain Sciences*, 33, 61–135.

Henrich, J., McElreath, R., Barr, A., et al. (2006). Costly punishment across human societies. *Science*, 312, 1767–1770.

Henrich, J., Boyd, R., Bowles, S., Camerer, C., Fehr, E., & Gintis, H. (2004). *Foundations of Human Sociality*. New York: Oxford University Press.

Hershkovitz, I. Weber, G., Quam, R., et al. (2018). The earliest modern humans outside Africa. *Science*, 359, 456–459.

Hickel, J. (2016). Global inequality may be much worse than we think. *The Guardian*. April 8. www.theguardian.com/global-development-professionals-network/2016/apr/08/global-inequality-may-be-much-worse-than-we-think

Hill, M. Jr., Hill, M., & Widga, C. (2008). Later Quaternary Bison diminution on the Great Plains of North America: Evaluating the role of human hunting versus climate change. *Quaternary Science Reviews*, 27, 1752–1771.

Hill, K., Walker, R., Božičević, M., et al. (2011). Co-residence patterns in hunter-gatherer societies show unique human social structure. *Science*, 331, 1286–1289.

Hodgson, G. (1993). *Economics and Evolution*. Ann Arbor: University of Michigan Press.

Hodgson, G. (2012). *From Pleasure Machine to Moral Communities: An Evolutionary Economics without Homo economicus*. Chicago: University of Chicago Press.

Hodgson, G. & Knudsen, T. (2013). *Darwin's Conjecture: The Search for General Principles of Social and Economic Evolution*. Chicago: University of Chicago Press.

Hoffman, D. et al. (2018). U-Th dating of carbonate crusts reveals Neandertal origin of Iberian cave art. *Science*, 359(6378), 912–919.

Hoggarth, J., Breitenbach, S., Culleton, B., et al. (2016). The political collapse of Chichén Itzá in climatic and cultural context. *Global and Planetary Change*, 138, 25–42.

Holbrook, T., Barton, M., & Fewell, J. (2011). Division of labor increases with colony size in the harvester ant Pogonomyrmex californicus. *Behavioral Ecology*, 22, 960–966.

Holbrook, T., Clark, R., Jeanson, R., Bertram, S., Kukuk, P., & Fewell, J. (2009). Emergence and consequences of division of labor in associations of normally solitary sweat bees. *Ethology*, 115, 301–310.

Hölldobler, B. & Wilson, E. O. (2009). *The Superorganism: The Beauty, Elegance, and Strangeness of Insect Societies*. New York: W. W. Norton.

Hölldobler, B. & Wilson, E. O. (2011). *The Leafcutter Ants: Civilization by Instinct*. New York: W. W. Norton.

Horowitz, S. (2015). Hayek, the family and social individualism. *Cato Unbound*. www.cato-unbound.org/2015/08/05/steven-horwitz/hayek-family-social-individualism

Hou, C., Kaspari, M., Zanden, H., & Gillooly, J. (2010). Energetic basis of colonial living in social insects. *Proceedings of the National Academy of Sciences USA*, 107(8), 3634–3638.

Hublin, J.-J., Ben-Ncer, A., Bailey, S., et al. (2017). New fossils from Jebel Irhoud, Morocco and the pan-African origin of Homo sapiens. *Nature*, 546, 289–292.

Huxley, A. (1932). *Brave New World*. New York: Harper and Row.

Intergovernmental Panel on Climate Change. (2014). Fifth Assessment report. www.ipcc.ch/pdf/assessment-report/ar5/syr/SYR_AR5_FINAL_full_wcover.pdf

Isenberg, N. (2017). *White Trash: The 440-Year Untold History of Class in America*. New York: Penguin Books.

Jablonka, E. (2016). Beyond Genetic Evolution: A Conversation with Eva Jablonka. Interview with D. S. Wilson in *This View of Life*.

Jablonka, E. & Lamb, M. (2014). *Evolution in Four Dimensions*. Cambridge, MA: MIT Press.

Janssen, M., Kohler, T., & Scheffer, M (2003). Sunk-cost effects and vulnerability to collapse in ancient societies. *Current Anthropology*, 44, 722–728.

Jarvis, B. (2018). The insect apocalypse is here: What does it mean for the rest of life on earth? *New York Times Magazine*, November 27.

Johns, P., Howard, K., Breisch, N., Rivera, A., & Thorne, B. (2009). Non-relatives inherit colony resources in a primitive termite. *Proceedings of the National Academy of Sciences*, 106, 17452–17456.

Jones, N. (2011). Human influence comes of age. *Nature*, 473, 133.

Joordens, J., d,Errico, F., Wesselingh, S., et al. (2015). Homo erectus at Trinil on Java used shells for tool production and engraving. *Nature*, 518, 228–231.

Kahn, A. (1966). The tyranny of small decisions: Market failures, imperfections, and the limits of economics. *Kyklos*, 19, 23–47.

Kaplan, H., Lancaster, K., & Hurtado, M. (2000). A theory of human life history evolution: Diet, intelligence, and longevity. *Evolutionary Anthropology*, 156–185.

Kasting, J. (1998). The carbon cycle, climate, and the long-term effects of fossil fuel burning. *Consequences*, 4, 15–27.

Keely, L. (1996). *War before Civilization*. New York: Oxford University Press.

Keller, L. ed. (1999). *Levels of Selection in Evolution*. Princeton, NJ: Princeton University Press.

Kelly, R. (1995). *The Foraging Spectrum*. Washington, DC: Smithsonian Press.

King, J., Warren, R., & Bradford, M. (2013). Social insects dominate eastern US temperate hardwood forest macroinvertebrate communities in warmer regions. *PLoS One*, 8(10). https://doi.org/10.1371/journal.pone.0075843.

Kintisch, E. (2008). IPCC tunes up for its next report aiming for better, timely results. *Science*, 320, 300.

Kirch, P. & Yen, D. (1982). *Tikopia Prehistory and Ecology of a Polynesian Outlier*. Honolulu: Bernice P. Bishop Museum Bulletin, 238.

Klaus,V. (2008). Current global warming alarmism and the Mont Pelerin Society's long term agenda (Mont Pelerin Society Tokyo 2008) www.montpelerin.org/wp-content/uploads/2015/12/01-Vaclav-Klaus-Current-Global-Warming-Alarmism-and-the-MPSs-Long-Term-Agenda.pdf

Knight, R. (2018). Can we be sure the world's population will stop rising? *BBC Technology News*. www.bbc.com/news/technology-19923200

Korb, J. (2007). Termites. *Current Biology*, 17, R995–999.

Krausmann, F., Erb, K-H., Gingrich, S., et al. (2013). Global human appropriation of net primary production doubled in the 20th century. *Proceedings of the National Academy of Sciences*, 110(25), 10324–10329.

Krech, S. (1999). *The Ecological Indian*. New York: W. W. Norton.

Kucharik, C. & Serbin, S. (2008). Impacts of recent climate change on Wisconsin corn and soybean yield trends. *Environmental Research Letters*, 3, https://doi.org/10.1088/1748-9326/3/3/034003.

Kuijt, I. & Finlayson, B. (2009). Evidence for food storage and predomestication granaries 11,000 years ago in the Jordon Valley. *Proceedings of the National Academy of Sciences USA*, 106, 10966–10970.

Kump, L. (2002). Reducing uncertainty about carbon dioxide as a climate driver. *Nature*, 419, 188–190.

Kump, L. (2011). The last great global warming. *Scientific American*, 305, 57–61.

Lambert, P. (2009). Health versus fitness. *Current Anthropology*, 50(5), 603–608.

Landes, D. (1969). *The Unbound Prometheus: Technological Change and Development in Western Europe from 1750 to the Present*. Cambridge: Cambridge University Press.

Larbey, C., Mentzer, S., Ligouis, B., & Wurz, S. (2019). Cooked starchy food in hearths ca. 120 kya (MIS 5e and MIS 4) from Klasies River Cave, *South Africa Journal of Human Evolution*, 131, 210–227.

Larsen, C. S. (2006). The agricultural revolution as environmental catastrophe: Implications for health and lifestyles in the Holocene. *Quaternary International*, 150, 12–20.

Lawler, A. (2018). Scarred bird bones reveal early settlement on Madagascar. *Science*, 361, 1059.

Lawton, G. (2018). Road kill. *New Scientist, September*, 1, 36–43.

Layard, R. (2006). *Happiness: Lessons from a New Science*. New York: Penguin Books.

Leacock, E. (1998) [1983]. Women's status in egalitarian society: Implications for social evolution. In J. Gowdy, ed. *Limited Wants, Unlimited Means: A Reader on Hunter-Gatherer Economics and the Environment*. Washington, DC: Island Press, pp. 139–164.

Lee, R. (1968) What hunters do for a living, or, how to make out on scarce resources. In R. Lee and R. Devore, eds. *Man the Hunter*. Chicago: Aldine. Reprinted in Gowdy, 1998, 43–63.

Lee, R. (1990). Primitive communism and the origin of social inequality. In S. Upham, ed. *Evolution of Political Systems: Sociopolitics in Small-Scale Sedentary Societies*. Cambridge: Cambridge University Press, 225–246.

Lee, R. (1992). Art, science, or politics? The crisis in hunter-gatherer studies. *American Anthropologist*, 94, 31–54.

Lee, R. (1993). *The Dobe Ju/'hoansi*. New York: Harcourt Brace.

Lee, R. (1998). *Forward to Limited Wants, Unlimited Means: A Reader on Hunter-Gatherer Economics and the Environment*, J. Gowdy, ed. Washington, DC: Island Press.

Lee, R. (1998). Non-capitalist work: Baseline for an anthropology of work or Romantic delusion? *Anthropology of Work Review*, XVIII, 9–13.

Lee, R. & Devore, I. (1968). *Man the Hunter*. New York. Routledge.

Liu, C., Tang, Y., Ge, H., et al. (2014). Increasing breadth of the frontal lobe but decreasing height of the human brain between two Chinese samples from a Neolithic site and from living humans. *American Journal of Physical Anthropology*, 154, 94–103.

Lister, B. & Garcia, A. (2018). Climate-driven declines in arthropod abundance restructure a rainforest food web. *Proceedings of the National Academy of Sciences*, 115(44), E10397–E10406.

Lobell, D., Burke, M., Tebaldi, C., et al. (2008). Prioritizing climate change adaptation needs for food security in 2030. *Science*, 319, 607–610.

Lordkipanidze, D., Jashashvili, T., Vekua, A., et al. (2007). Postcranial evidence from early Homo erectus from Dmanisi, Georgia. *Nature*, 449, 305–310.

Lüthi, D., Le Floch, M., Bereiter, B., et al. (2008). High resolution carbon dioxide concentration record 650,000 – 800,000 before present. *Nature*, 453, 379–382.

Lyons, K., Amatangelo, K., Behrensmeyer, A., et al. (2015). Holocene shifts in the assembly of plant and animal communities implicate human impacts. *Nature*, https://doi.org/10.10.1038/nature16447

MacDonald, G., Beilman, D., Kuzmin, Y., et al. (2012). Pattern of extinction of the woolly mammoth in Beringia. *Nature Communications*, (June 12).

MacLean, N. (2017). *Democracy in Chains: The Deep History of the Radical Right's Stealth Plan for America*. New York: Penguin Books.

Maes, D., Titeux, N., Hortal, J., et al. (2010). Predicted insect diversity declines under climate change in an already impoverished area. *Journal of Insect Conservation*, 14, 485–498.

Makarewicz, C. (2012). The Younger Dryas and hunter-gatherer transitions to food production in the Near East. In M. Eren, ed. *Hunter-Gatherer Behaviour: Human Response during the Younger Dryas*. San Francisco: Left Coast Press, pp. 195–230.

Margulis, L. (1970). *Origin of Eukaryotic Cells*. New Haven: Yale University Press.

Margulis, L. (1998). *Symbiotic Planet*. New York: Basic Books.

Mariette, M. & Buchanan, K. (2016). Prenatal acoustic communication programs offspring for high posthatching temperatures in a songbird. *Science*, 353, 812–814.

Marshall, L. (1976). Sharing, talking, giving: Relief of social tensions among the ! Kung. In R. Lee and R. Devore, eds. *Kalahari Hunter-Gatherers*. Cambridge, MA: Harvard University Press.

Martin, M. (1970). The biochemical basis of the fungus-attine ant symbiosis. *Science*, 169(16), 20.

Martin, P. (1990). 40,000 of extinctions on the planet of doom. *Palaeogeography, Palaeoclimatology, Palaeoecology*, 82, 187–201.

Martínez, M. & Moya, A. (2011). Natural selection and multi-level causation. *Philosophical Theory and Biology*, 3, 1–23.

Marx, K. (1846). *The German Ideology*. Moscow: Progress Publishers.

Marx, K. (1884/1909). *The Origin of Family, Private Property and the State*. Chicago: Charles H. Kerr & Co.

Matthew, S. & Boyd, R. (2011). Punishment sustains large-scale cooperation in prestate warfare. *Proceedings of the National Academy of Science USA*, 108, 11375–11380.

Matthews, D. & Caldeira, K. (2008). Stabilizing climate requires near-zero emissions. *Geophysical Research Letters*, 35, L04705.

Mattison, S. Smith, E., Shenk, M., & Cochrane, E. (2016). The evolution of inequality. *Evolutionary Anthropology*, 25, 184–199.

Maynard Smith, J. & Szathmáry, E. (1995). *The Major Transitions in Evolution*. Oxford: W. H. Freeman.

Mazzucato, M. (2014). *The Entrepreneurial State*. London: Anthem Press.

Mazzucato, M. (2018). *The Value of Everything*. New York: Public Affairs Press.

McAuliffe, K. (2010). If modern humans are so smart, why are our brains shrinking? *Discover Magazine*, 31(7), 54–59.

McCorriston, J. & Hole, F. (1991). The ecology of seasonal stress and the origins of agriculture in the Near East. *American Anthropologist*, 93, 46–69.

McCorriston, J. & Hole, F. (2000a). Barley. In K. Kiple and K. Ornelas eds. *The Cambridge World History of Food*, vol. 1, Cambridge: Cambridge University Press, pp. 81–90.

McCorriston, J. & Hole, F. (2000b). Wheat. In K. Kiple and K. Ornelas, eds. *The Cambridge World History of Food*, vol. 1. Cambridge: Cambridge University Press, pp. 158–174.

McDaniel, M. (2005). Big-brained people are smarter: A meta-analysis of the relationship between in vivo brain volume and intelligence. *Intelligence*, 33, 337–346.

McDaniel, C. & Gowdy, J. (2000). *Paradise for Sale: A Parable of Nature*. Berkeley: University of California Press.

McEvan, G. (2006). *The Incas: New Perspectives*. New York: W. W. Norton.

Melis, A., Hare, B., & Tomasello, M. (2006). Chimpanzees recruit the best collaborators. *Science*, 311, 1297–1300.

Michaels, R. (1915). *Political Parties: A Sociological Study of the Oligarchical Tendencies of Modern Democracy*, trans. Eden Paul and Cedar Paul. Kitchener: Batoche Books.

Michod, R. & Nedelcu, A. (2003). On the reorganization of fitness during evolutionary transitions in individuality. *Integrated Computational Biology*, 43, 64–73.

Mirowski, P. (2014). *Never Let a Serious Crisis Go to Waste*. London: New Left Books.

Mirowski, P. (2016). Is this water or is it the Neoliberal Thought Collective? *Naked Capitalism*. www.nakedcapitalism.com/2016/05/philip-mirowski-this-is-water-or-is-it-the-neoliberal-thought-collective.html

Mirowski, P. & Plehwe, D. eds. (2009). *The Road from Mont Pelerin: The Making of the Neoliberal Thought Collective*. Cambridge, MA: Harvard University Press.

Mithen, S. (2007). Did farming arise from a misapplication of social intelligence? *Philosophical Transactions of the Royal Society B*, 362, 705–718.

Mittnik, A., Massy, K., et al. (2019). Kinship-based social inequality in Bronze Age Europe. *Science*, early release 10 October. 10.1126/science.aax6219

Moffett, M. (2010). *Adventures among the Ants*. Berkeley: University of California Press.

Moffett, M. (2013). Human identity and the evolution of societies. *Human Nature*, 24, 219–267.

Monbiot, G. (2014). *Feral: Rewilding the Land, the Sea and Human Life*. Chicago: University of Chicago Press.

Monbiot, G. (2018). A despot in disguise: One man's mission to rip up democracy. *The Guardian*.

Montenegro, A., Brovkin, V., Eby, M., et al. (2007). Long term fate of anthropogenic carbon. *Geophysical Research Letters*, 34, L19707.

Mooney, S., Harrison, S., Bartlein, P., et al. (2011). Late quaternary fire regimes of Australasia. *Quaternary Science Reviews*, 30, 28–46.

Morgan, D. (2009). World on fire: two scenarios of the destruction of human civilization and possible extinction of the human race. *Futures*, 41, 683–693.

Moseley, M. (1992). *The Incas and Their Ancestors: The Archaeology of Peru*. London: Thames and Hudson.

Mueller, U. & Gerardo, N. (2002). Fungus-farming insects: Multiple origins and diverse evolutionary histories. *Proceedings of the National Academy of Science*, 99(24), 15247–15249.

Mueller, U., Rehner, S. & Schultz, T. (1998). The evolution of agriculture in ants. *Science*, 281, 2034–2038.

Mueller, U., Gerardo, N., Aanen, D., Six, D., & Schultz, T. (2005). The evolution of agriculture in insects. *Annual Review of Ecology, Evolution, and Systematics*, 36, 563–595.

Mueller, U., Kardish, M., Ishak, H., et al. (2018). Phylogenetic patterns of ant-fungus associations indicate that farming strategies, not only a superior fungal cultivar, explain the ecological success of leafcutter ants. *Molecular Ecology.* https://doi.org/10.1111/mec.14588

Muir, W. (1996). Group selection for adaptation to multiple-hen cages: Selection program and direct responses. *Journal of Poultry Science,* 75, 447–458.

Munro, N. (2002). Small game, the Younger Dryas, and the transition to agriculture in the southern Levant. *Mitteilungen der Gesellschaft für Urgeschichte,* 12, 47–71.

Murra, J. V. (1980). *The Economic Organization of the Inca State.* Greenwood, CT:

Nagaoka, L., Rick, T., & Wolverton, S. (2018). The overkill model and its impact on environmental research. *Ecology and Evolution,* 8, 9683–9696.

Naroll, R. (1956). A preliminary index of social development. *American Anthropologist,* 58, 687–715.

New Scientist. (2018). *How Evolution Explains Everything about Life.*

Nguyen, N. (2005). Global climate changes and rice food security. FAO, Rome. www.fao.org/forestry/15526-03ecb62366f779d1ed45287e698a44d2e.pdf

Nielsen, R., Akey, J., Jakobsson, M., et al. (2017). Tracing the peopling of the world through genomics. *Nature,* 541, 302–310.

Nissen, H. (1988). *The Early History of the Ancient Near East 9000–2000 BC.* Chicago: University of Chicago Press.

Norberg, J. (2016) *Progress: Ten Reasons to Look Forward to the Future.* London: One World Publications.

Norberg-Hodge, H. (1991). *Ancient Futures: Learning from Ladakh.* San Francisco: Sierra Club Books.

Nowak, M. & Highfield, R. 2011. *Super Cooperators.* New York: Free Press.

Nowak, M., Tarnita, C., & Wilson, E. O. (2010). The evolution of eusociality. *Nature,* 466, 1057–1062.

Okasha, S. (2006). *Evolution and the Levels of Selection.* New York: Oxford University Press.

Oreskes, N. & Conway, E. (2010). *Merchants of Doubt.* London: Bloomsbury.

Oxfam. (2016). An economy for the 1%. www.oxfam.org/en/pressroom/ pressreleases/2016-01-18/62-people-own-same-half-world-reveals-oxfam-davos-report

Palmer, T. (2020). Short-term tests validate long-term estimates of climate change. *Nature,* 582, 185–186.

Panter-Brick, C., Laydon, R., & Rowley-Conway, P. (2001). Lines of inquiry. In C. Panter-Brick, R. Laydon, and P. Rowley-Conway, eds. *Hunter-Gatherers: An Interdisciplinary Perspective.* Cambridge: Cambridge University Press.

Pappu, S., Gunnell, Y., Akhilesh, K. et al. (2011). Early Pleistocene presence of Acheulian hominins in South India. *Science,* 33, 1596–1599.

Peck, J. (2010). *Constructions of Neoliberal Reason.* Oxford: Oxford University Press

Peeters, C., Liebig, J., & Hölldobler, B. (2000). Sexual reproduction by both queens and workers in the ponerine ant Harpegnathos saltator. *Insectes Soc.*, 47, 325–332.

Pennisi, E. (2014). Our egalitarian Eden. *Science*, 344, 824–825.

Pennisi, E. (2018). Hybrids spawned Lake Victoria's rich fish diversity. *Science*, 361, 539.

Pigliucci, M. & Müller, G. (2010). *Evolution: The Extended Synthesis*. Cambridge, MA: MIT Press.

Piketty, T. (2014). *Capital in the Twenty First Century*. Cambridge, MA: Harvard University Press.

Pinker, S. (2011). *The Better Angels of Our Nature: The Decline of Violence in History and Its Causes*. London: Viking Penguin.

Pinker, S. (2017). The false allure of group selection. *Edge Magazine*. www.edge.org/conversation/steven_pinker-the-false-allure-of-group-selection

Pinker, S. (2018). *Enlightenment Now: The Case for Reason, Science, Humanism, and Progress*. New York: Viking.

Polanyi, K. (1941). *The Great Transformation*. Boston: Beacon Press.

Ponting, C. (2007). *A New Green History of the World*. New York: Penguin Books.

Porter, E. (2015). Education gap between rich and poor is growing wider. *New York Times*. September 22. www.nytimes.com/2015/09/23/business/economy/education-gap-between-rich-and-poor-is-growing-wider.html

Posth, C., Wissing, C., Kitagawa, K., et al. (2017). Deeply divergent archaic mitochondrial genome provides lower time boundary from African gene flow into Neanderthals. *Nature Communications*, July 4. https://doi.org/10.1038/ncomms16046

Prentiss, A., Foor, T., Cross, G., Harris, L., & Wanzenried, M. (2012). The cultural evolution of material wealth based inequality at Bridge River, British Columbia. *American Antiquity*, 77, 542–564.

Price, D. & Bar-Yosef, O. (2011). The origins of agriculture: New data, new ideas. *Current Anthropology*, 52 (Supplement), S163–174.

Price, G., Louys, J., Faith, T., Lorenzen, E., & Westaway, M. (2018). Big data little help in megafauna mysteries. *Nature*, 558, 23–25.

Pringle, H. (2014). The ancient roots of the 1%. *Science*, 344, 822–825.

Rand, A. (1957). *Atlas Shrugged*. New York: Random House.

Rand, A. (1964). *The Virtue of Selfishness*. New York: New American Library.

Ratnieks, F. & Wenseleers, T. (2005). Policing insect societies. *Science*, 307, 54–56.

Raupach, M., Marland, G., Ciais, P., et al. (2007). Global and regional drivers of accelerated CO_2. *Proceedings of the National Academy of Sciences*, 104, 10288–10293.

Reardon, P., Seidlitz, J., & Vandekar, S. (2018). Normative brain size variation and brain shape diversity in humans. *Science*, 360, 1222–1227.

Richerson, P. & Boyd, R. (1998). The evolution of human ultra-sociality. In I. Eibl-Eibisfeldt and F. Salter, eds. *Ideology, Warfare, and Indoctrinability*. New York: Berghan Books, pp. 71–95.

Richerson, P., Boyd, R., & Bettinger, R. (2001). Was agriculture impossible during the Pleistocene, but mandatory during the Holocene? A climate change hypothesis. *American Antiquity*, 66, 387–411.

Richerson, P. & Boyd, R. (2005). *Not by Genes Alone: How Culture Transformed Human Evolution*. Chicago: University of Chicago Press.

Riches, D. (1995). Hunter-gatherer structural transformations. *The Journal of the Royal Anthropological Institute*, 1, 679–701.

Ridley, M. (2011). *The Rational Optimist: How Prosperity Evolves*. New York: Harper Perennial.

Ridley, M. (2017). www.rationaloptimist.com/blog/free-markets-and-free-trade

Rightmire, P. (1996). The human cranium from Bodo, Ethiopia: Evidence for speciation in the Middle Pleistocene. *Journal of Human Evolution*, 31, 21–39.

Rindos, D. (1984). *The Origins of Agriculture: An Evolutionary Perspective*. New York: Academic Press.

Riveros, A., Seid, M., & Wcislo, W. (2012). Evolution of brain size in class-based societies of fungus-growing ants (Attini). *Animal Behavior*, 83,1043–1049.

Roberts, E. M., Todd, C., Aanen, D. et al. (2016). Oligocene termite nests with in situ fungus gardens from the Rukwa Rift Basin, Tanzania, support a paleogene African origin for insect agriculture. *PloS ONE*, 11. https://doi.org.10.1371/journal.pone.0156847

Rosen, A. & Rivera-Collazo, I. (2012). Climate change, adaptive cycles, and the persistence of foraging economies during the Late Pleistocene/Holocene transition in the Levant. *Proceedings of the National Academy of Sciences USA*, 109, 3640–3645.

Rosenthal, E. (2017). *An American Sickness: How Healthcare Became Big Business and How You Can Take It Back*. New York: Penguin Press.

Rosenthal, E. (2020). Who's profiting from your outrageous medical bills? *New York Times*, February 14.

Rowe, J. R. (1947). Inca culture at the time of the Spanish Conquest. In Julian Steward, ed. *Handbook of South American Indians, Vol. 2. The Andean Civilizations*, pp. 198–330, Washington, DC: Smithsonian Institute.

Ruff, C., Trinkaus, E., & Holliday, T. (1997). Body mass and encephalization in Pleistocene Homo. *Nature*, 387, 173–178.

Ruse, M. (1979). *Sociobiology: Sense or Nonsense*. Dordrecht: Reidel Publishing Company.

Rushton, P. & Ankney, D. (2009). Whole brain size and general mental ability: A review. *International Journal of Neuroscience*, 119, 692–732.

Ryan, C. & Jethá, C. (2010). *Sex at Dawn*. New York: Harper Perennial.

Safina, C. (2015). *Beyond Words*. New York: Henry Holt.

Sahlins, M. (1972). *Stone Age Economics*. Chicago: Aldine.

Sahlins, M. (1996). The sadness of sweetness: The native anthropology of Western cosmology. *Current Anthropology*, 37, 395–428.

Sahlins, M. (1998). *The Original Affluent Society*. Chicago: University of Chicago Press.

Sanderson, M. (1996). Biomass of termites and their emissions of methane and carbon dioxide: A global database. *Global Biogeochemical Cycles*, 10, 543–557.

Sanderson, E., Jaiteh, M., Levy, K. et al. (2002). The human footprint and the last of the wild. *BioScience*, 52, 891–904.

Scheidel, W. (2017). *The Great Leveler: Violence and the History of Inequality*. Princeton, NJ: Princeton University Press.

Shermer, M. (2008). https://michaelshermer.com/2008/01/why-people-dont-trust-free-markets

Schultz, T. (2000). In search of ant ancestors. *Proceedings of the National Academy of Sciences*, 97, 14028–14029.

Schultz, T. & Brady, S. (2008). Major transitions in ant agriculture. *Proceedings of the National Academy of Sciences*, 105(14), 5435–5440.

Schwab, I. (2018). *Evolution's Witness: How Eyes Evolved*. New York: Oxford University Press.

Scott, J. (2017). *Against the Grain: A Deep History of the Earliest States*. New Haven, CT. Yale University Press.

Seid, M., Castillo, A., & Wcislo, W. (2011). The allometry of brain miniaturization in ants. *Brain, Behavior, and Evolution*, 7, 5–13.

Shepard, P. (1998). *Coming Home to the Pleistocene*. Washington, DC: Shearwater Books, p. 132.

Sherwood, C., Subiaul, F., & Zadiszki, T. (2008). A natural history of the human mind: Tracing evolutionary changes in brain and cognition. *Journal of Anatomy*, 212, 426–454.

Shik, J., Hou, A. Kay, C., Kaspari, M., & Gillooly, J. (2012). Towards a general life-history model of the superorganism: Predicting the survival growth and reproduction of ant societies. *Biology Letters*, 8, 1059–1062.

Shiva, V. (1993). *Monocultures of the Mind: Biodiversity, Biotechnology and Agriculture*. New Delhi: Zed Press.

Shweder, R. (2010). Donald Campbell's doubt: Cultural differences of failure of communication. *Behavioral and Brain Sciences*, 33(2/3), 109–110.

Slezak, M. (2015) Megafauna extinction: DNA evidence pins blame on climate change. *New Scientist*. www.newscientist.com/article/dn27952-megafauna-extinction-dna-evidence-pins-blame-on-climate-change

Slon, V., Mafessoni, F., Vernot, C., et al. (2018). The genome of the offspring of a Neanderthal mother and a Denisovan father. *Nature*, 561, 113–116.

Smaje, C. (2015). Dark thoughts on ecomodernism. http://dark-mountain.net/blog/dark-thoughts-on-ecomodernism-2

Smil, V. (2013). *Harvesting the Biosphere*. Cambridge, MA: MIT Press.

Smith, A. [1776] 1937. *An Inquiry into the Nature and Causes of the Wealth of Nations*. New York: Modern Library.

Smith, H. (2019). Wallace Broecker, who helped popularize term 'global warming,' dies at 87. *Washington Post*, February 19. www.washingtonpost.com/local/obituaries/wallace-broecker-who-helped-popularize-term-global-warming-dies-at-87/2019/02/19/3f8bd7e0-3458-11e9-854a-7a14d7fec96a_story.html?utm_term=.d8e0aa12cbe4

Smith, P. (1972). Diet and attrition in the Natufians. *American Journal of Physical Anthropology*, 37, 233–238.

Sober, E. & Wilson, D. S. (1998). *Unto Others: The Evolution and Psychology of Unselfish Behavior*. Cambridge, MA: Harvard University Press.

Solway, J. & Lee, R. (1990). Foragers, genuine or spurious: Situating the Kalahari San in history. *Current Anthropology*, 31, 109–146.

Spencer, C. (2010). War and early state formation in Oaxaca, Mexico. *Proceedings of the National Academy of Sciences USA*, 100, 11185–11187.

Sperry, R. (1969). A modified concept of consciousness. *Psychological Review*, 76, 532–536.

Spikens, P., Needham, A., Tilley, L., & Hitchens, G. (2018). Calculated or caring? *World Archaeology*, 50, https://doi.org/10.1080/00438243.2018.1433060

Stanford, C. (2012). *Planet without Apes*. Cambridge, MA: Belknap Press.

Steffen, W., Cruzen, P., & McNeill, J. (2007). The Anthropocene: Are humans now overwhelming the great forces of nature? *Ambio*, 36, 614–621.

Storm, S. (2018). Financialization and economic development: A debate on the social efficiency of modern finance. *Development and Change*, 49(2), 302–329.

Stringer, C. (2003). Out of Ethiopia. *Nature*, 423, 692–694.

Stringer, C. & Galway-Witham, J. (2017). On the origin of our species. *Nature*, 546, 212–214.

Sullivan, S. (2013). Banking nature: The spectacular financialisation of environmental conservation. *Antipode*, 45, 198–217.

Sutcliffe, T. (2016). When Neanderthals replaced us. *Discover Magazine*, May 27.

Tainter, J. (1988). *The Collapse of Complex Societies*. Cambridge: Cambridge University Press.

Testart, A. (1982). The significance of food storage among hunter-gatherers: residence patterns, and social inequalities. *Current Anthropology*, 23, 523–537.

Thompson, W. (2004). Complexity, diminishing marginal returns, and serial Mesopotamian. fragmentation. *Journal of World-Systems Research*, X, 613–652.

Thorne, B., (1997). Evolution of eusociality in termites. *Annual Review of Ecological Systems*, 28, 27–54.

Tizo-Pedroso, E. & Del-Klaro, K. (2018). Capture of large prey and feeding priority in the cooperative pseudoscorpion Paratemnoides nidificator. *Acta Ethologica*, 21, 109–117.

Trinkaus, E. & Sébastien, V. (2017). External auditory exostoses and hearing loss in the Shanidar 1 Neanderthal. *PLOS One*, https://doi.org/10.1371/journal.pone.0186684

Tripati, A., Roberts, C., & Eagle, R. (2009). Coupling of CO_2 and ice sheet stability over major climate transitions of the last 20 million years. *Science*, 326, 1394–1397.

Trivers, R. (1971). The evolution of reciprocal altruism. *Quarterly Review of Biology*, 46, 35–57.

Trivers, R. (1985), *Social Evolution*. Menlo Park, CA: Benjamin Cummings.

Turchin, P. (2006). *War and Peace and War: The Life Cycles of Imperial Nations*. New York: Pi Press.

Turchin, P. (2013). The puzzle of human ultrasociality: How did large-scale complex societies evolve? In P. Richerson and M. Christiansen, eds. *Cultural Evolution*. Cambridge, MA: MIT Press. pp. 61–73.

Turnbull, C. (1965). *The Mbuti Pygmies*. New York: Simon & Schuster.

United Nations. (2019). World population prospects. https://esa.un.org/unpd/wpp/Publications

Vallas, S., Kleinman, D. & Biscotti, D. (2009). Political structures and the making of U.S. Biotechnology. In F. Block and M. Keller, eds. *State of Innovation: The U.S. Government's Role in Technology Development*. Boulder, CO: Paradigm Publishers.

Van Essen (2018). Scaling of human brain size. *Science*, 360, 1184–1185.

Van Valen, L. (1974). Brain size and intelligence in man. *American Journal of Physical Anthropology*, https://doi.org/10.1002/ajpa.1330400314

van Wilgenburg, E., Torres, C., & Tsutsui, N. (2010). The global expansion of a single ant supercolony. *Evolutionary Applications*, 3, 136–143

Veblen, T. (1907). Professor Clark's economics. *Quarterly Journal of Economics*, 22, 147–195.

Wade, M. (1976). Group selection among laboratory populations of Tribolium. *Proceedings of the National Academy of Science*, 73, 4604–4607.

Wagner, G. & Altenberg, L. (1996). Complex adaptations and the evolution of evolvability. *Evolution*, 50, 967–976.

Walker, A., Zimmerman, M. R., & Leakey, R. (1982). A possible case of hypervitaminosis A in Homo erectus. *Nature*, 296, 248–250.

Wallace, A. R. (1869). *The Malay Archipelago: The Land of the Orang-utan and the Bird of Paradise. A Narrative of Travel, with Studies of Man and Nature*, vol. 2. London: Macmillan.

Wallace-Wells, D. (2019). *The Uninhabitable Earth*. New York: Duggan Books.

Walpole, S., Prieto-Merino, D., Edwards, P., et al. (2012). The weight of nations: an estimation of adult human biomass. *BMC Public Health*, 12, 439.

Wcislo, W. (2012). Big brains, little bodies. *Science*, 338,1419.

Weiner, S., Xu, Q., Goldberg, P., Liu, J., & Bar-Josef, O. (1998). Evidence for the use of fire at Zhoukoudian, China. *Science*, 281, 251–253.

Weiss, H. (2017). *Megadrought and Collapse: From Early Agriculture to Angkor*. New York: Oxford University Press.

Weiss, H. & Bradley, R. (2001). What drives societal collapse? *Science*, 291, 609–610.

Weiss, H., Courty, M-A., Wetterstrom, W. et al. (1993). The genesis and collapse of third millennium North Mesopotamian civilization. *Science*, 261, 99–104.

Wexler, B. (2006). *Brain and Culture*. Cambridge, MA: MIT Press.

Wheeler, W. M. (1911). *The Ant Colony as an Organism*. https://doi.org/10.1002/jmor.1050220206

White, T., Asfaw, B., DeGusta, H., et al. (2003). Pleistocene Homo sapiens from Middle Awash, Ethiopia. *Nature*, 423, 742–747.

Williams, K., Hewitt, A., & Bodas-Salcedo, A. (2020). Use of short-range forecasts to evaluate fast physics processes relevant for climate sensitivity. *Journal of Advances in Modeling Earth Systems*, 12. https://agupubs.onlinelibrary.wiley.com/doi/epdf/10.1029/2019MS001986

Wilson, D. S. (1997). Human groups as units of selection. *Science*, 276, 1816–1817.

Wilson, D. S. (2010a). Multilevel selection and major transitions. In M. Pigliucci and G. Müller eds., *Evolution: The Extended Synthesis*. Cambridge, MA: MIT Press, pp. 81–94.

Wilson, D. S. (2010b). Truth and reconciliation for group selection. http://evolution.binghamton.edu/dswilson/wp-content/uploads/2010/01/Truth-and-Reconciliation.pdf

Wilson, D. S. (2015). *Does Altruism Exist?* New Haven, CT: Yale University Press.

Wilson, D. S. (2015). The road to ideology: How Friedrich Hayek became a monster. *Evonomics*. http://evonomics.com/the-road-to-ideology-how-friedrich-hayek-became-a-monster

Wilson, D. S. (2016). Beyond genetic evolution. A conversation with Eva Jalonka. https://evolution-institute.org/article/beyond-genetic-evolution-a-conversation-with-eva-jablonka

Wilson, D. S. (2016). Love Hayek, love Darwin. *Evonomics*. https://evonomics.com/love-hayek-love-darwin

Wilson, D. S., Ostrom, E., & Cox, M. (2013). Generalizing the core design principles for the efficacy of groups. *Journal of Economic Behavior and Organization* 90 (Supplement), S21–32.

Wilson, D. S. & Sober, E. (1989). Reviving the superorganism. *Journal of Theoretical Biology*, 136, 337–356.

Wilson, D. S., & Wilson, E. O. (2007). Rethinking the theoretical foundations of sociobiology. *Quarterly Review of Biology*, 82, 327–348.

Wilson, E. O. (1975). *Sociobiology: The New Synthesis*. Cambridge, MA: Harvard University Press.

Wilson, E. O. (1984). *Biophilia*. Cambridge, MA: Harvard University Press.

Wilson, E. O. (2008). One giant leap: How insects achieved altruism and colonial life. *BioScience*, 58: 17–25.

Wilson, E. O. (2012). *The Social Conquest of Earth*. New York: W. W. Norton.

Wilson, E. O. (2014). *The Meaning of Human Existence*. New York: W. W. Norton.

Wilson, E. O. (2016). *Half Earth: Our Planet's Fight for Life*. New York: W. W. Norton.

Wilson, E. O. & Hölldobler, B., (2005). Eusociality: Origin and consequences. *Proceedings of the National Academy of Sciences*, 102(38), 13367–13371.

Wilson, N. (2009). Cold, high and dry: Traditional agriculture in Ladakh. The Permaculture Research Institute. https://permaculturenews.org/2009/02/06/cold-high-and-dry-traditional-agriculture-in-ladakh

Wolpoff, M., Hawks, J., & Caspari, R. (2000). Multiregional, not multiple origins. *American Journal of Physical Anthropology*, 112, 129–136.

Woodburn, J. (1968). An introduction to Hadza ecology. In I. Devore and R. Lee, eds. *Man the Hunter*. Chicago: Aldine.

Woodburn, J. (1998) [1982]. Egalitarian societies. In John Gowdy, ed. *Limited Wants, Unlimited Means: A Reader on Hunter-Gatherer Economics and the Environment*. Washington, DC: Island Press, pp. 87–110.

Wong, S. (2018). Tiny termites dig a world of their own. *New Scientist*, November 24.

World Bank. (2012). Turn down the heat: Why a 4°C warmer world must be avoided. *Turn down the heat*. Washington, DC: World Bank Group.

World Wide Fund. (2016). *Living Planet Report 2014: Species and Spaces, People and Places*. Gland: World Wide Fund for Nature.

Wright, R. (2004). *A Short History of Progress*. Philadelphia: Carroll & Graf.

Wynne-Edwards, V. (1962). *Animal Dispersion in Relation to Social Behaviour*. Edinburgh: Oliver and Boyd.

Yan, H., Bonasio, R., Simola, D., Liebig, J., Berger, S., & Reinberg, D. (2014). Eusocial insects as emerging models for behavioral epigenetics. *Nature Reviews Genetics*, 15, 677–688.

Yan, H., Simola, D., Bonasio, R., Liebig, J., Berger, S., & Reinberg, D. (2015). DNA methylation in social insects: How epigenetics can control behavior and longevity. *Annual Review of Entomology*, 60, 435–452.

Zeder, M. (2011). The origins of agriculture in the Middle East. *Current Anthropology*, 52, S221–S235.

Zeder, M., Emshwiller, E., Smith, B., & Bradley, D. (2017). Documenting domestication: The intersection of genetics and archeology. *Trends in Genetics*, 22, 139–155.

Zerjal, T., Xue, Y., Bertorelle, G., et al. (2003). The Genetic Legacy of the Mongols. *American Journal of Human Genetics*, 72, 717–721.

Zimmer, C. (2017). In Neanderthal DNA, signs of a mysterious human migration. *New York Times*, July 4.

Zimmerer, K. (1993). Agricultural biodiversity and peasant rights to subsistence in the central Andes during Inca rule. *Journal of Historical Geography*, 19, 15–32.

Zimmerman, P., Greenberg, J., Wandi, S., & Crutzen, P. (1982). Termites: A potentially large source of atmospheric methane, carbon dioxide and molecular hydrogen. *Science*, 218, 563–565.

Zvelebil, M. & Rowley-Conwy, P. (1986). Foragers and farmers in Atlantic Europe. In M. Zvelebil, ed. *Hunters in Transition: Mesolithic Societies of Temperate Eurasia and their Transition to Farming*. Cambridge: Cambridge University Press, pp. 67–93.

INDEX